THE
ZEPPELIN STORY

Other books by W. Robert Nitske

The Amazing Porsche and Volkswagen Story
The Complete Mercedes Story
Rudolf Diesel
The Life of Wilhelm Conrad Röntgen
Travels in North America, 1822-1824, by
Duke Paul of Württemberg (a translation)
Mercedes-Benz 300SL
Mercedes-Benz Production Models 1946-1975

THE
ZEPPELIN STORY

W. Robert Nitske

SOUTH BRUNSWICK AND NEW YORK: A. S. BARNES AND COMPANY

LONDON: THOMAS YOSELOFF LTD

© 1977 by A. S. Barnes and Co., Inc.

A. S. Barnes and Co., Inc.
Cranbury, New Jersey 08512

Thomas Yoseloff Ltd
Magdalen House
136-148 Tooley Street
London SE1 2TT, England

Library of Congress Cataloging in Publication Data

Nitske, W. Robert.
  The Zeppelin Story.

  Bibliography: p.
  Includes index.
  1. Zeppelin, Ferdinand Adolf August Heinrich, Graf
von, 1838-1917. 2. Air-ships—History. 3. Aeronautics
—Germany—Biography. I. Title.
TL540.Z4N5 1977   629.133'24'0924 [B]   76-10875
ISBN 0-498-01805-9

PRINTED IN THE UNITED STATES OF AMERICA

CONTENTS

PREFACE

The idea for *The Zeppelin Story* first came to me when, on a visit to Stuttgart, I reminisced over Count Zeppelin with our good friend Prince Albrecht von Urach-Württemberg.

We both recalled the tremendous popularity of the aged Graf during the early days of World War I when any appearance of the white-capped airship pioneer caused an unbelievably tumultuous rejoicing by his fellow citizens.

Fürst von Urach recalled an amusing incident in the days long before that, when his father and the King of Württemberg were enthusiastic supporters of the then valiantly struggling airship builder. At one of the many regal social functions at the Royal Palace, when the youngster, curly hair and flowing dress, made before the group a well-wishing recitation written by his father, Count Zeppelin was so taken with the elaborate greeting that he picked up the child, kissed him, and then asked, "And what is your name, my little darling?" "Ich bin Albrecht," replied the embarrassed boy.

Now we laughed at the incident, but the fact that Count Zeppelin had mistaken him for a girl and kissed him was an embarrassment to my friend throughout his entire youth.

Such reminiscences suggested that it was worthwhile to recount the story of the untiring inventor and his zeppelins.

ACKNOWLEDGMENTS

I wish to thank Mrs. Rhoda Gilman of the Minnesota Historical Society for making readily available accurate details and supplying photo copies of her articles and old newspapers on Count Zeppelin's early activities in this country; Miss Elaine Nantkes for her generously given and valuable editorial assistance; and those firms and agencies that supplied the fine photographs: Daimler-Benz A.G., Stuttgart; Deutsche Lufthansa, Cologne; Goodyear Tire and Rubber Company, Akron; Library of Congress; National Archives, Navy Department; and Luftschiffbau Zeppelin, Friedrichshafen. Without the vast collection of memorabilia, facts, figures, and models at the fine Zeppelin Museum at Friedrichshafen, where we spent much time and reaped immense harvests, this story would have been impossible.

Thanks are also due for permission to quote to the following publishers: *"The Zeppelins"* by Ernst Lehmann and Howard Mingos, "Reprinted by permission from the Saturday Evening Post © 1927 The Curtis Publishing Company"; *"Zeppelin"* by Margaret Goldsmith ©1931 by William Morrow and Company, Inc.; and for quotations and illustrations *"Zeppelin in Minnesota: The Count's Own Story"* Rhoda R. Gilman, ed., in Minnesota History 40: 274, 275, 277, published in 1967 by the Minnesota Historical Society, St. Paul.

To my wife Betty I express my sincerest appreciation for her untiring help in preparing the manuscript, as well as gathering information for the book in Europe and later on, here at home. Much of its success is due to her suggestions and assistance in the entire project.

INTRODUCTION

Ever since man observed a bird soaring effortlessly in the air, he desired to fly. The mythical Icarus tried to reach the sun, but the wax that held his feathery wings together melted from the heat, and he plunged into the sea.

Leonardo da Vinci (1452-1519) drew sketches of gliders but obviously never pursued the idea farther. When Otto Lilienthal in 1891 made over a thousand successful gliding experiments, he utilized a glider but arranged the wings exactly opposite from a da Vinci sketch. However, these were heavier-than-air trials.

To achieve lifting a body into the air, Lana-Terzi believed (in 1670) that a lighter-than-air substance was needed and proposed to use the lighter air found in higher altitudes. But heated air proved practical, and successful balloon flights were first made in 1782. These various free balloons were at the mercy of prevailing winds and thus a means of controlling their directions was devised. Various types of dirigible balloons were constructed, but the rigid style developed by Count Ferdinand von Zeppelin proved to be the one most successful.

This retired general spent the balance of his rich life—as well as his fortune—in the task to make his zeppelins the ideal means of transportation over long distances and to link continents and bring their people closer together. The ideal airship was built after the death of the Count and was aptly named the *"Graf Zeppelin."* (This airship was 790 feet long; a Boeing 747 airliner is 231 feet long.)

After nine years of service and 590 flights, many of them on a regular transatlantic schedule, this consummate airship was retired in 1937.

Other air transport in those years of heavier-than-aircraft was limited to mail; flying boats made some trips across the oceans. The *China Clipper* of Pan American Airways in November and December 1935 flew from San Francisco to Manila and returned, carrying mail and the crew. Passenger-carrying aircraft, flying on a schedule, was still spasmodic. The airship flights were indeed the pathfinders and originators of air travel as we now know it. Only the *Hindenburg* disaster put an end to the era.

Periodically, new ideas in airship construction have been proposed, but none have become a reality. Some years ago we saw at the Transportation Exhibition, the *Verkehrsaustellung,* at Munich, a model of a three-bodied airship, but this project never progressed beyond the idea stage. Now, again, there is speculation of an airship revival.

Just how far these ambitious projects will go is impossible to predict. Unorthodox ideas have often brought amazing results, and the entire development of aircraft now in service was only fantasy not too long ago.

Nuclear power is obviously the ideal power source for a dirigible airship. The necessary shielding is extremely heavy, but the range and endurance are nearly unlimited. In 1953, Gordon Dean, chairman of the Atomic Energy Commission, pointed out that the one place where atomic power can come into its own is in the rigid airship because the airship could lift the required heavy shielding certainly more readily than could an airplane.

The Goodyear Aircraft Corporation in 1945 proposed an airship of ten million cubic-feet capacity. The airship would be 950 feet long, 142 feet in diameter, and would have a range of 6,000 miles. It could carry a payload of one-hundred tons. Deluxe accommodations would be for 112 passengers, but tourist accommodations could be made for 288 persons. With a fleet of six airships, a regular schedule of transatlantic flights, as well as Hawaii flights, could be maintained. These airships could operate forty-eight weeks of a year, with four weeks for overhauling during the off-season. Each ship would make ninety-six round trips on the 2,500-mile route, or forty-eight round trips on the 3,500-mile route from New York to London. (Airship service was to be a two-day service, steamship five days, and airplane less than one day.)

As reported in *Nucleonics* of December 1965, at the Boston University, College of Engineering, associate professor of aerospace engineering, Francis Moore, produced a complete preliminary design for a nuclear-powered airship. Using basically the design of the *Graf Zeppelin II,* the proposed nuclear airship would utilize helium gas. With modern weather radar systems, navigational problems would be minimized.

Such an airship would be 980 feet long and carry four-hundred passengers. It would be powered by reactors developed by the General Electric Company and Pratt & Whitney Company as part of the cancelled ANP (Aircraft Nuclear Propulsion) program. The weight of the airship would be 380 tons, plus sixty tons for the reactor, shielding, and turbines. In addition to the passengers, the airship would be able to carry ninety tons of mail or freight. The payload would equal the C-5A aircraft, which has a five-thousand-mile range, while the airship would have an unlimited range; and instead of requiring an eight-thousand- to ten-thousand-foot runway, the dirigible would have a very short take-off and landing ability.

Another proposal has come from the British Furness-Withey group's Manchester Liners, Limited. This freight line created a division, Cargo Airships Limited, which plans to build a 2.4 million-dollar prototype of a 1,200-foot long airship with a five to six million cubic-feet gas capacity of helium. The proposed fleet of several such airships will eventually be nuclear powered, but at first the ships will be powered by diesel engines, according to Max Rynish, as reported in *True* magazine. Utilizing twenty-foot bulk containers, loading of the five-hundred-ton payload could be done quickly and profitably by S-64 Sikorsky helicopters, which are capable of lifting thirty-eight tons. The airships would not land at all, but be held nearly motionless above their respective ports of call. Such a transportation system would be exceedingly costly, but perhaps not entirely impossible for a resourceful corporation.

To such imaginative proposals, as the nuclear powered or even the tri-bodied airships, Hans von Schiller, the veteran *Graf Zeppelin* commander, turns a cold shoulder. "How could one think of such nonsense. The project is aerodynamically absurd, and the tie-up of three separate bodies would constitute a totally impossible addition of weight." While agreeing that atomic energy is the ideal power source for a zeppelin, there are many problems. The weight of the necessary protective devices of a reactor would take too much space and would reduce the payload too much. At the present time, a reactor is much too heavy for an airship when one considers the weight of the reactor installed in a freight-carrying steamship. For an airship the reactor and especially the protective shielding would weigh even more: because of safety reasons added precautions would be necessary. "I am certainly no opponent of airship development, but one must keep his feet on the ground and not chase phantoms," von Schiller concluded in a letter to me.

THE
ZEPPELIN STORY

1

INTRODUCING THE COUNT

In a lowland region near the Baltic Sea in northern Germany, many years ago the storks gathered annually in preparation for migration. Still a favorite breeding ground for the large birds, the area contains hardly a house or a barn that does not have a wagon wheel fastened to its roof to provide a nesting place for storks, which are said to bring good luck to the family on whose property they nest.

During the Middle Ages, the Wendes, a Slavic people, immigrated into the region of the storks; they called the area *czapla,* meaning storks. Later the name became Cepelin, Sepelin, Zepelyn, and eventually Zepelin. A settlement by the name of Zepelin, near Bützow in Mecklenburg, was first officially mentioned in 1246. However, the name of a person called Zepelin did not appear in the chronicles until 1286. The Zepelin descendants apparently held the land continuously for more than five hundred years thereafter. Then, about 1600, the brothers Volrath and Johann Zepelin lost their estate, the Gut Thürkow, but they later recovered their holdings, which combined the acreage of over fifty farms.

At the turn of the eighteenth century the brothers Johann Carl and Ferdinand Ludwig Zepelin were invited by Duke Friedrich of Württemberg to enter his services. For some twenty years Ferdinand was in the army, having started his military career at sixteen as *Fähnrich,* or

ensign, in the dragoon regiment of the Duke. Ferdinand also took part in the Turkish War (1788-91), where he acquired a richly studded dagger—which was to become a favorite family heirloom—and advanced to *Rittmeister,* or captain. In the battle at Marengo in 1800 he was severely wounded, ending his active military service.

When Johann Carl died the following year, Duke Friedrich took Ferdinand Ludwig to his court as *Reichsmarschall* and gave him the diplomatic duties of the deceased brother to perform.

Others of the seven brothers had entered military service for various rulers and were listed in Danish, Russian, or Austrian regiments as Konstantin von Zepeline, Theodor von Zeplin, and Gottfried von Zeppelin.

At the court, the new diplomat Ferdinand Zepelin met the young Baroness Pauline von Maucler and married her in 1802, spelling his name from then on *Zeppelin* to accommodate the softer southern pronunciation of it. When Württemberg became a kingdom in 1806, Ferdinand Ludwig was made a *Graf,* or count, by his appreciative King Friedrich, and advanced to the rank of minister for foreign affairs. In his new position Count Ferdinand traveled to Paris after the Napoleonic Wars to negotiate with Napoleon. In 1813 he met with Prince Metternich in Fulda, and he went to Russia to confer with the Czar.

His king wrote to him, "In this miserable

situation we expect that you will do whatever is in your power to protect your king and your country against future ill treatment." Apparently the count distinguished himself in these delicate positions, for he earned the highest decorations from the sovereigns of Austria, Russia, and Prussia for these services.

In 1819, Count Ferdinand retired from the chores of the ministry to Münster, his estate near Cannstatt. However, when he was asked by King Wilhelm I to go to Vienna as ambassador in 1826, he went. He died in Austria in 1829.

Friedrich, the son of Ferdinand, also became a diplomat, but in the service of a Prince von Hohenzollern-Sigmaringen. Count Friedrich was a shy man who disliked the formalities of court life. He preferred music and played the violin, collected butterflies, wrote poetry judged by his son to be "delicate and beautiful," and was a friend of the contemporary poets Nikolaus Lenan and Gustav Schwab.

At Konstanz in 1834, Count Friedrich married Amelie Macaire d'Hogguer, the daughter of wealthy French immigrants from Geneva. About her future husband, the bride-to-be had written to her sister-in-law:

> . . .he loves flowers and he is a poet (and please do understand that I do not mean simply a verse-maker, but a genuine poet, when I say this). I shall not try to tell you how kind and good he is for I should never finish telling you if I once began.[1]

Three children were born to Friedrich and Amelie. A daughter Eugenie was the eldest, a son Ferdinand arrived two and a half years later, and another son Eberhard joined the family four years after that. The second child, Ferdinand Adolf August Heinrich, was born on 8 July 1838, in the home of his grandparents on an island in the Bodensee, or Lake Constance. The home, where the mother herself had been born twenty-two years before, on 10 January 1816, was situated at the precise point in the Bodensee where the Rhine leaves the lake, close to the city of Konstanz, and connected with it by a covered wooden bridge. The Romans had built a fortified castle on this island so that they could defend the newly won Konstanz from their enemies. Centuries has passed and the Roman fortifications had fallen into ruin; in their stead a summer house was built by the bishops of

Konstanz. Later, this house also disappeared, and the famous Dominican monastery, where John Huss lay imprisoned until his fiery death, was built on its site. Toward the end of the last century when the poor monks were driven out, Kaiser Joseph II had presented the island and all of the buildings on it to Monsieur Louis Macaire, the grandfather of Amelie, who established himself with two sons and a housekeeper quite comfortably in some of the monk's cells. And the large cellars, kitchen, and refectories were turned into an unromantic calico factory.

Actually, when the Free City of Konstanz was ceded to Austria in 1548, the emperor gave the entire island to the Jacques Louis de l'Or family, which had emigrated from Geneva to escape the religious and political turbulence.

Because of her delicate health, Amelie and her children spent considerable time at the parental home, although they had actually moved two years after Ferdinand's birth to Girsberg, which they bought from Duke Friedrich of Württemberg for 20,600 guldens. The history of that cloister estate went back to 1300. Kaiser Rudolf II was one of the earlier landowners, before the estate became the famed Abtei Zwiefalten. After the seculariza-

Count Ferdinand von Zeppelin as the author remembers him. (Courtesy, Lufthansa).

tion, this cloister became the property of the Duke, who then sold it in 1808.

Located between hills, the large estate acreage included vineyards and orchards. The main and auxiliary buildings were enclosed by a thick wall with two portals at the entrance. The castle with its onion towers, Schloss Obergyrsberg (they preferred the ancient spelling of the hill area), was placed atop a hill overlooking the huge lake. The wide driveway was lined with tall poplar trees, and a fountain with weeping willows graced this impressive approach.

The lake, once called *Brigantinus Lacus* by the Romans, had already reached considerable importance. The first steamer was launched in 1824, and now the fifty-mile-long lake boasted of much international steamship traffic. The southern shore belonged to Switzerland, with Austria-Hungary touching a small area on the easternmost end. The northern shore touched the Grand Duchy of Baden, while portions of the eastern end were part of the Kingdom of Württemberg.

His wife was happy when Count Friedrich retired early from the diplomatic service. During all of the ceremonies at court he had worn a diplomatic uniform with gold epaulettes and carried a black staff with a silver knob. Suddenly, one day, bored with all this pomp, he discarded the staff and fancy uniform and came to live in this former Dominican monastery. Later, unfortunately, Count Friedrich became ill and the damp air near the Bodensee did not agree with him. The family moved to Girsberg to escape the dampness.

Ferdinand was an attractive child, "somewhat spoiled and a bit vain," as he himself wrote years later, based on his mother's letter. "I was considered a pretty child, and my special adornment was a tight curl which looked like a rose and which no efforts with a brush would straighten out."

His mother wrote that when Ferdinand was five and a half years old, he was a blue-eyed little angel with blond, curly hair, and was the favorite of all his aunts and uncles. Strangers called him a little *Herzkäfer,* heart-bug, while in the family he was called little *Knöpfelschwab,* button-Swabian; and both names apparently suited him very well. Like his father, Ferdinand had a gentle disposition. His scientific studies had not yet begun, but he used his innate talents very successfully in herding cows, carrying wood, pulling weeds, hauling stones, and in similar tasks. He was considered *au fait* in regard to all the agricultural work being done on the estate, always knowing exactly on which field each particular laborer was working. He was particularly interested in new plows and intricate machines. He was a proud little *Württemberger* when he was presented with his first pair of boots.

The children were brought up in a most sensible manner. Ferdinand observed years later that the thought that he belonged to the ruling classes was not allowed to even enter his head. He was not conscious of that, as were so many others of the nobility in Germany. Even getting new clothes was a special occasion in the lives of the children. He recalled that one time when he wore a new suit with white pants, of which he was especially proud, Nemesis punished his vanity. On a visit to friends at Schloss Ratzenried the other boys tried to ride some goats. Naturally Ferdinand had to try it too, but it was not long until he fell into a mud puddle with his new suit.

Ferdinand's mother taught her children at home for the first few school years. A local teacher came twice weekly to assist in this task, but she strongly believed that an informal type of instruction was of greatest benefit to the youngsters, and that they should be subjected to the regular school disciplines only at a later age. However, Ferdinand and Eberhard had a full-time tutor when nine or ten years old.

The tutor noted that the little Count Ferdinand was a beautiful boy, strong and well built, and like his delightful mother, charming, kind and good. The youngster was highly gifted, and the tutor believed that his talents were of a practical rather than a theoretical nature. Always obedient to the tutor, the child was most eager to learn and was kind to everyone.

The development of the bodies of her children was as important to Amelie Zeppelin as was the development of their minds. They were told just what and how much to eat. This rule was strictly enforced, even when they visited friends and relatives. The children were advised exactly what they could eat there, and at large dinners they generally had to pass up several courses.

During the winter months the children were occupied in their playroom with handicrafts. Bookbinding and woodworking were favorite pastimes, and besides making books and small knickknacks for their own enjoyment, they made Christmas gifts for their parents and relatives.

Most of the time the children played out of doors. The spacious grounds surrounding their home offered all sorts of territory for enticing games, but the nearby lake was the favorite playground. At the age of six Ferdinand had already passed a swimming test to prove his ability to swim continuously for half an hour. Once during that summer, when a visiting cousin lost her ring while swimming, Ferdinand promptly retrieved it by expertly diving into the deep waters of the lake. Both boys thoroughly enjoyed the water.

On walks with their father the children learned to know nature. The parent was a willing teacher; he painstakingly answered numerous questions, and even encouraged more pertinent ones by cleverly suggesting interesting observations along the lakefront or in fields and forests of their estate.

Hikes into the more distant hills and into higher mountains were also occasionally undertaken because the father strongly believed that such training was essential to his children. On a hike to the Hoher Kasten Mountain the father and his two sons were overtaken by a bad storm that forced them to spend the night in a protective mountain-climber's hut. The next day, when the ascent was to be made, the father cautiously did not allow his six-year-old son to continue. Two men who had come to look for them carried the boy down ignobly in a laundry basket, to his immense embarrassment.

A few days after this demeaning episode, however, a thrilling adventure made up for the disgrace. On a hike into the forest, father and son found a wooden bridge damaged beyond repair, across the deep Tamania Gorge. Ferdinand was allowed to ride horseback on the secure shoulders of his father, who, astride a large log, slowly pushed himself and his load across the gorge. This unique procedure was the only possible means of reaching the other side of the deep crevasse. Ferdinand enjoyed this exciting ride to the fullest. Fear was unknown to him, and he felt completely secure on the shoulders of his father.

Ferdinand showed considerable presence of mind in emergencies. With a playmate that winter, he ran across an ice-covered pond on their estate when the thin ice broke and Ferdinand fell into the cold water. The other youngster began to cry out, but Ferdinand kept his head and was able to reach the opposite shore, where he held on to the edge of a solid portion of the ice. The other boy just stood there wailing. Ferdinand, utterly disgusted with such a silly attitude, spoke to the boy severely, telling him to lay flat on his stomach on the ice, slide forward, and reach out his hands so that Ferdinand could grasp them. So that his parents would not know of the mishap, Ferdinand tried to dry outside, but the eleven-degree cold was too much. The boys then went to a neighbor's house to borrow dry clothes and get the wet ones dried out. The neighbors, however, sent word to the parents, and Ferdinand was wrapped in blankets, taken home, and put to bed.

The next summer a situation developed in which the young Ferdinand had to use his ingenuity. Watching a small herd of cows in a pasture while the regular herder took time out, the youngster found that the cows, accustomed to a sterner tone and more vigorously applied switch, failed to heed his direction. The cows just kept walking toward the more lush-looking piece of ground belonging to a neighbor. The young cowherd knew that a leader was responsible for this, and he quickly surveyed the situation properly. Running ahead of the lead cow, he cut off her progress and forced her to turn around to the regular pasture. The other cows followed their leader.

Generally, the Zeppelin children led sheltered lives. Their small worlds did not often include neighboring children, and the three played congenially without disagreements. The delicate health of the mother limited visitors to their home, as well as visits to other places. The grandparental villa was the only exception.

When in 1848 their own home underwent extensive repairs, the mother and children stayed temporarily at Castell while the father stayed with the grandparents at Konstanz. The children were allowed to "visit" their father there.

During this period, the German Revolution had spread from the other states also to Württemberg, and Ferdinand eagerly watched these activities. He observed the insurgents, brightly colored rooster feathers in their hats, drilling in the streets. The boy heard the revolutionaries make speeches, and witnessed a particularly violent tirade made to the crowd by Struve, one of the revolutionary leaders, from the balcony of the schoolhouse. Another time he saw the actual arrest of a leader named Zerrleder in the midst of a large and angry crowd of people in the streets. All of these events stimulated the imagination of the young Ferdinand and were of immense interest to him.

The inflammatory speeches usually attacked the nobility class unmercifully and pictured these privileged people as architects of all the troubles in the land. Ferdinand believed these accusations to be irresponsible, for he knew the very people who were being pictured as evil influences of society, and he had found most of them quite charming.

Since the troublemakers had come from their aborted radical activities in Prussia, it was but natural that Prussian agents were sent to hunt them down. Eventually, the revolutionary uprising was crushed by troops of King Wilhelm of Prussia, who later was elected Kaiser of the newly created Federation of Germany. Although rulers of the southern German states welcomed the help of the king to maintain their positions of authority, the people considered these northern Germans as intruders. Temperamentally, citizens of Baden and Württemberg were quite different from the efficient Prussians who had come to save the royal and ducal governments from overthrow by the revolutionary elements.

Some forty years later Ferdinand wrote that during these days two officers were billeted in the house of his grandparents. When the Prussians came, his father was obliged to give up his two rooms to the officers. While packing his personal things the father put something red into his luggage. One of the officers asked him if that was some of the red stuff they were making there now, to which his father answered calmly that it was his red sash of the Johannisorden, the Order of Saint John. The watching Ferdinand was much less calm than his father, and his childlike spirit was tremendously incensed at the inquisitorial manner in which they had asked this question. "Generally, the Prussians were not popular in Konstanz. Their walk and their facial expressions, in fact, their whole manner, displeased the population," he stated.

Ferdinand also played a minor but rather exciting role when troops were stationed at the Swiss border to guard that frontier and to check on any suspicious traffic across the line. His uncle Wilhelm, an Austro-Hungarian officer who had been blinded during the storming of Brescia in 1848, lived in Switzerland, just across the border. Ferdinand's father wished to communicate with his brother, but could not get past the border guards without being searched; thus the youngster was

asked to carry a letter to his uncle. With the letter hidden in his long stocking, astride his white pony, he was allowed to cross the border unmolested.

It was probably inevitable that the efforts of the first tutor were doomed to failure. A tall slender teacher, J. Kurz of Ravensburg, presented the precocious children with many occasions of merriment. His name, Kurz, meant short; yet he was a lanky towering man. He was unable to accomplish much constructive teaching with the boys, who failed to take him very seriously.

Ferdinand said that the tutor was "a very upright creature." Kurz generally spent hours telling his pupils fascinating stories, and they liked him. But he was not able to cope with them outside the schoolroom.

Riding the white pony, Kurz made a strange impression. Ferdinand observed that he sat astride the animal with his legs hanging down so that his feet touched the ground; he looked like Don Quixote. Once he rode to Konstanz to the pottery market, and before he knew what had happened the pony walked directly into the stalls where pottery was displayed. Many pieces of pottery were broken. A great deal of laughter and much abuse were showered on the hapless rider. Kurz eventually subdued the pony and, most dejectedly, led his mount back to Girsberg by the bridle. The laughter of the unsympathetic children accompanied him along the way.

Once during a heavy snowfall, the teacher became completely stuck in a drift, and servants were called to shovel him free. Although he had probed for an easier trail to get the children and himself out of a predicament, his charges thought it a highly hilarious situation.

Under the guidance of Kurz, the children published their own "newspaper." Written neatly on pages torn from their school notebooks, Ferdinand called his "The Girsberg Air-Newspaper," perhaps an early indication that he found the air of great interest and importance.

When the renovation work on their own home at Girsberg was finally completed, the family returned. Soon, however, the mother's illness became progressively worse.

With the children's elementary schooling concluded, the parents carefully selected a teacher to take over the tutoring. Robert Moser, who later became well known as an educator and theologian in Württemberg, took over the tutorial task in

1850. He quickly surveyed the situation and wrote:

> I entered the Manor House with fear in my heart, but before I had reached the staircase leading up the veranda, two boys came out to meet me. They escorted me to the rooms I was to occupy. It was quite obvious that they had been awaiting my arrival eagerly and that they were looking me over from head to foot.[2]

Moser was a good educator. He realized that the usual classroom curriculum was of little interest to these active and precocious youngsters, so he emphasized the studies of natural sciences, geography, and history. "I tried to teach my pupils how to think independently, and I did all I could to make their lessons a pleasure and not a torment for them."

As a theological candidate, Moser was proficient in Latin and Greek, but these subjects were of only secondary importance to his charges. The tutor's knowledge of French was so inadequate that he had difficulty in communicating with the grandparents of the children. Religion was a dominant subject, as was to be fully expected.

By stressing the geography and history of distant lands, Moser considerably widened the horizon of his pupils; and he stimulated their already well-developed powers of perception. After field trips, he had his charges write in detail of their observations gathered during these excursions.

But the good teacher did not neglect play altogether. Ferdinand showed a deep interest in puttering and building, and together they worked in the playroom, which then looked as if it were a carpenter shop. All sorts of water wheels were constructed and then tested in a nearby creek or even in the lake. For indoor recreation, pupils and teacher often played chess, a rather difficult game for such youngsters, but they seemed to enjoy it.

When Ferdinand was thirteen, a longer journey was undertaken in which the teacher and the three children visited in several cities with close and distant relatives. Seemingly the trip was a huge success, for in an elaborately decorated document prepared as birthday gift for his father, Ferdinand wrote of the magnificent sights and challenging encounters of the journey. The title though impressive, was longspun: "The most peculiar points, castles, ruins, waterfalls, rivers, mountains, etc., which we have seen and visited together on our journey through Württemberg, as well as the characteristics of the most peculiar personalities which we learnt to know, described and presented alive and true." As part of this thirty-six-page essay, Ferdinand wrote:

> As soon as we had arrived [at the factory at Esslingen], we saw and heard an Alpine locomotive which was letting out steam with a terrible noise. We saw completed locomotives as well as separate parts, and the functions of this machinery were explained to us. We were also taken into a large hall in which were a great many iron machines. Most of the parts at which the men were working were parts of the machinery for the new steamer *Wilhelm*. The chief wheel which they showed us revolved around itself three hundred times an hour. It is incredible what man can accomplish with the help of nature.[3]

When Robert Moser finished his tutoring after three years, he had given the boys a solid foundation in Christian ethics and in the basic academic fields. Moser had found the aristocratic home a happy one. He recalled that the entire household was permeated with an atmosphere of peace and harmony, creating a most salubrious and most healthy influence in the development of the children. There had never been any quarreling or scolding in the family, and no swearing or cursing or storming about. Serenity reigned everywhere in this happy home. If any one of the children was reprimanded, it was done with a loving spirit and great gentleness. In such an atmosphere it was only natural that the tutor also used only kindness and consideration in the education of his charges. He felt that "the incredible gentleness and repose that characterized Count Ferdinand were chiefly due to the exemplary spirit that prevailed in his parent's home."

The precarious health of the mother had deteriorated to such an extent that she was sent to a sanatorium at Montpellier to recuperate, and the children went to stay at Konstanz. The change of air failed to do much good for the mother and did not bring about the hoped-for recovery or arrest the failing health. Amelie Zeppelin died in 1852; her death was a terrible blow to her family.

Amelie's children, who had loved their mother deeply and were so dependent upon her, were dreadfully grieved at this calamity. "It was probably under the influence of my grief," Ferdinand wrote later, "that I decided to become a missionary when I grew up, but my father wisely resisted this decision very firmly. Perhaps he was right."

The following year Ferdinand was enrolled in the Realschule of the Gymnasium at Stuttgart, entering the top class. The emphasis here was on physics, chemistry, and mathematics, subjects for which Moser had prepared them during the preceding years.

After graduation the young man, on 21 October 1854, entered the military academy, the *Kriegsschule,* at Ludwigsburg, a few miles north of Stuttgart, from where he graduated in March 1857.

The twenty-year-old Count Ferdinand von Zeppelin became a lieutenant in the Eight Württemberg Infantry Regiment, attached to the quartermaster corps of the general staff. He soon found the military routine boring, however, just as he had not been too fond of the discipline in the academy, where he had become as unimportant as all of the other cadets, equal in dress and duties. Being an individualist, he did not easily take to the rigid discipline and strict conventional attitudes of the military officer. His interests seemed broader than merely military affairs, and he planned to enroll in the University at Tübingen.

About a year after he had received his commission, he petitioned the war office for a leave of absence for that purpose. The leave was readily approved, and Count Zeppelin went to the charming university town on the Neckar River. For a year he studied there. He attended classes and lectures in engineering, political science, and chemistry. He spent some time in the laboratories making experiments and in the libraries reading books mainly on engineering, as he recalled later.

During this time, on the international scene, Napoleon III demanded the Savoy and the Nice areas of Italy, and on New Year's Day of 1859 he brought pressure on Austria with his Italian alliance. The subsequent ultimatum did not indicate a war, but achieved that effect when the other powers rejected the demands. The attitude of Prussia in the war between France and Austria was uncertain, but seemed to lean in favor of Austria. Mobilization of the armed forces followed, and in 1859 Count Zeppelin left Tübingen to join the corps of engineers stationed at Ulm. For a count to join the lowly engineer corps was an unusual thing to do, and Count Zeppelin reaped many critical comments from his relatives and friends on that odd decision. But it was a typically independent action of his, quite unexpected of a young man in his position, but perhaps influenced by his superiors in recognition of his special knowledge in that field.

Through exceedingly bad generalship the Austrian forces lost the initiative and were beaten in several battles by the smaller forces of the French armies. Neither side wanted Prussia to enter the war, and peace negotiations were quickly begun. The recently mobilized regiment at Ulm never got into action at all.

However, Count Zeppelin's superior officers were pleased with his aggressiveness and efficiency; therefore, in 1862, just before the Villa Franca peace, he was promoted to first lieutenant and transferred back to the general staff. Routine work took over once more.

2

OBSERVING THE CIVIL WAR IN THE UNITED STATES

When at the beginning of 1863 the detailed orders for the junior officers of the general staff of the Württemberg army were posted, the young lieutenant, Count Ferdinand von Zeppelin, was deeply disappointed in the proposed unimaginative tasks. He felt that several important questions on military matters could further be explored; for, only shortly before, he had read a provocative book by von Rüstow on the superiority of the militia over the professional soldiers as employed under the rigid Prussian military system.

To convince himself of the rather dubious supremacy that the author had advanced, Count Zeppelin conceived the idea of observing the behavior of the volunteer armies engaged in the Civil War in the United States of America.

His father was strongly opposed to the whole idea, believing it to be nothing but a youthful infatuation. Disappointed, the young count accepted the parental verdict and tried to forget it, but as he wrote to his sister, he "carried the scheme as a bride in her heart."

Eventually, however, the father became convinced that the son intended to combine serious work with the pleasure of the journey, and the parent felt that continued opposition was useless. Nevertheless, the father pointed out that really nothing important would be shown him, and that only superficialities could be observed by the young but eager officer. He certainly would not be allowed to participate in interesting military events. The father also expressed deep concern about the many possible difficulties that could befall the young man in the far-distant land, especially in the war zone: contracting of illness, receiving a serious wound, being suspected of spying, or incurring many other such dangerous risks.

To support his request for furlough activity, Count Zeppelin sought the aid of a cousin, Baron Maucler, cabinet chief of King Wilhelm I, vacationing at that time in Nice on the French Riviera. The Count forwarded a letter outlining his proposed plan; he wrote:

I believe it to be my duty to use this opportunity through travels to secure information that I can possibly utilize for my fatherland at some time. Despite the totally chaotic situation there, North America still offers the richest rewards at the present time. The investigative observer could find the solution to problems that also will be of value to us, in the organization, leadership, and provisioning of the armies there, particularily since these are being administered under highly unfavorable and quite unusual conditions. The Americans are especially inventive in the adaptation of technical developments for military purposes. I do not have to mention the benefits which such a journey promises to have for the general enlightenment.[1]

Even before the letter of request was received by the baron, the king had given permission for a year-long furlough, as earlier urged by the influential cousin.

That Count Zeppelin was indeed in a hurry to get to the United States without delay was indicated when one of his best friends, the Freiherr von Woellwarth, asked him to be best man at his forthcoming wedding: the Count could not attend because of his impending trip. His letter of regret consisted of a forty-eight-line verse, which began:

Ich bin Soldat, Mann rascher Tat.
Ich muss im Kampf, Muss im Pulverdampf
Prüfen den Mut
Und im Gefahren Ruhigen Blick bewahren. . . .
(A soldier in fact, a man quick to act.
In powdercloud grey, in battle array
Courage I prove.
And in exposure, I show composure. . . .)[2]

After a short layover in London, on 30 April 1863, at Liverpool, the twenty-four-year-old Count Ferdinand von Zeppelin boarded the Cunard liner *Asia* for the crossing of the Atlantic Ocean.

The *New York Times* of 7 May 1863 listed a Count de Zeppelin as one of the many passengers of the Cunard steamship *Australiasian*, which had docked the previous day at New York and which had left Liverpool, England, on 25 April. (This differed slightly from accounts stated by Count Zeppelin in 1914.)

After his arrival in the New World, Count Zeppelin did not remain in New York for any considerable time. He was anxious to get into the war; and, after a brief visit in Philadelphia, he took passage to Baltimore as *Le Comte Zeppelin, Charge d'affaires de S.M. le Roi de Wurttemberg* on a French corvette. The following account, told by a French naval officer, was published in the *Paris Temps:*

In 1863 the French corvette *Tisiphone,* which had been riding at anchor in the harbor of New York for quite some time, sailed for Baltimore. But just before the ship left port, a man of about twenty-five, who wanted to sail to Baltimore, came as a passenger on board. Because warships, naturally, never carry

ordinary passengers, it seemed most obvious that this young man was an especially favored person. This fact became even more obvious when we noticed that our captain received him with particular courtesy. That evening the young passenger dined with our captain, and it was quite late when he joined me and the other officers of the vessel in our cabin. He was young and gay and inquired if he might offer his hosts some good Rhine wine which had accompanied him on board. Then he unpacked twelve bottles of wine, and quickly all of the assembled company became very merry.

Soon one by one of the officers were obliged to leave to go on ship's duty, until finally our passenger was left alone with only a young midshipman who had no duty that night. The two men drank and talked until early dawn. After they had finished all of the wine, both went for a walk around the ship, ending finally on the highest point of the mast. They climbed it to prove to each other that they were both perfectly sober and entirely steady, despite the large quantity of wine. That the midshipman could climb the mast did not indicate any particular valor, for the weather was just lovely and the sea was completely calm. But it was an astonishing feat indeed for the passenger to perform such an act of daring. He admitted to the midshipman that as a cavalry officer he had never before had an opportunity to climb a ship's mast and that this was, in fact, his first ascent into the sphere above the earth.

Count Zeppelin disembarked at Baltimore and went to the nation's capital.

As the Count wrote fifty-one years later in the periodical *Der Greif,* the city of Washington definitely did not make a grandiose impression upon him. He expected the capital city of a country to consist of really spectacular sights, but Washington offered no special attractions. The unpaved streets were dusty, and the sidewalks consisted merely of wooden boards. Most of the houses were low, wood structures. Only few were built of stone, one being the well known but considerably less than palatial White House, the residence of the president. It was situated amidst a garden but close to the street. The capitol building, however, appeared mighty and imposing, but this effect was lost almost entirely because the building stood in an area surrounded completely by wasteland, rather than in the center of a built-up city.

In the streets were many soldierly dressed men, wearing quite short pants, light boots, and a soft wide-brimmed or a straw hat. Few women were to be seen, suggesting to him that the purpose of life in Washington was not fun.

The capital was thronged with Europeans looking for positions in the Union army, because "the news had gone abroad that in America there was a great demand for officers of military training and experience. This demand could not fail to attract from all parts of the globe adventurous characters who had, or pretended to have, seen military service in one country or another."

Count Zeppelin stayed at the elegant Willard Hotel, located at the end of a long boulevard that passed the White House. Since he previously had made reservations, he was given a spacious corner suite on the second floor, with windows offering him splendid views of the colorful picture of the streets. Because the hotel was the stopping place for most of the higher-ranking officers, couriers were coming and going constantly.

The Count promptly contacted the Hanseatic ambassador, to whom he carried a letter of introduction. Herr Doktor Rudolf von Schleiden, who had been at his post for several years, was known to nearly all persons of importance. Well versed with local conditions, he indeed proved to be an experienced and influential friend. He took the young count to introduce him to the Prussian ambassador, Baron Gerold, at an evening reception at that embassy.

But the introduction to Washington high society was not without its own peculiar incident. In later years Count Zeppelin liked to tell the story, perhaps embroidering it a bit to emphasize the hilarity of the event, although at the time it was less than funny to the serious young military officer.

When the young Count's name was announced to the assembled guests in the salon, a slight sound of laughter reached his ears; he was, of course, flabbergasted and highly embarrassed by this odd reception of the distinguished group. Soon, the ambassador explained the curious circumstances to him. Only a few hours before the arrival of Count Zeppelin, the conclusion to a distressing episode involving an Austrian nobleman had been reached.

Some four weeks before, a certain count had appeared at the office of the Austrian ambassador, Count Trautmannsdorff, claiming that, after crossing the ocean, his steamship had been wrecked; as a survivor, he had lost all of his belongings, as had all of his fellow passengers. The obliging ambassador arranged generous credit with his own banker so that the temporarily impoverished count could reestablish himself again and could live comfortably until funds from home could be provided.

The count, who had a most engaging personality, was readily accepted in the society of the capital and enjoyed its liberal hospitality. To show his appreciation for these abundant pleasantries, he gave a costly, superb state dinner, to which many members of the diplomatic corps were invited.

In the meantime, Count Trautmannsdorff had, of course, made inquiries in Vienna, and on this very same afternoon when Count Zeppelin was a dinner guest, word had been received that a Count S. indeed existed and was even, at present, at his country estate; the Washington count obviously was an imposter—in fact, perhaps an escaped convict with a criminal record.

Count Trautmannsdorff felt it too embarrassingly painful to confront the imposter himself, and so asked the Prussian Baron Gerold, who was present, to do it. While both of these gentleman were still discussing the strategy to be used, the bogus count was announced. The Austrian ambassador quickly left the room, and the Baron handed the questionable count the incriminating letter. After carefully reading the note, the count bowed low and excused himself rather abruptly, left the room, quickly asked the servant for his carriage and jumped hurriedly into it, and was driven to the friendly banker of the ambassador, where he asked for and was given another emergency loan of six hundred dollars. Then, seemingly, he disappeared forever.

The guests at the dinner reception were talking about this sad but exciting event of the day, when Count Zeppelin, another newly arrived count with a German name, was introduced. The assembly could hardly be blamed for finding the similarity quite hilarious. Fortunately, Count Zeppelin had not experienced a shipwreck on his way, as he jokingly pointed out when telling of the affair.

Through the good offices of the Prussian ambassador, soon after his arrival in Washington, Count Zeppelin secured an audience with President Lincoln on 21 May. For that occasion, he dressed formally in a long frock coat and tall silk hat, although the meeting itself was quite simple, without pomp and ceremonies.

When the Count was shown into the study of the president at the White House, "there rose behind his writing desk this very gaunt, tall figure with a large head and long, ill-kempt hair and beard, with strikingly prominent cheek bones, and shrewd yet friendly looking eyes." The president expressed his gladness at the coming of the Count, spoke of his purpose, and wished him good success for his studies.

In an interview in 1915, Count Zeppelin recalled that President Lincoln was exceedingly concerned about the cruelties of the war, "now referred to as atrocities. People had the same impression then as now. This was expressed in the popular song of the time, 'When this cruel war is over.'"

Count Zeppelin was immensely impressed with the austere simplicity of the whole scene, so unlike an audience with highly important heads of state in Europe, and yet he was deeply in awe "as he felt always before the Kaiser."

A rather disturbing occurrence, which could never have happened in the presence of any so prominent a personage in the Count's own country, was that, during the entire short audience, the private secretary, Reed (whom he identified at another time as young Stewart, the son of the secretary of the interior) sat atop the desk and swayed in uniform rhythm, his moccasin-clad feet dangling way below his short pants legs.

Before the audience was granted, President Lincoln had written to Secretary of State William H. Seward and Secretary of War Edwin M. Stanton, making inquiries about Count Zeppelin, asking if the request for a military pass should be granted. Such a passport, signed by President Lincoln, was then given the count, allowing him full freedom of movement within the areas of the Northern armies. The only others who ever received such courtesies during the war were the duke of Joinville, the duke of Chartres, and the count of Paris. The pass remained cherished by the Count and was one of his prized possessions.

Understandably, a somewhat different version of the audience with President Lincoln exists. In his *Reminiscenses,* Carl Schurz recalled that, while in Washington awaiting the confirmation of his nomination for brigadier general and assignment to General John C. Fremont for duty, he was approached by several persons who wished him to exert his influence in their behalf. Schurz then tells of a Major Hoffman and Captain Spraul, both of whom were appointed aides-de-camp as a result of his influence. Schurz also mentioned an imposter who claimed to be a nobleman and officer of the *Uhlanen* of the Austrian army. This man was, however, merely a son of a washerwoman and had served as a valet to an actual uhlan officer, whose papers and uniform he had stolen. (Perhaps this was another version of the Count S story.)

Finally Schurz relates the story of another nobleman who sought his intercession. Schurz was convinced of the "genuineness" of this young man.

He was a young German count whose identity was vouched for by a member of the Prussian legation. Moreover, there was no boastfulness at all in his talk. He had a long row of ancestors, whom he traced back for several hundred years, and being greatly impressed with the importance of this fact, thought it would weigh heavily in securing him a position in our army. If he could only have an audience with the president and lay his case before him, he believed the result could not be in doubt.

He pursued me so arduously with the request for a personal introduction to Mr. Lincoln, that at last I succumbed and promised to introduce him, if the President permitted. The President did permit.

The Count spoke English moderately well, and in his ingenious way he at once explained to Mr. Lincoln how high the nobility of his family was, and that they had been counts for so-and-so many centuries. "Well," Mr. Lincoln interrupted him, "that need not be in your way, if you behave yourself as a soldier." Whereupon the poor count looked puzzled, and when the audience was over, asked me what in the world the President could have meant by so strange a remark.[4]

It is quite understandable that Carl Schurz did not care to name the count in question. He was not going to embarrass him further. While not accurate in the detail regarding a post in the Union army, it is generally assumed that the reference was definitely to the young Count Ferdinand von Zeppelin, although he himself never even mentioned Schurz in this connection. But there is serious doubt that the incident ever happened, for with his superb storytelling ability and high sense of humor Count

Zeppelin surely would have enjoyed telling this amusing episode about himself.

Count Zeppelin met Lieutenant General Daniel Butterfield, chief of staff of the Army of the Potomac, who was then on a furlough in Washington and who advised him how best to get to the army in the field. Now, anxious to get to the front, the Count procured his equipment with all possible speed.

He had a tailor make him a uniform, which differed from the regulation model quite considerably, but was well adapted to the existing climate. For instance, the heavy Russian epaulettes, then part of the Prussian uniform, were eliminated entirely, and instead of the stiff gold-braided black-velvet collar a soft folding collar was substituted. On this collar the star of the rank of first lieutenant was attached. Later, the Count noted that his lieutenant's insignia was amazingly similar to that of the American general, and he was often mistaken for such an exalted officer. Although he was not prepared for such rapid advance in rank, even in America, as he later reminisced, he never changed the insignia.

To secure a suitable horse, he had the assistance of former Prussian Cavalry Guard Colonel von Radowitz who, after leaving his German post, had joined the Union army. Now he was the chief procurer of horses for that army and was said to have made a tidy fortune from that activity. Instead of the usual English saddle, Count Zeppelin chose an American wooden saddle as used by the army. He found these saddles so excellently constructed that they exerted hardly any pressure whatever. The stirrups also were different from those he was used to. They were of the Mexican style, made of wide wooden strips with a leather cap for protection. These caps had the twofold advantage of protecting against the cold and keeping twigs from getting into the stirrups when riding through thick underbrush. On his return to Germany Count Zeppelin brought his saddle with him and turned it over to the Prussian War Ministry for further study.

For the horse, Count Zeppelin needed a groom, and he found a good strong black man, Louis Taylor, who had worked for Dr. von Schleiden. Taylor proved a faithful and skilled servant. The Count liked to have the man around, although at times he felt that Taylor's prolonged presence in the small tent was unbearable.

And he engaged a cook. But later, when a battle seemed eminent, the cook suddenly disappeared, leaving that chore to Louis. Then, later, just as suddenly, the cook returned and took over his duties as if nothing had ever happened.

Before he left Washington, Count Zeppelin made the acquaintance of a person whom he considered to be one of the most interesting men in the government—the secretary of the treasury, Salmon P. Chase. At a dinner at the secretary's home, Chase told the Count in greatest detail how he had planned to pay for the war with greenbacks. Utilizing the vast silver deposits of the country, Chase intended to mint dollars and retire a greenback for every silver dollar then in circulation. However, as long as Count Zeppelin was in the United States, he never once saw a silver dollar in circulation. And since there were no smaller denominations circulating, he observed that people often used a dollar bill torn in half for exchange. In New York, he even saw street-car tokens and beer tokens used as legal tender.

Count Zeppelin boarded a small steamer to sail for the Army of the Potomac. Aboard, he found a gay group going on a visit over Sunday to friends and relatives in that army. This seemed indeed a most unusual kind of social outing to the observer. The social life he had experienced in Washington appeared hardly affected by the war, perhaps because the army was made up of enlisted civilians and not of professional soldiers. The dancing and general gaiety aboard the vessel was only briefly interrupted when the steamer met an unidentified ship crowded with casualties from the fighting front.

The steamer went as far as Aquia Creek. From there a narrow-gauge railroad train with open flatcars—the passengers sitting on the sides, their feet dangling over the edges—took Count Zeppelin into the vicinity of Falmouth, Virginia, where the army headquarters was located.

Headquarters was a huge camp in a sparsely wooded region with tents lined up in long rows. Finding it impossible to get properly oriented in this chaotic tent forest, Count Zeppelin never felt really at home in it. Since the servant and his baggage as well as an extra horse, furnished him by the government, would arrive on the following day, the Count set out to take his letter of introduction to the commander of the Army, General Joseph Hooker. But the general had gone to Washington over Sunday, and Count Zeppelin could not report to him. This made it impossible to find lodging and food for himself. Besides, his English was rather poor and he could not make himself properly understood. Finally, Captain Frederick Rosenkranz, a Swede, who understood and spoke German well, offered to share his tent.

On the very first day with the Northern army, the count experienced, what he called "the romance of war." Toward evening, when the thunder of the artillery could be heard from the direction of Rappahannock, Captain Rasdereshin, a Russian, asked the count to accompany him to the scene of firing. He offered the use of one of his horses. It was to be an impressive ride for the young German officer, to find himself in the seemingly endless forests of Virigina and to experience the baptism of fire.

Soon shells hit nearby with some regularity, to which the two men were unnecessarily exposed. They had arrived at the scene of battle and had to make a decision. Count Zeppelin suggested to the Russian that, since they really could do nothing, they had better ride a bit to a side of the established firing line from where they could also watch the affair quite well. Later he remarked that it actually took more courage to get away from the danger than to remain passively exposed to it.

Soon it became evident that no major action was going to take place and, with utter darkness approaching, the artillery firing stopped completely.

Captain Rasdereshin explained that, instead of returning to camp, he had to ride along the riverbank some distance to a small fishing shack where he had some business to attend to. He asked the Count to ride back to camp alone and to arrange things so that his own absence would not be noted. Somewhat perplexed by this odd request, Count Zeppelin said that he never overcame the suspicion that the captain, whom he really never liked, was engaged in some espionage activity.

Count Zeppelin rode off alone, along the edge of a forest, as he had been advised, and after about seven miles he came upon a line of sentries who were able to direct him to the headquarters.

It was a wonderful, starry night, but the German experienced a feeling of loneliness in this foreign land. He tried to follow the tracks of a column. In the relative darkness, he met no living creature, but fully expected to come face to face with some ferocious wild animal in this new and unknown primeval forest. Eventually he was challenged by a sentry. Replying with the parole that Rasdereshin had given him, he was told to follow some telegraph wires. He finally reached the headquarters camp and the familiar tent where Captain Rosenkranz welcomed him.

Rosenkranz was a superb-looking soldierly man with brown hair and open face, and seemed completely trustworthy. He hinted that he had connections by relationship with the Swedish royal house.

After a few days Captain Rosenkranz confided in Count Zeppelin that he had in his possession several letters with addresses and return addresses deleted, which had been given to him by the headquarters of the army for translation into English. The letters were actually for the Count from his homeland. He had longingly awaited them and had believed them lost. Many days later he received these translation copies, made by the captain, but the originals were never delivered to him.

When General Hooker returned from his short Washington trip, Count Zeppelin reported to him and presented his pass. He was well received, offered a drink of whiskey, and assigned a private tent. Count Zeppelin observed that the general seemed to have been a better drinker than an efficient army general, although he was one of the better educated officers, having attended the United States Military Academy at West Point. Because for a long period he was unable to achieve any notable military successes, General Hooker fell from the grace of the government and was recalled. There appeared but few expressions of regret.

Count Zeppelin quickly became acquainted with the headquarter's officers, usually over a drink in their tents, to which every known person walking past was generally invited. An important headquarters officer whom he got to know quite well was Lieutenant General Daniel Butterfield, whom he had already met in Washington. In private life, General Butterfield had been postmaster of San Francisco, and he was an able organizer, especially well suited for his post. Count Zeppelin later related that the general paid particular attention to the weather forecasts, and he greatly became attached of an excellent and rather costly aneroid barometer that the Count had purchased in London before he sailed for America.

The general had first seen the barometer in the German officer's tent and was so enthralled that he quickly borrowed it to keep in his own tent for better observation. Eventually, when Count Zeppelin left the army, he asked Butterfield for the return of the instrument, but as on previous occasions, the general found an excuse to postpone the return. Finally, when the Count strongly insisted, the general went to get the barometer, while the Count waited in his own tent. After a long time, when the general did not return, Zeppelin went to get the barometer himself. He then discovered that Butterfield had left with the instrument, apparently by crawling through the rear end of the tent. Anyway, his barometer was never recovered, the Count said.

Count Zeppelin also became acquainted with the General Quartermaster, Colonel Dickinson, another West Point graduate, who was a sober, solemn, and friendly officer. Able officers were Captain Russel and Captain Dahlgreen, the son of Admiral Dahlgreen of the Confederate forces. Here, as in many instances, one member of the family fought for one side while another was in the service of the other. After having been severely wounded, Captain Russel was sent to Newport to recuperate, where Count Zeppelin saw him again. Soon after that, Russel returned to the saddle and before long was killed while leading his cavalry regiment into battle.

At many of these congenial get-togethers with other officers, usually in their own tents, the talk over a drink would be of personal experiences rather than of exploits or strategy in the war. Light, funny stories and anecdotes were the rule; the story of two spies caught at Rappahannock often made the rounds. Count Zeppelin also like to repeat it often: One of the captured spies was a Yankee, the other a German. Both men had been quickly court-martialed and sentenced to death. They were to be executed by hanging from a sturdy branch of a tree extending over a rushing stream. The idea was to cut the branch with the dead victim dangling on it, so that a burial would become unnecessary. The Yankee offered his last five dollars to the executioners, pleading, "For God's sake, use a bad rope." Sure enough, the rope broke easily, and the Yankee spy being a good swimmer, saved himself by swimming vigorously across the river to the friendly shore and to safety. When the German saw that, he begged the soldiers to use an extra strong rope for him, because he could not swim a stroke.

The commissary tent was a popular meeting place for officers. At one time Count Zeppelin met there, standing on a barrel of beer, a short captain of the Volunteer Artillery of New York, dressed informally in straw shoes, short pants made of ticking, and a wide-brimmed hat; he was holding a filled glass and making an inflammatory speech in broken English for the Union cause. Upon closer inspection, Count Zeppelin recognized him as a former First Lieutenant von Kusserow, who had entertained him most cordially in 1857 in Ehrenbreitstein and Koblenz. Now the German was serving the American North. Many years later, both officers met again in Berlin, then both in the Prussian service.

One day, Count Zeppelin rode to visit the headquarters of the Eleventh German Division at Fairfax Court House, commanded by General Schurz: to Germans known as the liberator of the poet and art historian Gottfried Kinkel. Schurz tried to appear every inch a soldier, which he decidedly was not. He liked to stand, posed in a theatrical manner with his wide overcoat draped over his arm in typical soldierly fashion, perhaps to cover up his ignorance of military matters. At any event, the officers under his command held no high opinion of him.

Schurz invited the Count to join him at his staff meeting and at the dinner, where, with the general presiding, military operations were openly discussed. At the meeting, the commanding general stated in a rather pathetic manner, Count Zeppelin noted, some of his proposed activities for the next day. He summed up what would happen to the Northern armies and what his own orders would be. Then a young officer from across the table called: "But General, that is nonsense. You wouldn't do such a foolish thing."

Count Zeppelin was stunned at such shameful insubordination. It could never have happened in the Prussian army. General Schurz merely joined the laughter that greeted the outburst, and the entire matter was settled with a loud laugh. The young officer, named Dilger, had been only a junior lieutenant in the Baden army in Germany before enlisting in the Union forces, where he now commanded a battery. Riding a white charger, Dilger had made a name for daring bravery for himself and had earned the title of "White Horse Harry."

One day, intelligence reports reached headquarters that General Robert E. Lee had begun to march with the left wing of his troops in a northwesterly direction. The Army of the Potomac was ordered to follow that line in a parallel march so that it would remain between the enemy troops and the northern cities: Washington, Philadelphia, and New York. On that move, while the infantry troops and the artillery stopped to build a bridge to span a river of several-hundred feet, members of headquarters swam their horses across. This in itself was not a too unusual practice, the Count observed, except that the *Höchstkommandierente,* the highest commander, himself also did it.

After a strenuous march the troops reached Fairfax Court House in the afternoon. Here, dispatches told them that Lee's army had already solidly entrenched itself northwest of Manassas Gap.

General Alfred Pleasonton, who was with his cavalry unit at Aldie, about twenty miles away, was ordered to make an accurate reconnaissance and ascertain details on the enemy. An officer was selected to take these orders to the general. A detachment of covering cavalry was given to him. Count Zeppelin asked to be allowed to accompany this small group, and his request was granted.

Toward evening, the column rode off, and soon the darkness became so thick that one could not even see his own hand in front of him, let alone the ill-defined narrow lane in the dense forest. The riders let the horses find the path, being glad that their steeds were quite adept at that task. Soon they came to a most difficult spot where branches of low trees and brush hit the riders in the face, where the horses stumbled over fallen tree trunks, and where the extremely rough going made the progress slow and painful. Somehow they got ahead and kept together.

When the column returned by the same route two days later, the explanation became evident. In the darkness they had crossed a tough barricade built by the enemy troops, and now in the daylight they were convinced that horses could never cross those obstacles. In the dark of night this impossible terrain had been overcome, but that day they decided to ride around the obstruction.

At about three o'clock in the morning the column arrived at Aldie, solidly occupied by the cavalry troops of General Pleasonton. After a considerably long search, the officer carrying the dispatch finally located an adjutant, lying on a cot fully dressed in his uniform with boots with spurs. When the adjutant left to take the officer to the

general, Count Zeppelin promptly fell down on the bed to sleep until four o'clock when the troop started to move.

Major General Pleasonton was an excellent, vigorous, and militarily well-educated leader. He was also a graduate of West Point. But outwardly the general did not at all look like a good soldier, because some two years before at the outbreak of the war, he had vowed not to cut his hair until the rebels would have been beaten. Now his long hair hung down in fancy curls, way over his collar.

On 9 June, the general told Count Zeppelin that he had made contact with the cavalry of the Confederate army under the command of the daring leader General J.E.B. Stuart. Stuart, a former Austrian officer, held Ashby's Gap. The plan was to attack Stuart hard, so as to get a view into the Shenandoah Valley, where Pleasonton expected to see enemy columns poised to march against the Northern armies.

Contact with the enemy was quickly made. Both cavalry groups advanced under the protection of their own artillery. Then regiments from both sides attacked with loud yelling, first riding in a trot. At a certain distance giving their horses the spurs, which were attached to their left boots only, they rode at full gallop into each other's lines. The cavalrymen fought each other furiously with drawn sabers, then withdrew in groups briefly, only to reassemble and attack again. The many head-wounds sustained attested to the fierceness of the battle.

The attack was repeated several times, until the general retreat of the Southern troop behind a shelter made by a small river. Artillery and infantry held that section and fired from fixed positions.

Count Zeppelin had taken part in the attack. Riding at the extreme end of the right wing, he got into the enemy lines, turned around to escape, but was followed by a troop of riders of the rebels. Luckily his horse was faster than those of his pursuers, and the revolver shots sent after him did not hit him. This was to him most welcome, he said, and while he would have liked to have made some studies of the army of the South, it would have been highly doubtful that his angry captors would have let him do so. Most likely they would have either shot him or hung him to a tree right there, although he did not use his sword, and even secretly carried, sewn into his inside coat pocket, a

Count Zeppelin, kneeling in center, with a group of Union army officers of the Army of the Potomac. Photographed by Alexander Gardner. (Courtesy, Library of Congress)

letter of recommendation to General Lee, given to him by the general's charming niece whom he had met in Philadelphia.

General Pleasonton moved then with his staff to a lower spot to find a suitable place for the crossing of the river. Some of the officers he had sent away with messages. When he again tested the river for a suitable fording place, most of his staff had found it prudent to lag behind. Count Zeppelin, seeing this, rode up to the general and explored the section of the river, not having the modesty to suppress his military eagerness, although he was to be purely a spectator and was not to partake whatever in any action of military nature. However, the general was so pleased with the active participation that he asked the Count,

through other parties, to enter into the services of the Northern States and to personally become his adjutant.

After crossing the narrow river, the retreating enemy forces were relentlessly trailed, and after passing through Middleburg from a northerly direction the cavalry troops reached Ashby's Gap. However, a forcing of that pass was impossible, for the running battle had already lasted some nine hours. It had been the largest purely cavalry battle of the entire war.

With the troop returned to the bivouac area, Count Zeppelin rode alone over the battle area to Aldie. He had not eaten anything since leaving Fairfax Court House. He was so hungry and exhausted that he did not pay any attention to the moans of a man who had been left in a ditch, assumed dead by the medical men. After riding with dulled senses a distance further, he realized eventually what he had done and rode back to the wounded soldier, whom he promised to send help.

Arriving at dusk at Aldie, Count Zeppelin found that the troops he had joined that morning had retreated to Fairfax Court House. Since Aldie was completely out of provisions, only a glass of milk was available to him. Finally, at Fairfax Court House, his trusted black servant, Louis, fixed some simple pancakes for him. The Count could not recall that he had ever eaten anything in his life with such eagerness as those hotcakes, taking them out of the pan and swallowing them practically without chewing. While Louis was busy with the next batch of pancakes, Count Zeppelin ate a piece of bread; he was never so famished.

Count Zeppelin told of no other battle experience of his. This, seemingly, was the only brief encounter he had with enemy troops, and typically, it involved one of the finest cavalry units of the whole war period, the command of the dreaded "Jeb" Stuart.

In the *Photographic History of the Civil War,* there is a photograph taken by Braden, showing Count Zeppelin standing with papers in his hand under a large shade tree and talking to Captain Rosenkranz. Other officers relaxing in front of them on the ground are Colonel Dickinson, Colonel Ulric Dahlgreen of General George Meade's staff, and Major Ludlow, who commanded the Colored Brigade. The location of the photograph is not identified, but the text indicates that it depicted the group "gathered together in an idle hour to chat about the strategy of the war." Count Zeppelin, it suggested, was "then on a visit to America to observe the Civil War."

Apparently Count Zeppelin left the Army of the Potomac when General Hooker resigned his command on 28 June 1863. To his father the count wrote that when his own horse had begun to limp badly and he had to turn in his army horse, he felt it reason enough to leave. He returned to New York. He told of having witnessed the draft riots there on 13 to 15 July, when about one thousand people were killed in New York and Boston. The Congress had voted the first conscription act on 3 March, drafting all men between the ages of twenty and forty-five, unless exempted by paying three hundred dollars for a substitute.

Count Zeppelin stayed in New York for a day or so, and then took a train for the West.

3

EXPLORING VIA TRAIN, BOAT, AND BALLOON

From Detroit, Michigan, Count Zeppelin wrote to his "Beloved Father" on 24 July 1863 that he wanted to gather as many actual impressions as possible of the cultural history of this part of the world.

He described three impressions in detail, calling them his "real-life pictures." His first picture was an observation at a railroad station. Through the window of his compartment he saw two Indian girls of about twelve to fifteen years of age and a small boy offering beadwork for sale from a small basket. Count Zeppelin had seen Greeks, Turks, Chinese, Negroes, and mulattoes, but never a human being belonging to a "savage" tribe, and he was astounded at the great difference in appearance, a truly startling one at first sight.

These Indian children were neither ugly nor overly tall, nor were their faces disfigured by tattooing, as he fully expected. All three were well-proportioned, their height being equal to that of other children at the same age. Large deep dark eyes sparkled from copper brown and rather pretty faces, with a friendly and astonishingly intelligent expression. An unmistakable stamp of the wilderness was evident in the children, and the Count speculated as to what it may have been. "Give a tame and a wild pigeon to a man who had seen neither before, and would he perhaps take one for the other? Certainly not."

The second impression occurred while the train traveled through a dense, seemingly impassable forest area. There the Count saw, in an open spot, a man with his axe trimming long trunks of felled trees, which he would use to build a protective fence for his livestock, straight through the dense forest jungle. Further on, Count Zeppelin noted such fences surrounding partially cleared openings in the forest, with only tree stumps left standing a few feet off the ground, and where oxen, cows, and sometimes horses were grazing. Next came a plot completely stripped of all timber, with a small wooden house standing in the middle of it. Depending on the size of the lot, usually there were one or even more small wooden barns or sheds. Fields of maize and potatoes surrounded these out-buildings, but usually only small areas were given to wheat and grain. These individual European settlers had thus started to till the ground for production.

The third real-life picture involved the cities of Buffalo, Erie, Cleveland, Toledo, and Detroit, all of which were regular stopping places for the train. These towns had come into existence as if by magic during the very recent past, mainly to satisfy the demands of traffic on the great waterways. Even the small streams, which looked like tributaries on the maps, were actually large deep rivers joined by canals with the Ohio and the Mississippi

River system, and even with the Hudson River. Around the original locations of a few fishing and boating shacks, workshops and stores had been built. Then came the railroad lines, generally a single track with a discarded car serving as a station, some still in use in the smaller places. Larger railroad depots were recently built on slender pilings over the edge of the water. Boats and trains carried goods to and from the depots in all directions. These depots were now flanked by big buildings with large painted signs advertising the great bargains offered.

Count Zeppelin particularly mentioned Buffalo, which he remembered mainly for the good strong beer he sampled at the brewery of Albert Ziegele. "Reminiscent of Drake's rarest brew! It was heady stuff, and I was not accustomed to it. It made my knees so wobbly that I had to sit down on a sofa to rest, and a guest took advantage of my condition and made off with my umbrella," he told Karl H. von Wiegand in 1915.

He visited the magnificent Niagara Falls. As he told later, he crossed to the Canadian side for a better look at the really spectacular sight "of the full circle of the rainbow of the mist." Below the American falls he swam across the still rapidly running stream, and this daring deed years later gave rise to exaggerated stories by Markus Werder who told of the Count's truly death-defying heroic feat of having crossed the falls at their actual tumultuous drop.

The train ran along the southern and western shores of Lake Erie. The lake was so large that Zeppelin could not see the opposite shore, and he found the sight rather dull and uninteresting, not at all as powerfully attractive as the open sea. Yet he liked the idea that it seemed actually endless. Then they crossed an almost open plains area.

Toledo, Count Zeppelin recalled, was founded from two villages, and so named in 1837. Now it was one of the major markets for farm produce. The principal goods were copper, iron, fruit, and an enormous amount of maize, coal, wood, salt, flour, and timber.

Cleveland, a city since 1796, had a population of sixty thousand, with many attractive houses of wealthy merchants, many good schools, and numerous stylish churches, but it lacked the cozy character of German towns.

The journey had taken three days, but despite the uniformity of the landscape it had not been monotonous. The Count was greatly impressed by the grandeur of the American continent. After traveling so long at the speed of an American locomotive, he felt that this could go on and on and that there was really no end to it all. But he realized how this flat open country was mercilessly exposed to the storms born in the Gulf of Mexico, which would rage unhindered northward until they finally died over the ice fields of the north. Still, Count Zeppelin found it all exceedingly interesting, and he wrote that "this is definitely more impressive than the stretch from Biberach to Ravensburg."

At Detroit, the Zeppelin party, which included the Russians Davidow and Ponomarew, boarded the steamer *Traveller* to explore Lake Huron and Lake Superior. The steamship, built in 1852, and known for its elegant accommodations, speed, safety, and gentlemanly officers, ran regularly between Detroit, Michigan, and Superior, Wisconsin, on "a grand excursion to the romantic regions of Lake Superior."

When the steamer stopped at Ontonagon, Michigan, on 1 August 1863, the local *Lake Superior Miner* reported that every stateroom was occupied, and among the passengers were counts, consuls, and other foreigners. The trip was memorable for an incident that Count Zeppelin recalled years later, as reported in the *St. Paul Daily News* of 9 February 1915. He flirted there "with some beautiful American girls, who were as anxious to get acquainted with me as I was with them. They finally broke the ice by flipping apple seeds into my face, and then we had a jolly talk."[1]

To his father, however, Count Zeppelin wrote that he felt enormously well and had gained some weight. He also mentioned some impressions during that lake trip. "Usually one comes upon a settlement in a charming harbor," he wrote, "where nature has provided vast areas of densely growing grass." He could see some large buildings where cast-iron was worked and the metal washed and melted. A few simple dwellings were generally also there, always with a church. This, to the Count, was the real wilderness, a thousand miles from civilization, yet he found it not entirely uncivilized nor wild. "Here man has discovered beneath the unproductive soil exciting treasures of iron, copper, and silver," he observed.

Count Zeppelin visited at Pere Marquette and stayed briefly in Superior. Some of his friends there suggested that the name of the town be changed in his honor. However, this movement was of such minor proportions that the *Superior Chronicle* never mentioned it in its pages in 1863.

From Superior the party planned to travel with two Indian guides up the St. Louis River by canoe to explore the source of the Mississippi, then on to St. Paul. Their excess baggage was to be shipped by boat to Chicago, which the party hoped to reach after stopovers at La Crosse, Madison, and Milwaukee. The trip was to take two weeks, but it was eighteen days later when the Count wrote again to his father.

"The time of remarkable and delightful events were troubled by the thought of leaving you for so long without news," he wrote. While at the edge of the wilderness, three weeks before, he had encountered his last mail carrier, an Indian paddling down the swift St. Louis River, whose speed and haste were such that he did not hear the calls and almost capsized the Count's light birchbark canoe and his party.

At Crow Wing they had seen the last newspaper, and the Count read that Russia had given such a sharp answer to a note by Austria, France, and England that these powers were forced to present an ultimatum. Count Zeppelin wrote, "Indeed Russia cannot and will not retract. With the delays of diplomacy, I do not see how war can break out before next spring, as much as they [Petersburg] would like it. God grant that you may laugh at my political observation!"

(The affair had developed because Napoleon III had intervened in behalf of the Poles who had started an insurrection in January 1863 against Russia. Count Zeppelin was anxious to know the outcome of this exchange of communications, which seemed to lead to war. If so he had to get back into service for his country. Instead, for an entire month he was totally uninformed on this tense situation, except for the reports in the press. Eventually, when Napoleon withdrew his support for the Polish revolutionaries, the Russians quickly squelched the uprising, and the "inevitable" war never developed.)

Regarding the war in America between the states, Count Zeppelin wrote that it was indeed difficult to judge the matter when his father suggested that perhaps a peace settlement with the help of European influence could be worked out between the fighting states. "A reconciliation

Drawing by Count Zeppelin of Minnesota route (Courtesy Minnesota Historical Society).

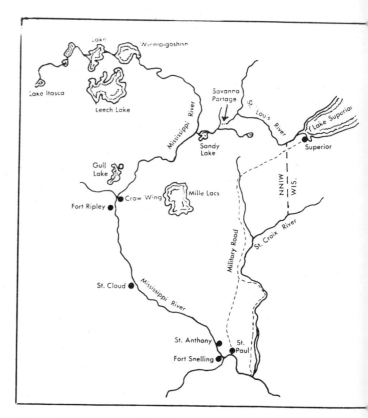

Map of Minnesota, visited by Count Zeppelin (Courtesy Minnesota Historical Society).

cannot be thought of yet," Count Zeppelin believed.

The only thing which could bring about a quick ending would be an uprising of the blacks, or possibly a war with England, and so on. If no such unforeseen powerful events should occur, the war would be prolonged without important decisions until November of next year, when a new president and along with him a new era in politics will emerge from the contest between the parties in the North. Either a more determined war strategy will then come, which would give the already weakened South the last blow; or concessions will be made to the secessionists. In any case it will still be a long, long way to a solution of the troubles underlying this war.[2]

From the St. Louis River to the Mississippi, the party took the historic Savanna portage route, used by fur traders and Indians alike ever since the earliest times. Seasoned frontiersmen could travel it in about five days. But in 1863 this overland route was little used anymore because of the opening of the much shorter and better military road five years before. According to reports of the time, the summer of 1863 was one of the driest in the upper Midwest region, and low water probably made the route more difficult by necessitating longer portages. The Old Savanna Portage was widely known by travelers as one of the worst in the entire region because of its length, mud, and mosquitoes.

To his father, Count Zeppelin wrote:

I regret I can not give you a description of our fortnight in the wilderness— the experiences are too many, the impressions too varied! There is the feeling you have when you know you are all alone in the midst of primitive, unspoiled nature. You can laugh, cry, shout, shoot, throw yourself into the rushing current of a river; you can set fire to the woods, and no human soul cares about it. You are all alone with the Creator in his magnificent temple.

There is the soil on which you walk, the vegetation, the animal life inhabiting the woods — from the bear to the much much worse mousquitos (sic). There is the strange way of traveling by canoe, and when the highest ridge of land is reached, of carrying it across over your head. There is the rocky island in the midst of a rushing stream, as described by [James Fenimore] Cooper in his novels, and the stillness of a lake on whose shore the Indian erects his fleeting wigwam. The swampy savanna is there with its high grass. There are the hardships of the march: heat; thirst, when water is lacking because of the unusual drought; hunger, when ammunition and provisions come to an end. Because of the lowest water ever, we traveled at a slower pace than planned.[3]

Even after the group had reached their destination, the Russian companions still claimed that muskrat was a fine dish, but for his part, Count Zeppelin had failed to enjoy the *Wasserratten* (water rats).

The party had traveled through thick forests on Indian paths not wider than a hand, and only a skilled eye could detect them. Above all, there were the Indians themselves, their peculiar ways and strange customs, their wild calls and songs, their strange war stories, their dwellings, their phenomenal skills. One of the guides had shot a duck in flight at sixty paces with one shot and one bullet. "And what is more," the Count wrote, "there is the language which can create the word *schingkubabo* for eggs." (But the actual Chippewa word for it was *wanan,* according to Frederick Baraga, in his 1853 *Dictionary of the Otchipwe Language,* or *wahwun,* as Edward F. Wilson heard it and stated in his *The Ojebway Language* of 1874.) At a camp of Chippewa Indians, the exploring party watched a war dance performed to celebrate a victorious fight with the Sioux.

Where they came onto the Mississippi, after crossing Sandy Lake and canoeing down a small stream, they found the river to be rather wide but shallow. Soon they came to Crow Wing, a small settlement of about two hundred people, most of whom traded with the Indians. They found a tavern, but its dilapidated condition caused them to prefer sleeping in the open. In fact, during the entire trip Count Zeppelin had slept ten full weeks outside a house — three on boats and railroads, four in tents, and three under the open sky — as he wrote to his father at home.

The party of explorers then traveled from Crow Wing to St. Anthony by stagecoach, passing Fort Ripley and St. Cloud on the Mississippi River. The trip took two days, and in order to see the famed Minnehaha Falls and Fort Snelling before reaching their destination, they hired a carriage to take them to St. Paul. According to the *Minneapolis Journal,* the entire trip had taken twenty-one days.

Count Zeppelin registered on 17 August at the International Hotel in St. Paul. Among the fifty-six guests registered that day, as reported in the daily newspapers, the *Pioneer* listed a "Count Reppelin" and the *Press* a "Zepperlin." His companions signed as "Mr. Donsemaren, Russia," and "Mr. Dauydan, Washington."

In a letter to his father, on stationery of the

International Hotel, on 18 August 1863, the Count wrote that he had made the acquaintance of a Professor Steiner, "the famed aeronaut," who had invented a new kind of balloon suitable for army reconnaissance.

A portion of flat ground across from the four-story brick hotel on Seventh Street and Jackson was closed off by this traveling balloonist. The title "Professor" was purely ornamental, the usual one bestowed on such persons at that time. John H. Steiner, of Philadelphia, was a well-known balloonist, having survived a narrow escape from drowning in Lake Erie in 1857. He had also engaged in a balloon race with the Frenchman Eugene Godard in Cincinnati in 1858, and he made the first ascension from Toledo the following year. In 1861 Steiner joined the balloon corps of Thaddeus S.C. Lowe and served along the upper Potomac, at Cairo, and on Island 10 in the Mississippi, below Cairo. In December 1862, Steiner, who, as was Lowe, a civilian employed by the Union army, left the corps because of delays in receiving his compensation. As a traveling balloonist, Aeronaut Steiner had contracted with the town to make a series of ascensions, including one "grand, or cloud" flight, and a number of lesser "army flights" for the enjoyment "of ladies and gentlemen who wished to make short aerial trips of one thousand feet in the air." The contract fee usually defrayed the actual expenses, and a small admission was charged to enter the enclosure to view the balloon. Passage was five dollars per flight.

The balloonist made several ascensions but experienced some difficulties with the gas supply. On 19 August, with fair weather, twenty ascensions were made, but on each the balloon could take only one passenger aloft instead of the usual four to six persons. The corpulent governor, Alexander Ramsey, proved too heavy even for that, permitting the balloon to rise but a few feet off the ground. Instead, the ten-year-old daughter Marion went aloft; fifty years later, as Mrs. C.E. Furness, she remembered "how horrified my mother was on learning that my father had permitted me to go up in the balloon." After that, Steiner allowed "some single ascensions made, the ascensionists taking the responsibility on their own shoulders. Of course, Captain Steiner gave them all the necessary information as to the conduct of the balloon."

As Count Zeppelin recalled later, the next day, 20 August, captive flights were resumed, but the gas supply became so exhausted that even the empty basket could not be lifted off the ground. Steiner, as well as the newspapers reporting it, were utterly disgusted with the gas-company officials and their failure to furnish sufficient gas to ensure a successful demonstration flight. The balloon required forty-one-thousand feet of gas, but the gas works could supply only thirty-six-thousand feet.

Incurring a loss of three to four hundred dollars, Steiner deflated his balloon bag and traveled to Grand Rapids to assist another aeronaut. When a reporter saw the professor later at La Crosse, Wisconsin, he wrote that "he had just received twelve barrels of iron filings and was busy in arranging his machinery to make hydrogen gas. He is not going to depend on gas companies as he did once."

Later, Steiner actually patented several improvements in gas generators, but as the reporter observed, "it will be many a long day, I fear, ere we will have any more attempts at aerostation in St. Paul."

Count Zeppelin did not fly an experimental balloon in a daring maneuver off the tower at Fort Snelling, nor did he barnstorm under the alias "Count Steiner" with such a contraption as a daring aeronaut, as some writers have suggested. He did ascend in a balloon, however, and he later stated: "While I was above St. Paul, the idea of aerial navigation was strongly impressed upon me, and it was there that the first idea of my zeppelins came to me."

About the actual details, the Count was a bit vague when he stated in an interview to von Wiegand in 1915 that:

I made my first balloon ascension at St. Paul, and not on the civil war firing line, as has been frequently said. A major of the Union Army, whose name I have forgotten, was there and had a captive balloon. I wanted a real sensation and arranged for the use of the balloon, he to cut the rope and me to make a long flight, after I had gotten up the limit.

I bought all the spare gas that the St. Paul gas works would let me have and was able to get up several hundred feet, but gas was of such poor quality that I could not get the bag filled sufficiently to essay a long flight.[4]

Count Zeppelin had ascended with Steiner to an

altitude of some six or seven hundred feet, finding the ground exceptionally well suited for demonstrating the importance of the balloon in military reconnaissance. Apparently, the balloonists could see the entire Mississippi Valley below them from the vantage point over St. Paul, built on a bluff overlooking the vast expanse of the river basin.

The Count observed that the ridge of hills running parallel with the river formed an excellent defensive position against an aggressor marching up through the valley. From the high position of the balloon, the defender's troops could completely be surveyed. Should one wish to harass the troops with artillery fire, the battery could be informed by telegraphic signals where their projectiles should hit. In fact, such a technique had been used with great success by the army. No method was better suited for viewing quickly the terrain of unknown enemy-occupied regions.

John Steiner had made several flights while with the Union armies, and especially at Edward's Ferry, Maryland, where he had been able to move over the entire enemy position, and through good binoculars could recognize every single man. Smaller bodies of troops, hidden in thick forests, could remain undiscovered by the balloonist, and a strong wind could easily endanger such a reconnaissance flight. But the aeronaut had already planned for an improved design, giving the balloon a very long thin shape and reducing the capacity until it would be just enough to lift two persons. With the addition of a strong rudder, the balloon would be hindered less by the winds and could reach its destination more smoothly and more securely. However, such an improved design was not yet created; it existed only in the mind of Steiner, as the count duly reported in a letter to his father.

The Union army had a regular unit to operate its two balloons attached to General George C.

The *Intrepid,* the Union army observation balloon, is being inflated at Gaines Mill, Virginia. (Courtesy, Library of Congress).

McClellan's Army Corps. Consisting of about fifty men, the group was in charge of the two generators, drawn by four horses each, the two balloons, also drawn by four horses each, and the acid cart, drawn by two horses. The two balloons took about three hours to inflate, holding respectively thirteen-thousand and twenty-six-thousand cubic feet of gas. Captain Lowe had introduced balloon observations and had accomplished some truly remarkable ascents. He also had remarkable experiences, as that at Fair Oaks on 31 May 1862.

The captain found it impossible to ascend with the smaller *Constitution* because the lifting power was not strong enough to carry the heavy telegraph equipment needed for successful communication to the ground force. Lowe wrote:

I was at my wit's end as to how I could best save an hour's time, the most precious and important hour of all my experience in the army. I saw the two armies coming together nearer and nearer and there was no time to be lost. It flashed through my mind that if I could get the gas which was in the smaller *Constitution* into the larger *Intrepid,* which was then half filled, I would save an hour's time, and to us that time was worth a million dollars a minute.[5]

Captain Lowe finally used a ten-inch camp kettle with the bottom cut out, through which he transferred the gas from the smaller to the larger balloon.

The Confederate army had only one balloon, made entirely out of silk dresses donated by southern ladies. General James Longstreet wrote about it:

We had no gas except in Richmond, and it was the custom to inflate the balloon there, tie it securely to an engine, and run it down the York River Railroad to any point at which we desired to send it up. One day it was on a steamer on the James River when the tide went out and left the vessel and the balloon high and dry on a bar. The Federals gathered it in and with it the last silk dress in the Confederacy.[6]

Count Zeppelin stopped briefly in Milwaukee on his return east, where he noticed many homes flooded because of the extremely high water in Lake Michigan.

Chicago he found to be:

living evidence of the fast, powerful development of the West. Thirty years ago there was nothing here, today the city numbers more than 160,000 inhabitants. Railroads and canals cross the bustling streets in all directions. The characteristics of a higher level of civilization are more plentiful here than in other places newly created by commerce. In Chicago churches, theaters, museums, large hotels, and splendid stores are numerous. Only art does not set up its workshop amid the hurrying and the pushing; the Yankee's heart has no room for it![7]

When he arrived in New York, Count Zeppelin had gone from Chicago to Cincinnati, Harpers Ferry, Baltimore, and Philadelphia, "all beautiful and noteworthy places." Letters, long awaited from home, were to be held for him by Leopold Bierwirth, the German consul, but he found none there. He was most anxious to know if Russia's reply had caused his furlough to be canceled and if he had to return to his military post at once.

From New York the Count wrote that he had found America to be definitely a land of tremendous contrasts. A strange peculiarity was that while everything aristocratic seemed definitely opposed to the fundamental ideas of the country, he believed that nowhere else was as much fuss made over the travels of a simple count. At every stop, people rushed to be the first with an invitation, and if he accepted, often a large gathering, appearing in frock coats and low-cut dresses, came to take a look at "this wonderful little monster." It was easy to reconstruct the entire journey through America as a distinguished foreigner from the newspaper files.

Another peculiar American characteristic was that while in Europe, people generally speculated in making a good match; "here in America they speculated in everything but that," he wrote. While the ability to make a profit when dealing with others is a concern of vital importance, the Count found from his own experience, and confirmed by others, that "nowhere in the world is so much reliance placed on the word of a man in business matters."

Count Zeppelin remained in the United States for another two months. He traveled to Newport, Rhode Island, where he remained for some time, and returned at least once to Washington. The French ambassador gave him permission to travel aboard the French gunboat *Tisiphone* to

Charleston, South Carolina, where he observed the military operations of blockading that important port. On 31 October, the Count reached New York aboard the steamer *Arago;* nineteen days later, on 18 November 1863, he sailed for Europe on the Cunard liner *China.*

Tensions had abated, and no war had resulted from the Polish situation, but three years later the Austrian War and in 1870 the Franco-Prussian War were to break out.

4

THE CRAZY COUNT

The twenty-six-year-old Count Ferdinand von Zeppelin returned to his army post and reluctantly adjusted himself to the daily routine of dull army life in peacetime.

When in 1866, war between Austria and Prussia broke out, the Count saw at last a promise of some exciting activity. The rulers of the smaller German states feared to support Prussia lest they strengthen it and greatly impair their own sovereignty in a regenerated Germany. Thus, Bavaria, Baden, Saxony, Hannover, and Württemberg joined the Austrian side in the conflict.

In March Count Zeppelin was promoted to captain and became a personal adjutant to King Karl I of Württemberg. In this position he took part at a relative safe distance in the minor battles of Tauberbischofsheim and Würzburg.

During the battle of Aschaffenburg, however, the adjutant saw some action. An important message had to be carried to the headquarters of the Hessian army, encamped across the Main River. The bridges at Aschaffenburg and Stockstadt were in the hands of the enemy, and it seemed impossible to cross the fast-flowing swollen river by boat. On 14 July Count Zeppelin was ordered to investigate and to find a way to get the message across, if indeed there was a way to do so.

As the Count told of the exploit later:

I had accepted the order to establish some communication between the Hessian and the Württemberg armies. I had galloped along the banks of the river despite intense heat. My horse collapsed. I was wearing the heavy uniform and high riding boots. As there was no other way of conveying the message, I jumped into the stream to swim across. An entire enemy brigade passed by. The current was very strong, and in midstream I was completely exhausted and sank to the river bed but kicked myself up to the surface again and caught my breath. I believed that my last hour had come. I continued these efforts, and after sinking several times, finally reached the opposite shore and shallow water.[1]

As an afterthought, he added, "Even in drinking water, a person should use moderation."

After delivering the dispatch to the Hessian headquarters, Count Zeppelin returned to his own command post in the same manner. Taking off his heavy boots and uniform would have eased this so strenuous undertaking considerably, but apparently it never occurred to him. It certainly would have been most unbecoming to an officer.

When the king heard of this act of daring, he congratulated the Count on his bravery and courage in the face of such danger and awarded him the high order, the Württemberg Knight's Cross of Military Merit.

Before any important battles in this war developed, on 3 July, the illustrious Prussian strategist Count Helmuth von Moltke engaged the Austrian army at Königgrätz in Bohemia and utterly crushed it. A truce followed, and the war was over in August.

Seemingly there was little or no animosity between the opposing powers in this war, for shortly thereafter Crown Prince Wilhelm of Württemberg was sent by his father on 22 March 1867 to serve for a year as a lieutenant in the Prussian Guard. The guard was an elite regiment elevated to this special honor by King Friedrich the Great, and it was the custom for young officers of the nobility to fill the several posts available. As crown prince, Wilhelm was, of course, entitled to have a captain as his personal adjutant, and the choice of Count Zeppelin seemed indeed a happy one.

Life in Potsdam consisted of the usual rounds of dull barracks duties, or the uninteresting mess-table conversations with fellow officers. Even the social activities, receptions, and dances at the elegant palaces there or at Berlin bored Count Zeppelin, and he soon procured an appointment to the superb Prussian General Staff at Berlin to do special work.

This new appointment took him to the headquarters in the capital several times a week, away from guard routine. It also allowed him to attend all military maneuvers in various parts of the country. At one of the Bavarian maneuvers, held late in 1867 at Lechfeld near Augsburg, Count Zeppelin had a narrow escape.

While riding across the rough country with a distant cousin, who was a general, the two horsemen got into a swampy area. A farmer in the field nearby tried frantically to warn the officers that this particular swamp they were heading for was dangerous and that they must ride around the section. Despite this warning, Count Zeppelin rode on and urged his horse to jump, but the animal was unable to clear the wide ditch. The front feet hit solid ground, but the rider and his mount sank into the morass. Quickly realizing his predicament, the Count pulled himself up over the head of his horse onto firm ground, and with his cousin's help was able to rescue his bogged-down animal. The older cousin admonished his foolhardy relative for this stupid stunt, but the Count merely shrugged it off. He was fast becoming known as the *verrückte Graf,*

the "crazy count," by his fellow officers, and obviously he liked it. He believed that taking chances, even foolish ones, were acts of bravery, and he gloried in them.

Upon his return to Potsdam from a short leave, Count Zeppelin surprised his comrades and close friends when he announced that he intended to marry the Freiin Isabella von Wolff, whom he had met several years before at the wedding of his brother Eberhard. Isabella was a cousin of his brother's wife and came from an old noble Latvian family of Alt Schwanenburg.

The friends of Count Zeppelin were amazed to hear this seemingly confirmed bachelor even speak of marriage because he had never displayed any particular interest in women. There appeared to be no time for romances in his life, which was taken up with travels, adventures, and daring feats. But the wedding took place on 8 July 1869.

A daughter, Helene, always called Hella, was born to the couple in 1879. In 1909 Hella married Lieutenant Alexander von Brandenstein of an old family of Hesse. At the wedding, the King of Württemberg made the bridegroom a count, and he took the name of Brandenstein-Zeppelin. Countess Hella died in December 1967 at the age of eighty-eight.

Life in the guard, even with special privileges of the general-staff activities, soon became boring to Count Zeppelin, and again he requested a transfer of duties. Because of his close family connections with the royal house of Württemberg, this was not difficult to arrange.

Thus, in 1868, the Count obtained an appointment to the Military Intelligence Department. This work gave him an opportunity to travel through certain sections of France, where he openly and most thoroughly studied the fortifications, especially of cities along its eastern border. He wrote a detailed report on his observations for the headquarters of the department. These papers were carefully filed away for future reference, and only two years later they were of tremendous importance to the German armies in the Franco-Prussian war.

With preparations for the war again going on all around him, Count Zeppelin, as aide to the king, was destined to remain in the country away from the excitement he craved. He was, in fact, ordered to stay at the royal palace at Friedrichshafen.

As he told later, while he was standing alone on

the terrace of the formal garden overlooking the lake and bemoaning the fact that as a professional soldier he was not allowed to enter into the excitement of combat, he became aware of the rustle of a silk dress behind him. He was startled to see Queen Olga, who asked him what the matter was, and he told of his misfortune. The compassionate queen arranged his immediate transfer.

Count Zeppelin reported to the general staff of the Württemberg cavalry, a part of the Third Army Corps under the command of the crown prince of Prussia. Count Zeppelin hoped for some activity, and the opportunity came quickly.

On the evening of 23 July 1870, only a few hours after the formal declaration of war, the cavalry, then stationed with a division of the Baden army at Karlsruhe, wanted a patrol to reconnoiter enemy territory. Count Zeppelin volunteered to lead a selected group of four officers and seven enlisted men.

Cavalry troops had never been used for fast reconnaissance by the Prussian army, but rather only behind columns of marching infantry. The old-fashioned use of these troops by the French army had them unattached to one of the mobilized army units near the border. Neither of these powers used cavalry troops as a separate fighting force, as Count Zeppelin had observed them in the Union army in America.

The aim of the patrol was to ascertain the scope of mobilization of the French forces close to the German border. Rumor had it that General MacMahon had amassed two or three divisions poised to attack the Pfalz (Palatinate).

The twelve horsemen set out that Sunday morning from Hagenbach, crossing the border without incident. Lieutenant Herbert Winslow, an Englishman, knew the terrain well from a previous hunting trip. The *modus operandi* of the patrol was to gallop through any hindrance that might block their way. The farmers in these small communities showed no concern over these riders, as galloping horsemen were a daily occurrence. The slight difference in the German uniforms from those of the French troops was not noticeable in the speeding riders.

The German patrol galloped through Lauterbourg, taking the few guards completely by surprise. The streets of the community were deserted, for most of the people were attending church services. The patrol cut the telephone line along their route, and rested at noon for a short time at Neuweiler where obliging farmers supplied clover for the horses and offered bread and wine to the men.

Reaching Trimbach, some ten miles inside French territory, the Germans met a French lancer patrol from Niederbronn, and a skirmish developed. Lieutenant Winslow was killed, becoming the first German casualty of the war. The horse of Count Zeppelin was injured, but the Count was able to take the mount of a local gendarme who had joined the fight.

Instead of returning to Karlsruhe after being detected by the French, the German invaders went even deeper into hostile terrain. They rested that night in the forest. When the following morning they reached Woerth, some twenty miles across the border, news of their presence had already preceeded them. Still, the reconnoitering Germans learned that only a cavalry detachment and no infantry troops were stationed in the district.

The day was exceedingly hot, and the patrol felt quite tired. Some of the officers wanted to return with what information they had gathered, but Count Zeppelin urged that they try to get more news about the French army positions.

The group stopped at the Scheuerlenhof, an inn near the village of Gundershofen, to rest their horses and to eat a hasty lunch. In their leisure, they were surprised by two French patrol squadrons. In the ensuing action, several of the Germans were killed, and the whole German patrol was thoroughly dispersed. Count Zeppelin barely escaped in the confusion.

During the fight he lost all of his maps. Now totally lost, for the next two days he rode aimlessly through the country, trying to get nearer to the border, but also trying to keep out of the way of any other patrolling French troops. Occasionally he was able to buy some milk and bread from a farmer at the edge of some settlement. Eventually, nearly exhausted, he reached the border near Schönau. Leading his tired horse by the bridle and stumbling along the narrow road, he met a Major von Friedburg, an officer on his way to join his Baden regiment, who took him into his carriage. Here, Count Zeppelin fell limply against the shoulder of his rescuer and slept for several hours.

Count Zeppelin was the only member of that patrol to return to the headquarters of his army.

All other officers and men were killed either at the Scheuerlenhof or after escaping from it. Still, the mission was considered to have been successful, and many honors were heaped upon the Count because of his bravery and cleverness in escaping when others had failed. The Württemberg Royal Cross, First Class, was awarded him for this exploit.

A lesson learned from his observations in the United States was promptly put into effect. Had the cavalry patrol carried their carbines instead of having them holstered on their mounts, the surprise at the Scheuerlenhof would not have been as devastating as it was for the unarmed Germans. Count Zeppelin also suggested that the cumbersome drum signals in the field be replaced by easier recognizable hand or saber motions.

Later in the war, during the siege of Paris, the German general staff was headquartered at Villiers. Count Zeppelin then was able to observe first hand how cleverly the besieged French military forces used free-moving balloons. Occasionally, an unfavorable wind would drive one of the balloons across the lines, and it would be captured by the Germans.

Count Zeppelin was immensely interested in this whole subject and thought much about the utilization of ballooning during the war. It seemed regrettable to him that there was but so little control of a free balloon, severely limiting it for practical military use.

The balloons employed by the French were, according to the brothers, Albert and Gaston Tissandier in *Les Ballons du Siège de Paris,* used mainly as communication between the beleaguered capital and the provinces where the main forces of the military were stationed. Often the balloons carried a large flock of carrier pigeons from Paris into the provinces; then the birds were sent flying back to Paris with messages in minute capsules attached to their legs.

Balloons played an important part in that siege, which lasted from 23 September 1870 to 28 January 1871. No fewer than sixty-four balloons left Paris, carrying 164 persons and 381 pigeons. Not all of the balloons got through safely, of course. The Prussians captured six, and an occasional one strayed far from its intended destination, as did the *Ville d'Orleans,* which rose from Paris on 21 November 1870, caught a strong wind current, and descended fifteen hours later near Christiana (now Oslo) in Norway. Another balloon was found three years later in Port Natal, Africa.

But the most fascinating balloon feat was the escape of Leon Gambetta. Then minister of war, he had counseled the cabinet to leave Paris and establish the government in a provincial city. However, the officials were fearful that their departure would allow a revolution to break out in the capital. Some government officials left to form a provisional government in Tours and to organize new resistence throughout the provinces. When such plans lagged, Gambetta decided to go to Tours himself, and on 7 October he left Paris by balloon to descend safely near Rouen. It was one of the most decisive developments of the war, and could easily have prolonged the conflict, had not the French army been defeated and destroyed at Metz on 27 October. With that substantial fort fallen, the newly created army could not come to the rescue of Paris, but Gambetta's escape was highly significant. The spectacular event made a greater impression on Count Zeppelin than did any other incident during the Franco-Prussian war.

With his regiment back in peaceful Württemberg after the war, Count Zeppelin now eagerly read all he could find about balloons and thought of how to control these free balloons. The pamphlet *Weltpost und Luftschiffahrt* (*World Post and Airship Journey*), by Heinrich von Stephan, gave the Count the final impulse to actually draw plans for his dirigible airship, as he stated in 1913.

Heinrich von Stephan was appointed general postmaster of the North German Confederation in 1870, and became minister when that position was later created. The published booklet consisted of speeches made before the Scientific Society in Berlin in 1873, in which von Stephan had summarized the development of the postal systems. He described the various means of transporting the mails (by horses, wagons, railroads, and steamships) and suggested that the experiments made with balloons and other means of flying ever since ancient times held great promise for the future. "Providence has surrounded the entire earth with navigable air. This vast ocean of air still lies empty today and wasted, and is not yet used for human transportation," von Stephan wrote.

Count Zeppelin read and reread this small booklet, and felt certain that the time would come when a steerable balloon was a reality. He drew plans of such a dirigible balloon. As he said, "My goal is clear, my calculations are correct." But he never published these goals and calculations of his dream airship.

When in 1874 Count Zeppelin had a riding accident and the sustained injuries placed him in a hospital at Strassburg, he found ample opportunity to read and to think about the balloons. His wife later stated that he first told her about plans for a rigid type airship during this hospitalization. His diary shows an entry on "balloon vehicles" on 24 April 1874.

5

AERO-PIONEERS

The end of the Franco-Prussian War in 1871 signaled the beginning of the Confederation of German States under the King of Prussia, Wilhelm I, and now kaiser of a united Germany. This political alignment also brought a new arrangement in military structures.

Captain Count von Zeppelin was assigned in 1872 to the Fifteenth Schleswig-Holstein Regiment of lancers, stationed at Strassburg. But when in 1874 he was promoted to the rank of major, he was able to arrange a transfer to his old regiment, the Twenty-sixth Dragoon Unit at Ulm. In 1882, Count Zeppelin was made a colonel and given command of the Nineteenth Uhlan Regiment at Stuttgart.

Soon after this, however, the Count became restless once more and bored with the dull routine of peacetime military duties. Through his influential connections at the court he was able to secure a transfer of service.

The king, aware of the Count's diplomatic abilities, appointed him in 1885 to be the military attache of the Württemberg legation in Berlin. After the various kingdoms, duchies, and free cities of Germany had united in the Confederation, each sent ambassadors to the capital. These representatives generally constituted the upper parliamentary house of the new empire. Count Zeppelin became a member in 1887.

A number of intellectuals and military leaders gathered at the Zeppelin home on the Vosstrasse, and the Count made the acquaintances of many great German scientists, including the leading physicist, anatomist, and physiologist Professor Hermann Ludwig Ferdinand von Helmholtz, the most illustrious of the group of scientific giants of the period.

During those years many trial balloons ascended in various parts of Europe, stimulated by the stunning use to which the French had put this unusual means of transportation. F.A. Gower, an American living in France, had steered his fish-shaped balloon in 1883 across the channel, using petroleum in a bronze steam engine developing five horsepower. Unfortunately at a later experiment Gower was drowned in that same channel, but his pioneering work left a definite impression on Count Zeppelin.

By 1884, the German army had a regular balloon detachment, and in 1887 the military budget included funds for the support of this group, consisting of a major, a captain, four lieutenants, and one regular-sized company of enlisted men.

At the start, the unit had no balloons of its own. A free balloon was leased for the weekly training periods from a lady acrobat, Kätchen Paulus, who ascended with it every Sunday in a popular outing place for Berliners: the Hasenheide. At one time, members of the general staff were invited to attend a parachute demonstration, a jump executed from a height of nine hundred feet by a daredevil who appeared daily at the vaudeville palace *Wintergarten*.

Count Zeppelin showed more interest in the activities of the French Colonel Charles Renard, who had built a steerable balloon for his government in 1884. This elongated balloon consisted of a large air sack filled with lifting gas and regulated by means of ventilators. A long wooden frame was attached to the lower portion of this balloon, holding that part quite rigid. At the end of the framework, Renard placed a large wooden screw for propulsion. However, the heavy electrical motors proved extremely cumbersome and too low in power output to propel the balloon sufficiently. Other engines, such as combustion power units, were not sufficiently developed, but they eventually promised to be lighter and more powerful. Count Zeppelin believed in the principle of rigidity in balloons, correctly speculating that otherwise they would not be steerable.

In a report on the "Possibility of Airships" to his King, Count Zeppelin as a military representative in 1887 pointed out that if airships were to be of any real value for military purposes, it would be imperative that they be maneuverable against very strong air currents. They would have to be able to remain aloft without landing for at least twenty-four hours, so that they could reach long distances and perform extensive reconnoitering missions. Such airships would be so constructed that they could carry a heavy load of men, ammunition, and supplies. These three basic demands would make necessary extensive balloon compartments for the required lifting gas. In other words, truly large airships would be needed for such purposes. The following main factor in the development of dirigible airships was the shape best suited to cut through the air. This had to be determined by experience, and ways would have to be found to rise in the air without having to throw off ballast, and to descend without having to let out and waste large quantities of expensive gas. If it were possible to solve these problems, the report continued, the importance of airships would certainly be immeasurable for the future. Not only would they become of immense value in war, but they would also be used for civil transportation. Count Zeppelin predicted that "airships could accomplish the shortest journeys across mountains, across the sea, or between any two given points. They will also be used on expeditions of discovery to the North Pole or to Central Africa."

There was no immediate reaction to this report, and it was probably filed for reference, without the king actually having seen it at all. No comments and no action were suggested by anyone.

Although Count Zeppelin had been appointed by his sovereign as ambassador plenipotentiary to Prussia, diplomacy and politics did not interest him too much. He preferred the military activity and reserved his option to join the troops in the field in event of another war. Two years later, in 1889, the Count left his diplomatic post in Berlin and in January 1890 as brigadier general took command of the Thirtieth Cavalry Brigade at Saarburg, near Trier.

Soon after the spring maneuvers of 1890, when Count Zeppelin expected to be placed in command of a division, his name was placed instead on the retired list of army officers. This totally unexpected sudden retirement was quite a blow to the fifty-two-year-old Count, for it was a rather unusual procedure for any commander to be retired immediately after the maneuvers. Speculations for this action abounded. Major August von Parseval, the builder of the airship named after him, wrote that the retirement came about because the independence and more especially the views of Count Zeppelin were not always in conformity with conventional standards, and Parseval speculated that the powers in command used this as a convenient reason to retire him.

The strong character of the Count undoubtedly often clashed with the orthodox thinking of the High Command, and it may well have been a case of insubordination that prompted the retirement. It has also been suggested that the Count insisted on applying more of his observations of the cavalry actions in the United States to his troops during the maneuver and that his superiors objected to it. But that had been twenty-seven years before, and the best practices of any army had been adopted by that time by most other armies anywhere.

The Zeppelin family moved into a comfortable, large house in the Keplerstrasse number 19 in Stuttgart and spent the greater part of the year in the Württemberg capital and the summers on their Girsberg estate on the Bodensee. What seemed a potential life of leisure for the retired general was actually the beginning of a busy activity for the airship enthusiast. He found time to read a veritable library of available published material on ballooning.

The Count found ample time to refamiliarize himself with the science of aerostatics, which deals with the balance of gaseous fluids and the equilibrium and buoyancy of bodies immersed in such fluids. While this law applies to gases and bodies at rest, these principles also rule some gases and objects in motion.

He learned, for instance, that a body submerged in air actually experiences a buoyant force that causes the body to rise. Thus, a lighter-than-air craft is able to float in the air whenever the weight of the gas container and all attached objects, plus the weight of the lifting gas, equal the weight of the displaced air. (The airship is governed by aerostatic principles, while airplanes are subject to the laws of aerodynamics.)

Count Zeppelin was well aware of the terminology of lighter-than-air craft. He read that a balloon is made of light, nonporous material filled with heated air or gas lighter than air, actually an aerostat without a propelling system of any kind.

A captive balloon is one restrained by a cable attached to the ground, while a free balloon is one whose ascent and descent can be controlled by the utilization of ballast or loss of lifting gas. It is dependent upon air currents. Observation balloons were usually captive balloons, generally manned so as to control their altitude and make the desired surveillance.

While the earliest balloons were merely spherical, the steerable types had an elongated form for improved maneuverability. Every different purpose demanded a different design the count realized.

(In later years, the captive barrage balloons, for instance, which rose and flew only as far as lift and mooring cable allowed, were in the shape of an elephant-eared bag, with a ballonet on the underside. This added scoop was designed to preserve the shape of the envelope by the pressure of the wind. The so-called kite balloons are elongated captive balloons, fitted with lobes to keep them headed into the wind and affording increased lift because of the inclination of the axis to the wind.

Sounding balloons are often small and carry instruments aloft for meteorological purposes. Some weather balloons are now made of polyethylene material and are forty-stories high. In 1947 the U.S. Navy launched its Skyhook program to study the stratosphere. In 1959 a balloon was sent up 149,000 feet to collect data on cosmic rays, and a year later a balloon satellite, Echo I, was launched into orbit around the earth to act as reflector for long-range radio signals.)

In 1670 the Jesuit Francisco Lana-Terzi of Brescia, observing that smoke or other gases lighter than air rose into the sky, reasoned that a vessel from which the air had been removed would also rise and even carry something aloft. He conceived a vehicle consisting of four copper balls from which all air had been removed, the balls thus actually weighing less than the air they would displace. Theoretically correct but never tested by Lana because of his religious convictions, the device actually would have been too heavy to lift off the ground. A substance lighter than air would have to be used to accomplish liftoff. (The Archimedic physical law of fluids applies also to balloons, or airships. They can carry the difference between their own weight and the weight of the air they displace. To fly at any desirable altitude, their weight must be considerably less than the weight of the air they displace. This difference is called "free lift." A cubic meter of air weighs normally

Professor Lowe observing the Battle of Fair Oaks from his balloon on 31 May 1862. (Courtesy, Library of Congress).

47

1.3 kilograms, only 1/800th that of water.)

The German physicist and author Georg Christoph Lichtenberg stated about 1750 that "the world could not be very old because man can not yet fly."

Perhaps the first man to demonstrate that a vessel could really rise into the air was the Jesuit Bartholomo Laurenco de Gusmao of Brazil. Having joined the religious society, he left a year later because of his air-mindedness. In about 1720 de Gusmao built a balloon and demonstrated his invention in Portugal before a most distinguished audience, which included royalty. His balloon rose to the ceiling in the huge ballroom where he and his audience were assembled.

Some twenty-five years later, a brochure on the "Art of Navigation in the Air" was published in Avignon by Pater Joseph Gallien. But to ensure his future as a religious man, the serious thesis was to be considered merely a "physical and geometric amusement." To be able to rise, a vessel would not only have to be airless, but would have to contain air lighter than that found at sea level, perhaps from higher altitudes: "the upper part of the atmosphere, out of the region of hail." Gallien calculated that a vessel of one hundred cubic-feet capacity would have a lifting power of 7.5 billion pounds.

The problem of lighter air was solved when in 1766 Henry Cavendish discovered hydrogen gas, but because of its unavailability, early balloonists resorted to hot air instead.

In their paperbag factory at Annonay, one of the owners noticed one day that a paper sack rose mysteriously into the air. It had been placed over a pot of boiling water and filled with steam vapor. Subsequently, the brothers Joseph Michel and Jacques Etienne Montgolfier in 1782 constructed a balloon and placed it over an open firepit. The silken bag filled with smoke and heat and rose up. A year later the brothers built a balloon holding 13,430 cubic feet of hot air, attached a basket with some animals, and sent it into the air. Reaching an altitude of some six-thousand feet and eventually a distance of 7,668 feet, they discovered upon descension that the rooster had a broken wing. It was believed that the air pressure was responsible for the damage, but others reasoned that the sheep with it had become frightened and had caused the injury by stepping on its wing.

When King Louis XVI was invited to witness a demonstration ascension with the two brothers, he forbade them to undertake such a risk. Instead, two condemned criminals were summoned to become the first passengers; but too much opposition to that scheme made the king change his mind. Two noblemen shared that high honor.

It is told that when the demonstration before an audience of high-church dignitaries and government officials took place, one asked, "Of what use is such a thing?"; to which the astute Benjamin Franklin replied, "Of what use is a newborn babe?"

A detailed report was made at the Palace la Muette, "immediately after the attempt with the aerostatic machine of M. de Montgolfier on November 21, 1783." The document was signed by members of the Académie de Sciences Francaise, the Duc de Polignac, Duc de Guines, Comte de Polastron, Comte de Vandreuil, d'Hunaud, Benjamin Franklin, Faujas de St. Fond, Delisle, and Leroy.

The record stated that the skies were covered here and there with specks of clouds. A slight wind blew from the northwest. The machine was filled within eight minutes and was ready to start its journey. The Marquis d'Arlandes and M. Pilâtre de Rozier stood on the platform. At the first attempt, however, a slight wind took the ornately decorated balloon, which then, instead of rising vertically, rose sideways. Despite the holding of the ropes by the ground crew, the balloon was dashed against some tall trees surrounding the palace square. The craft was returned to the scaffold and again filled with hot air. Two hours later, precisely at 1:54, it rose majestically to a height of about 250 feet, and the proud passengers raised their hats in greeting to the assembled spectators on the ground. Everyone there felt fear and admiration. The balloon rose to an altitude of at least three-thousand feet, and the balloonists became indistinguishable; as the craft floated over the Seine and the military academy and the hospital, all of Paris could see it. Satisfied with their test flight, the balloonists decided to land; but because they found themselves over the houses of the city, they rose again and finally landed in a meadow near the Moulin Croulebarbe. They still had about two-thirds of their supplies and thus could have stayed aloft for a much longer time than the twenty to twenty-five minutes they spent in the air. The machine was seventy feet high, had a diameter of forty-six feet, contained sixty-thousand cubic feet of hot air, and could carry a load of sixteen-thousand to seventeen-thousand pounds. This first passenger flight was a spectacular success.

Another Frenchman, Jacques Alexandre César Charles, familiar with the theories of Lana and knowing of the discovery of hydrogen gas, also built an aerostatic machine. Filled with hydrogen gas, it could lift a greater load and could stay in the air longer than the balloon of the Montgolfiers. It was but three months after the first successful flight of the two noblemen that the *Charlière* took to flight. The hydrogen gas was made in several barrels from which pipes ran into a large tube connected to the balloon. A valve was placed in the balloon bag, and ballast consisting of several bags of sand was carried to control the ascent and descent of the craft.

Pilâtre de Rozier then constructed a balloon that incorporated the two tested principles. He filled the upper part of his balloon with hydrogen, like the *Charlière,* and the lower portion was filled with hot air, *à la Montgolfière.* But the open flame ignited the upper part of the sphere and the pioneer Rozier was burned to death.

The Montgolfier balloons carried an open fire in their now solidly fixed gondola, and the rise and fall of their craft was controlled by that fire. A larger flame would cause it to rise, while a dampened fire would cause the balloon to lose altitude. It was a relatively safe system.

Improvements were made. Rubberized silk fabrics were used with nettings and bag suspensions, a valve was mounted for discharging of gas, and oval shapes were tried out to improve directional stability and to assist in steering. Even oars were used for that purpose. With a crew of six men manipulating the silk-covered oars, the Robert brothers flew, or perhaps rowed, their melon-shaped dirigible balloon for seven hours during 1784. As means of propulsion and steering, such methods as gunpowder charges, movable wings, riggings of sails, or a rotating screw acting as a primitive propeller were used.

In Italy, the brothers Augustin and Charles Gerli built and flew a balloon in 1784 by sustained heating; and Miolan and Janinet utilized jets of hot air to propel themselves in their balloon.

In 1785 General Jean Baptiste Meusnier used an elongated form instead of a sphere for better maneuverability, and utilized goldbeater's skin instead of silk for greater durability. He also devised a manner of regulating the rise and fall of the balloon by using a separate gas bag enclosed in an outer envelope that would hold its shape when the supply in the smaller bag was either increased or decreased by a pumping device attached to the lower end of the balloon. The general also suggested the use of an air screw for propulsion. However, the inventive Meusnier was killed during the revolution before he could try his many improvements.

Within two years from the time of the first ascent of humans, thirty-five trips had been made and fifty-eight persons had been taken aloft, all without mishaps to the passengers. Some of the pioneering balloonists, trying out new methods, perished when their systems failed them.

Some intrepid men toured Europe with their balloons and demonstrated them to the people. Jean-Pierre Francois Blanchard gave a fine performance. He used a smaller balloon with a sheep tied to it and let it rise. Then, he and his wife took off in a larger one and cleverly maneuvered it to the rendezvous with the smaller balloon. When the contact was made, he cut the rope holding the sheep, and it floated gently, attached to a silken parachute, to the ground. It was a startling performance, and Blanchard was a superb showman. Blanchard also was the first man to fly across the English Channel, from Calais to Dover, but he finally met his death when in 1809 at his sixtieth ascent something went wrong. He had an astonishing career.

The French military used a balloon for observation purposes during the battle of Fleurus in 1794, the first such use anywhere.

On the day of his coronation, Napoleon ordered an elaborately decorated balloon to ascend in celebration of this great event. Legend has it that the balloon rose indeed to travel all the way to Italy and collapsed on the graveside of Nero. This was believed to be a bad omen for the new emperor of France.

After a pause of several decades, balloon activities accelerated again. On 24 September 1852, Henri Jacques Giffard successfully flew his elongated hydrogen-filled balloon in a directional flight. He used a three-horsepower steam engine to drive a screw suspended from the gondola for propulsion and steering. His airship was twenty-four meters long with a diameter of twelve meters.

Giffard believed that size was an important factor, but the engines of that day were too heavy to ensure success of his ideas. In 1855, the second airship, measuring seventy meters and containing 4,500 cubic meters of gas, was tested. But the gas reacted peculiarly, and the ship's nose rose straight into the air, which broke off the gondola, thereby saving the inventor. The balloon rose rapidly, only to burst into an explosive flame. Later, further experiments with hydrogen in the laboratory caused an accident, and Giffard gave up all work with that gas. In time, he again constructed some free balloons. Giffard also invented a safety valve for steam engines, which brought him recognition and wealth. Unfortunately, he soon became totally blind. Unable to cope with this misfortune, he took his own life in 1885.

Count Zeppelin considered Giffard to be a genius and technically highly educated, although he was the son of a locksmith. Henri Giffard had studied the many technical and physical problems of ballooning in his spare time while working for the French railroad.

In 1856 the inventive Jean Baptiste Justin Lassie proposed that his nine-hundred-foot-long, ninety-foot-diameter patented "gimlet balloon" be spun on its axis by three hundred men on a treadmill. No further information seemed available on this intriguing project, except the drawing that accompanied the request for a patent.

A similarly inventive Richard Boyman also obtained a patent for his metal balloon. The six-hundred-ton giant was to be 1,300 feet long with a diameter of two-hundred feet, and an elaborate system of blowers powered by a steam engine were to supply the propulsion. However, it never rose off the drawing boards.

But by 1868 the French government had issued fourteen patents for balloon constructions, including those for propulsion mechanisms.

The German Ensmann, in 1858, proposed to utilize rockets to propel an airship balloon; another inventor, a mechanic from Nürnberg, believed that a steerable balloon could be constructed of a light metal. Neither of these propositions were, of course, applied in practical applications.

By 1874 a total of 3,700 flights had been made, including a night journey by the Frenchman Camille Flammarion who took aloft a container filled with glowworms for illumination of his instruments. There had been sixteen deaths among the pioneers.

Captain Gaston Tissandier and his brother, Albert, in 1882 built an airship with pointed ends, powered by an electric motor and reaching a speed of six miles per hour. Two years later the brothers were able to steer their airship to fly a figure-eight and land at their starting place.

A Russian inventor in 1883 built an airship with a tubelike skeleton and named it the *Russia.*

Two French captains, Charles Renard and Arthur C. Krebs, in 1884 constructed an airship, powered by an electric motor, and flew their *La France* at a speed of fourteen miles per hour. The Chinese silk-covered ship traveled a distance of five miles.

One of the most significant innovators was the Brazilian Alberto Santos-Dumont, who first studied and then experimented with a nonrigid spherical balloon shape in Paris. A steerable balloon in 1898, equipped with a 3.5-horsepower engine, rose successfully but was soon caught in trees of the Jardin d'Acclimation. However, two days later, the ascension succeeded perfectly. The next year, when the experimenter tested his Santos-Dumont No. 2, the hydrogen gas contracted, the envelope shrank, and a strong gust of wind doubled it up. The No. 3 balloon functioned better, and the inventor learned much about dirigible ballooning from it. Santos-Dumont flew his No. 4 frequently at the 1900 Exposition. When Henri Deutsch offered one-hundred-thousand francs to the first person who could fly from the Aero Club around the Eiffel Tower and back within half an hour, Santos-Dumont worked diligently on his No. 5 steerable balloon.

Having successfully rounded the *Tour d'Eiffel,* the balloon flew into strong winds and was unable to land as planned. Driven back after his engine stopped, the inventor crashed the balloon into trees of the Rothschild estate. After repairs, another attempt was made, but this also ended in failure. Within twenty-two days the No. 6 was built. With a balloon displacing 22,239 cubic feet and powered by a four-cylinder engine of twelve horsepower, the intrepid inventor made an attempt to capture the Deutsch prize on 19 October 1901. Encountering considerable difficulties on the return trip, after rounding the tower, he nevertheless achieved the requirements and collected his prize. Alberto Santos-Dumont built more dirigible balloons of similar construction type and was a prominent personality in aeronautics in France. Altogether he had constructed fourteen airships, as told in his book, *My Airships,* published in 1904.

The Austro-Hungarian engineer David Schwarz in 1893 in St. Petersburg built an all-metal airship, using an outside aluminum frame. However, because of an unexpected construction failure, the airship never flew. During inflation, it collapsed entirely. Still, Schwarz constructed another similar airship in Berlin, after he was forced to leave Russia. With a conical bow and rounded stern, the forty-seven-meter-long aluminum hull, braced by aluminum frames, enclosed one huge undivided gas bag. After the death of Schwarz, his wife carried on his work, and his rigid airship, powered by a combustion engine of twelve horsepower, actually flew in Berlin in 1897, but it was not considered to have been very successful.

The second aluminum airship of David Schwarz of 1897. (Courtesy, Daimler-Benz).

The book dealer Karl Wölfert of Leipzig in 1887 had tested a dirigible airship near Dresden. A frame of bamboo poles gave it rigidity. Equipped with a two-horsepower engine that drove a cloth-covered wooden screw for forward propulsion, it had a similar device for lifting the steerable airship. When in Cannstatt the engine power proved insufficient to raise the craft and the inventor, a smaller man volunteered to take Wölfert's place. After shedding all unnecessary clothes, the passenger rose with the balloon and traveled nearly three miles to Kornwestheim. With no wind, the craft was steerable. But a stronger engine was too heavy for the airship to lift. Finally, with a larger airship, the *Deutschland,* Wölfert successfully flew at the industrial exhibition, the *Gewerbeausstellung,* at Berlin in 1896. The following year the airship

crashed, killing Wölfert and his mechanic Knabe.

Already in 1879 Wölfert and George Baumgarten had tested a model in Leipzig and the *Deutsche Verein zur Förderung der Luftschiffahrt,* the German Society for the Furthering of Airship Travel, was founded. But further tests of this airship, whose gondola was rigidly connected to the balloon with bamboo poles, were not encouraging in 1882, and the inventor waited another five years until a better construction type.

During that time Otto Lilienthal of Anklam, Pomerania, stated:

> . . .experiments in gliding by a single individual, resembling closely the gliding pattern of birds, is the only method which permits us to develop gradually our proficiency in the art of flying. We have to begin with a very simple apparatus and in a very incomplete form of flight.[1]

Lilienthal had watched young storks learn to fly, and he noted that they always faced into the wind when taking off. He studied engineering, which later proved of immense help to him and gave him a scientific approach to the problem. He constructed a pair of wings fastened to each other and attached them to himself. The wings were made of cotton twill stretched on a light frame of willow wood, curved front and back. This glider weighed about fifty pounds and had a surface of 160 square feet. For this experiment, Lilienthal used a conical hill that rose fifty feet, which enabled him to glide in every direction, depending on the wind.

Otto Lilienthal eventually succeeded in gliding as far as three-hundred yards. Then he constructed a biplane glider with a two-hundred-square-foot surface. But the problem of balancing became even greater now. Lilienthal then equipped a monoplane glider with an engine driven by carbonic acid gas. Again he intended to flap movable parts of the wings when airborne. But before testing this powered plane, Lilienthal took one of his many gliders out to test a new rudder in a high wind. In 1896 during that trial, he lost his balance at a height of about one hundred feet and was killed. He was a true pioneer in the art of flying.

Count Zeppelin followed the experiments of Lilienthal with utmost interest and said about the activities:

These trials to make a solo flight using two large wings like birds is most important. Should Lilienthal find many imitators in this endeavor it is highly conceivable that just as bicycles are now fitted with a small motor, a similar small engine could be attached to the pair of wings. Such an apparatus might form the basis for larger flying machines in the future.[2]

The public generally looked upon the several flying efforts as daring stunts or risky sporting affairs. Even later, when in 1897 the Scandinavian scientist Salomon August Andrée announced an attempt to cross the North Pole in a balloon, it was considered a daring feat of sportsmanship. The scientist set out on this exploratory voyage, only to disappear forever.

The reputation of Count Zeppelin was that of a daring and sometimes recklessly foolhardy man, and it was only natural that when he was observed to make peculiar experiments on the Bodensee with Kober, onlookers seemed certain that he was indeed a rather "crazy count."

In 1892 the Count had engaged the young engineer Theodor Kober to assist him in the planning of an airship. Engineering was not yet a recognized science, and aerodynamics was entirely unknown. Whatever knowledge was needed in the construction of an airship had to be learned by testing various ideas, based on well-educated guesses.

Theodor Kober was perhaps as technically experienced in that science as any man anywhere. He had been working with the balloon factory of Riedinger in Augsburg, where the airship of Wölfert had been built. Both men, Count Zeppelin and Theodor Kober, undertook to test the several elements needed to complete a dirigible airship. Studies were made with an engine coupled to sundry types of screw propellers, attached to the sides of a boat. Observers at the shore wondered just what this eccentric experiment was all about, and speculations on the sanity of the Count were abundant.

A Viennese actor named Tyrolt, who appeared on the stage of a Stuttgart theater during this time, told that he was dining with a friend in the main dining room at the Hotel Marquardt and, there, noticed a particularly vivacious elderly gentleman at a corner table explaining something to the officers seated with him. Tyrolt asked his companion whether he knew that enthusiastic man.

Being a good-natured Swabian, the companion obviously felt sincere pity for the gentleman referred to, and said: "That poor man is deranged. He is Count Zeppelin, and he wants to fly through the air."

Other tests were perhaps not as unorthodox as those made with the screw propellers. Proper weight distribution of the gondolas was of prime importance. Two gondolas were considered: one for the command post of the airship and another for the power unit. A third gondola for the passengers would have to be considered later, but first the main problems were to get the airship aloft and to master the handling of it. Payload, passengers, and freight would have to wait for the time being.

After almost three years of testing components, plans for an airship were complete. The *Luftschiff* was estimated to cost about three-hundred-thousand marks to construct. However, the cost of the first one would be considerably more than that, perhaps even a million marks (about 250,000 dollars). There were no halls large enough in which to build such a huge airship, and no factory facilities to fabricate most of the component parts. And a movable, floating hangar to launch the airship was essential since the craft had to be turned against the wind in order to rise into the air.

Count Zeppelin realized that such a project would cost considerably more money than he himself was able to provide or borrow. The problem of financing that ambitious scheme seemed a decisive stumbling block. Private bankers would not even consider the matter, and so Count Zeppelin hoped to enlist the interest of some government agencies. He contacted the war ministry and the general staff, but his journey to Berlin proved unfruitful. The reception was extremely friendly, but when the Count explained his mission and requested that the agency itself give official sanction and financial aid, none wanted to become involved in the radical project. To some of his friends the idea seemed sensible for the future, but not for now.

Since none of the ministries would underwrite the project, Count Zeppelin decided to enlist the help of the Kaiser by suggesting that a commission be appointed to investigate the feasibility of the plan and then to submit the findings to the government officials. But since no real experts in this new field of airship technic existed, such a commission could, at best, include eminent theoretical authorities in the field of physics, electricity, meteorology, and machine building. Aeronautic experts were limited to balloonists, and even they depended on air currents when aloft.

An opportunity presented itself when on New Year's Day the reception of outstanding citizens was held in the imperial palace. When shaking hands with the Kaiser, the Count took time to explain his request.

A committee was duly appointed with the esteemed Professor Hermann von Helmholtz as chairman. Two other professors of the technical high school, Müller-Breslau and Slaby, were also members of the committee, along with the free balloonist Gross and a representative of the war ministry. The group met first in March 1894.

Count Zeppelin was certain that a scientist of the stature of von Helmholtz, even skeptical at first, eventually would be won over after giving the study his unbiased evaluation. The Count was hopeful of the favorable decision. Thus, it was a decided disappointment when the commission made its report to the government.

The body of learned men stated that they did not believe that the idea of a dirigible airship merited any government involvement. The surprise of the report was that Professor von Helmholtz, who had at first dismissed the idea as impractical, had actually voted against the majority of the group. He felt that the project indeed merited further consideration, but that a definite decision should not be made for several years. The professor suggested that it was *sehr beachtungswert,* most worthy of consideration, and *nicht unausführbar,* not impossible to execute. But the proposed airship was too light, the commission felt, and it

seemed impossible to construct a sufficiently strong one, based on the design calculations submitted.

Because of the opinion of this renowned scientist, and despite the adverse decision of the majority of the committee, the ministry of war declared that it would postpone its final decision until Count Zeppelin had defined certain portions of the proposed plan in greater detail. The Count and Kober set at once to the task. But before that work was completed and handed to the ministry, Professor von Helmholtz died on 8 September 1894. The negative reply was a forgone conclusion. The plans were adjudged *praktisch unverwertbar,* practically worthless.

Count Zeppelin was stunned. It seemed impossible to him for a group of scientific experts to turn down the project; but that was exactly what they had done to his dreamship. The Count remembered what Stephan had written about Fulton's steamship idea: "In 1802, the commission appointed by Napoleon to investigate the plans for Fulton's steamship had reported these plans to be 'visionary and impracticable.' " This was precisely what the commission had done to his project. Count Zeppelin had tried to take the same route that Fulton and Napoleon had taken, but he hoped for an entirely different result. However, the present group of scientists had followed the very reasoning of that earlier commission of unimaginative people who did not recognize a visionary and quite practicable plan either.

To newspaper reporters who came to interview him, the Count said, "I do not blame anyone for considering me a fool, but I feel that it is my duty to go on with my work steadfastly and to hold to my idea, which I know is right."

6

THE FIRST RIGID AIRSHIP

On 13 August 1898, patent number 98580, Class 77 Sport, was issued retroactive as of August 31, 1895, to Count Zeppelin for his "steerable air-vehicle with several carrying bodies arranged behind each other" (*Lenkbaren Luftfahrzeug mit mehreren hintereinander angeordneten Tragkörpern*). An accompanying drawing on one page showed a figure of this long cylindrical airship; eight other drawings illustrated the skeleton and other arrangements. The text covered three pages.

Actually, this steerable airship consisted of three parts. The first section, pointed at the front end and flat on the other, was to carry the engine in the attached gondola. The center part, flat on both ends, was meant to carry the payload or the passengers, while the third section, pointed at the rear end, was also to carry freight. All sections were to be rigid and attached to each other by a flexible method, similar to three joined sausages. Each of the three sections had smaller inside balloons filled with lifting gas, and these cells were made of a cloth material. The skeleton consisted of aluminum cylindrical rings and longitudinal members, covered with durable cloth material.

Early in 1896, Count Zeppelin spoke before an invited audience, which included many dignitaries and members of government ministries as well as technical experts, outlining in detail his plans for an airship. Soon after this Stuttgart speech, the Count wrote a lengthy memorandum to the Society of German Engineers, warning them not to expect from him either the discovery of new natural laws or the exposition of new scientific formulas. He pointed out that he was one of the most recent recruits to their field of science. "My observations are confined basically to the practical application of theories that are already known in the newest branch of technical science, namely aeronautics." However, Zeppelin believed that in this field his efforts had already clarified a number of uncertainties.

Asking for definite consideration of his project by the society, the Count believed that he was correct in his calculations, but he suggested that if the scientists could prove him wrong, he would be sincerely grateful to be shown just where he was wrong.

The Society of Engineers took the matter under consideration and in October reported favorably on the project, recommending that the directors of the society take further steps in the realization of the proposed plans for the airship.

When, on 31 December 1896, the society issued a statement to the newspapers commenting favorably on the proposal and urging the general public to make financial contributions toward the building of an airship, Count Zeppelin was overjoyed. Early the next year, the Society of Engineers appointed a commission to cooperate with the Count in the construction of the dirigible airship.

The wide publicity given the project in newspapers all over Germany resulted in enough contributions so that the *Aktien-Gesellschaft zur Förderung der Luftschiffahrt,* or Company for the Furthering of Airship Travel, was founded in Stuttgart, with a capital of about eight-hundred-thousand marks (two-hundred-thousand dollars). This company had as its main purpose the development of the still necessary preliminary tests not yet completed and the selection of a suitable location and building of facilities to construct the first airship.

As a location, Manzell was chosen. This small village near Friedrichshafen on the Bodensee offered a vast, entirely flat expanse of territory for flight tests, and had a more constant wind and weather history than any area under consideration. The fact that the king encouraged this choice with generous terms was also of considerable influence in the final selection of the site.

Called Magni Cella in the earliest times when it was the cell of Magnus, the apostle to the Alemans who had come from Ireland and traveled up the Rhine to stay in this bay some two-thousand years before, Manzell now would house Count Zeppelin in similar fashion—away from all social obligations and cares, deeply involved in the problems of construction of his airship, and as disinterested in worldy affairs as the Monk Magnus once was.

After completing the original drawings and preparatory plans, including specifications and costs for the airship, Theodor Kober was in charge of the construction work. The basic elements were maintained: huge size of the airship, a sleek form and aluminum skeleton, divided and individual gas cells, arrangement of several independent gondolas and their seaworthiness, solid connections of the gondolas to the rigid skeleton, and connections between the gondola cars. Much of this original design was, of course, not original at all, but had been used previously by other builders. Some of the features, such as separate gas cells, were definitely new, but even those had been suggested in 1807 by a German, August Wilhelm Zachariae. Other construction features had been improved immeasurably over those tried by earlier builders of airships.

Count Zeppelin believed that size was important, although for the opposite reason of other perhaps more-learned men. The Count disputed the assumption that air resistance grew in proportion to the exposed surface. He explained that he had observed in nature that this was not a fact, for when one threw a large rock into the water it would sink at once, while a smaller stone would be carried somewhat by the current and be influenced much more by movements. Even if this reasoning was contrary to the accepted belief of all physical-science theorists, he firmly held to his position.

Engineer Kober had called attention to the engine that Wölfert had used in his steerable balloon, so Count Zeppelin met with the inventor and manufacturer Gottlieb Daimler in Bad Cannstatt to discuss this matter. Carl Wölfert had equipped the *Deutschland* with two joined four-cylinder engines and had flown his balloon at the *Gewerbeausstellung* in Berlin in 1896.

The procurement of materials presented. many problems. The vast amount of aluminum needed for the skeleton could be purchased only from one supplier in Germany: Karl Berg of Eveking, near Lüdenscheid. Berg was the first importer and fabricator of that metal and had furnished the material for the airship of Schwarz. Count Zeppelin required large quantities for his tubular girders and other parts of the frame. The aluminum parts were manufactured and assembled at Eveking, then taken apart and shipped by rail to Friedrichshafen, where they were reassembled. Serious supply problems were encountered in other unique materials for the construction of the first airship.

To test the reaction to actual flight of his new engineer, Count Zeppelin went with Kübler to Switzerland where he ascended with Captain Eduard Spelterini in his balloon. Subsequent events suggest that Kübler was not impressed with the thrill of being aloft in the air.

A huge workshop hangar was constructed in 1898 at Manzell on the Bodensee and on 17 June the actual building of the airship began. It was hoped that the airship could make its preliminary test flights in the late summer of 1899. Especially since nearly all of the available funds had been spent, Count Zeppelin reasoned that a successful flight would bring additional financial contributions. He speculated that it might even cause a new and favorable approach to reluctant government officials and reconsideration of the whole proposition of airship utility.

It was November when the assembly of the rigid frame was finished and the installation of the gas bags, which caused some unforseen difficulties, was completed. But some slight damage to the turning mechanism of the movable floating platform necessitated postponement of the maiden flight.

Unpredictable winter weather prevailed, and Count Zeppelin did not want to endanger the initial flight in any way. A sudden storm over the lake could make it impossible to get the airship out of the hangar or, once out, damage it beyond repair and destory forever the years of diligent toil. Thus it was decided to wait prudently until weather conditions would be perfect for the test. So the Count and his co-workers waited patiently for the most opportune time to undertake the first test flight of their airship.

For various reasons, the actual test flight did not take place until 2 July 1900. Weather conditions were predicted to be ideal. All of the preparations for the maiden flight had been made with the greatest care. Some minor miscalculations had been corrected; others were not. For instance, it was believed that an airship could be filled with

gas in five hours, but actually that task consumed a much longer period. Because the men had been at work almost constantly for the two preceding days, they were given off until Monday afternoon.

That Monday the sun rose on a beautifully cloudless and nearly windless summer day. From noon on, Count Zeppelin seemed to be everywhere among the feverish activity of each and everyone of the entire organization. He carefully checked the various anchor ropes, the engines, the gas capacity indicators, and a hundred other significant items. Nothing was left to chance, and each one of the co-workers felt the piercing, knowledgeable eyes of the general looking over their shoulders. Satisfied that every detail was in order, the Count walked out onto the platform on the outer edge of the hangar for a last look at the blue sky and the placid sea.

Count Zeppelin lifted his white cap, bowed his head, and said a prayer of thanksgiving and asked for the successful launching of his dream. Turning to the shore, he noted that, because of the wide

The *LZ 1* at her maiden flight on 2 July 1900, just above the floating platform. (Courtesy, Daimler-Benz).

publicity this coming event had received in the daily press, crowds had gathered to witness this auspicious occasion and filled nearly every available vantage point along the lake. Scientific observers, newspaper reporters, and government officials had been invited, and simple farm folk had come from nearby areas to see this miraculous sight.

One of the interested spectators at the launching was Rudolf Diesel, who had successfully constructed his own engines. Count Zeppelin suggested to him that Diesel engines of light weight were indeed desirable to power his airship, but that they would have to be better proved operationally before he could use them with confidence.

The hangar was turned into the gentle wind current, and the small steamer *Buchhorn* was attached to the platform on which the airship rested. At a signal, the steamer, its smokestack protected by a screen so that no sparks would come in contact with the hull of the dirigible airship, pulled the platform with the huge airship out onto the lake. Besides the Count, the Baron von Bassus and Eugen Wolf went along, as did the machinists Eisele and Goss.

The blunt nose of the airship moved ever so slowly out of the hangar over the placid water, its body resting securely on the long float. The crowd was surprised at its 128-meter (418 feet) length. Then, at 8:03, the airship rose almost unnoticeably, gently into the air, and when it had risen to a sufficient height on the tow ropes the engines were started to turn the propellers, and the ship moved away under its own power at increased speed. It seemed to glide effortlessly in majestic splendor, and, when an altitude of 1,312 feet was reached, this yellowish-colored, long, cigar-shaped balloon sailed smoothly into the distance.

After a flight of about eighteen minutes, the dirigible balloon landed at 8:21 off Immenstaad, a distance of about four miles.

The *Buchhorn* soon came to take the airship in tow and pulled it to its hangar at Manzell. Count Zeppelin was satisfied that his ship had proved its airworthiness, even if for only a short period at the scheduled test flight. The sliding weight lever had broken, and it was thought to be more prudent to land the airship than to take a chance on wrecking it should an emergency arise.

An uncovered walk connected the two gondolas, and from this catwalk a lead weight of 550 pounds hung on a wire cable. When the weight was pushed toward the rear, the stern of the airship sank and the ship climbed, but when the weight was pushed toward the front of the ship, the nose sank and the airship descended. There was no elevator rudder nor stabilizing surface, and only a tiny rudder was placed on each side of the bow and the stern.

Evaluating the flight, Count Zeppelin recognized the several shortcomings. The engines, developing thirty-two horsepower at the maximum revolutions of eight-hundred per minute, but running to an average of twenty-four horsepower only, were not powerful enough to keep the nose of the airship headed into the mild wind, and apparently the steering mechanism was unable to turn the airship sufficiently, although several slow turning maneuvers were successfully accomplished. Measurements showed the wind velocity to be five meters per second (11.25 miles per hour). By reversing the engines, the Count tried to turn the dirigible, but the airship failed to respond properly against the moderate air currents. A cruising speed of about eight miles per hour was reached. Since there had been no reason to travel further, Count Zeppelin decided to bring his airship down safely.

The Daimler airship engine of 1900: four cylinders, 12 horsepower. (Courtesy, Daimler-Benz).

57

He had observed the reaction to the almost imperceptible wind current and was glad that it had been so slight on this first test flight. Unfortunately, at the very spot where he landed on the lake, a navigational signal on a stake penetrated the hull and caused a leak in one of the gas cells.

Of course, Count Zeppelin was secretly disappointed in the performance of the airship, but he had made his point. The dirigible airship could rise, stay aloft, and be guided. As an initial demonstration of that basic fact, it was considered a successful performance.

However, comments in the newspapers were not at all favorable. Many journalists had expected much more than this simple initial exercise by the first airship of Count Zeppelin.

The prestigious *Frankfurter Zeitung* of 3 July 1900 reported:

> Yesterday we experienced a disappointment, probably greater than any ever experienced in this large lake district from Hegau to Saint Gallen. The entire countryside was ceremoniously invited to attend a performance to which not even the overture could be played successfully. Although Count Zeppelin's experiments were extremely interesting and perhaps even important, they have undoubtedly proved conclusively that a dirigible balloon is of practically no value.[1]

The following day's issue stated that the "dirigibility of a balloon is most problematic."

The "unsuccessful overture" referred to the miscalculation of the time taken to fill the cells with gas. Instead of taking five hours, as hoped, the operation took twenty-five hours and upset the launching schedule, to the dismay of all persons present.

The general tone of the other newspaper reports was similar. One paper told its readers that the airship rose exceedingly slowly with apparently good balance, but while in the air a few times one end or the other dipped in an alarming manner. The practically breathless spectators feared that the passengers in the gondolas would tumble out and the entire balloon would turn from a horizontal to a vertical position and crash down. But every time a fair balance was again achieved, "and now the close friends and enthusiastic proponents of the Count insist — rightly or wrongly — that all of these movements were made intentionally or quite arbitrarily." All movements were of course unexplainable to the anxious spectators, who believed that there were no intentional movements at all and that the airship was being buffeted by the wind and was unable to do anything about it.

Another newspaper reported that the airship offered a truly majestic sight to the onlookers and that it held its balance well, but that the load-carrying ability was too low for the size of the airship. The performance was relatively poor when compared to that of the Frenchmen Renard and Krebs who, fifteen years before, had been able to land their airship at the place of departure; Count Zeppelin's airship, however, was stranded a distance from its hangar.

The airship had been a subject for discussion in most parts of Germany before the initial flight, but the publicity in every newspaper now made it the main topic of every conversation. Generally, the public felt that the flight had been successful, reporters were doubtful, but engineers and scientists were considerably less enthusiastic, and most of them were actually convinced that it was not a practical invention.

Count Zeppelin believed that the problem of poor steering could be overcome, and he and his chief construction engineer, Kübler, worked diligently on a corrective rudder and elevator design. To correct any deficiencies in the engines, Wilhelm Maybach, the chief engineer of Daimler, who had come in July to supervise the installation of the two engines, stayed in Manzell.

Basically, the overall design was held to be correct. Count Zeppelin was absolutely convinced that a rigid airship would prove more practical than the nonrigid type with but a single chamber for gas, an insecure and inefficient design feature. A rigid frame maintained the shape of the airship; the several independent gas cells would not collapse when some of the gas escaped; the buoyancy of the balloon would not be destroyed; and practical control and safety would be retained. That is why seventeen individual free-hanging balloons were used inside the shell skeleton, which was, in turn, covered with a smooth cotton cloth, stretched tight to lessen friction. The airspace between minimized the temperature change of the gas. Because of the weight of the frame, the overall size had to be large enough to reduce the proportion of weight of the airship and increase its payload. The stern was tapered for improved speed, and the diameter of eleven meters (thirty-six feet) was in keeping with a thin long shape for reduced resistance to wind currents. The engines and aluminum screw propellers were placed close to the hull to exert their force near the center of the airship, and the two rudders—one fore and one aft—could easily be turned without impairing the stability of the rigid balloon. The Count felt certain that there was nothing wrong with the basic design of his *Luftschiff-Zeppelin One,* or *LZ 1.* Perhaps a better way could have been devised to attain the correct balance while in flight. But the weight attached to the girder or keel below the framework and running the entire length of the airship and controlled by a wire cable between the gondolas seemed the only possible solution to that difficult problem.

Two more test flights were scheduled to be carried out during October, and on the 17th of that month the airship took off again. The improved steering mechanism seemed markedly superior to the former system, and the airship responded well during several maneuvers. The speed of the airship was increased to about eighteen miles per hour. The flight lasted eighty minutes, until the engines stopped. The airship descended rapidly from an altitude of one-thousand feet onto the lake where the waiting motor launch cruised to take it in tow, assisted by the lake steamer *König Karl.* The crowd on the shore, considerably smaller than that of the first flight, was enthusiastic over this demonstration flight, but attending officials were still skeptical. The Society of Engineers was not completely convinced of the practicality of the dirigible balloon; the war-ministry representatives believed that the airship was much too slow to be of any use in wartime; and the post-office-department officials were entirely disinterested in it for their purposes.

The third test flight, held on 24 October, lasted but twenty-three minutes. The prevailing wind (eight meters per second, or eighteen miles per hour) had proved to be too strong for the available engine power, and the airship experienced difficulties in maneuvering.

All of the funds at hand had now been spent. There was not sufficient money left to purchase another supply of hydrogen gas for the airship. No new financing appeared feasible to the Count, and reluctantly, on 15 November 1900, he agreed to the forced dissolution of the joint-stock company.

The airship was dismantled and the hangar torn down. The 120,000 marks (thirty-thousand dollars) realized from the liquidation sale paid off some of the investors.

This setback was a hard blow to Count Zeppelin. Writing to a sick friend at that time, he added, "I, too, have become an invalid. My heart is broken."

The following January Count Zeppelin was asked to give a talk to the German Colonial Association, the *Deutschen Kolonial Verein,* in the huge Philharmonia Hall in Berlin. This appearance was a consequential one. The Count was presented with the *Roten Adlerorden,* the Order of the Red Eagle, by the chief of staff, General von Hahnke. Representing the Kaiser, the general delivered a personal letter from him. Written on 15 January 1901, at the Neue Palast in Potsdam, it read:

We have been informed of your ascents in the airship of your own invention, and it is our desire to express to you our recognition of the efforts and determination which have enabled you to accomplish your self-appointed task despite the numerous difficulties you have encountered. The obvious advantages of your system — the subdivision of the elongated balloon into smaller separate compartments, the distribution of the ballast, the power by two separate motors, and the first known application of a vertical steering mechanism — all of these features have supplied your airship with the greatest independent speed as well as with the greatest dirigibility known so far. The results you have attained signify truly epoch-making progress in the construction of airships. Further, these results will be a valuable basis for other experiments in the future. As an expression of our appreciation for your successful experiments we have ordered the counsel and advice of the Aeronautical Detachment always to be at your disposal. We have also ordered an officer of the Aeronautical Detachment to be detailed to you whenever you may think this necessary for your future experiments. As an outward proof of our recognition we herewith confer upon you the Order of the *Roter Adler* (Red Eagle), First Class. Wilhelm II, I.R.[2]

Highly gratified by the splendid reception of his talk before the large audience and especially at the interest shown by the Kaiser in his airship, Count Zeppelin returned quite elated to his Stuttgart residence. He wrote to the Kaiser, thanking him for the medal and for the interest shown, and offered to discuss future plans of his airship in greater detail at the emperor's convenience. But there is no record of an invitation from Berlin or Potsdam.

In March, still in an exultant mood, the Count again appealed to the Society of German Engineers. He composed the memorandum with his chief construction engineer Kübler.

Again, the appointed group discussed in great detail the various aspects of the airship construction, and again argued on the rigidity question. One of the points brought out was that a semirigid airship was much better suited for the military, since it could easily be dismantled and shipped, by rail, to whatever far destination it was to be employed. A totally rigid airship was too cumbersome to control in the air and much more sensitive to winds, it was suggested. Lieutenant Hans Gross was definitely against the type constructed by Count Zeppelin, and favored the semirigid types. He fully agreed with Victor Silberer of the Austrian Air Technical Association who stated that the airship was a failure and the construction of this type would lead to nothing but a huge fiasco.

Seemingly a strong point of disagreement was made by Professor Hugo Hergesell of Strassburg, a well-known meteorologist and ardent supporter of the rigid-airship type. He pointed out that only a rigid-type airship could stay aloft if its power failed. A semirigid type needed much more power to maintain its shape; with failure, it would lose its rigidity, the form would collapse, and it would fall to the ground. The Zeppelin airship, with its aluminum skeleton, was always maneuverable, while a semirigid construction could maneuver properly only when its form was fully inflated by the gas it carried. A less-than-full supply of gas would be disastrous to the semirigid type. No such problem faced a rigid airship. The individual gas cells were well distributed over the entire length of the airship, and a loss in any one of them would not cause the stem or stern to collapse, as in the semirigid form. The air space between the several gas cells and the outer covering acted as a temperature control, keeping a definite and equal temperature of the gas. This caused the maintenance of an adequate gas supply, so necessary for long-duration flights. And, the professor stated, the first Zeppelin-designed airship had achieved the speed of others that had been tested and improved over the years, indicating that improvement in that category could also be expected with further development. These points were later widely publicized.

The official reply by the society to the memorandum of Count Zeppelin was not encouraging. The feeling of the group was that, while the airship had flown satisfactorily, the demonstration did not at all promise sufficient future development of the airship and certainly did not warrant further investment by the society. Later, the honored Ernst von Siemens, in his *Erinnerungen,* or *Reminiscences,* pointed out how much mental energy had been wasted in the fruitless efforts to build the airship. As an electrical engineer of note, Siemens had no understanding of aeronautical problems, Count Zeppelin felt, and thus excused his critical judgment on that point.

But Count Zeppelin was not entirely dismayed by this new failure of official support. The ministries had turned him down, and so had the Society of Engineers, but seemingly his close friends and the general public had not completely lost faith in him. They had encouraged him when all seemed hopeless, and now that he had again reached this apparently final refusal by prominent groups, he decided to turn to this much larger group of people to expand his financial appeal. He mailed over sixty-thousand letters to selected names all over Germany.

"I appeal to the German people," the request for donations stated, "to sacrifice themselves for my undertaking and to support me in my persevering duty. Any sum will be welcome." As a subtle suggestion, a postal money order form was included in every mailing.

But only a small sum was donated, about fifteen-thousand marks (about four-thousand dollars), far too little to start the construction of an improved airship, which had been designed and now awaited only the assurance of sufficient financing. Clearly, some other means of support had to be found.

When Count Zeppelin was asked to write an article for the *Woche,* a mass-circulating weekly periodical, he was delighted. Already, a printed version of the thesis by Professor Hergesell had appeared in July 1903, and a few weeks later, a "Call on Germans," or *Aufruf an Deutsche,* was published by Captain H.W.L. Moedebeck. The Count realized that the widest publicity possible was needed to ensure a successful program of contributions.

In his *Notruf zur Rettung der Flugschiffahrt,* or *Distress Call to Save the Airship Travel,* Count Zeppelin recounted his initial idea (conceived some twenty years before), his work on it for about thirteen years (ever since he had been retired from the military service), and the fact that he himself had invested nearly all of his fortune in it. He lamented that time was a fleeting thing:

A short span of time, and weather, storm and waves, will make the stored material worthless. My last experienced helpers will not be available anymore. The last means that I may be able to offer will be exhausted. The advancement of age or even death will set a definite limit to my work.[3]

To shock his readers into action, he proposed, quite audaciously, that if his supporters did not hurry with their contributions, it may become too late to send his new dirigible airship to the World's Fair at St. Louis, where it could be admired by people from the world over. The preposterous proposal did not take into consideration that it was believed impossible by all, except the Count, that an airship could fly across the Atlantic Ocean or any other similar formidable obstacle. Still, this monumental effrontery seemed to bring results, and the imaginative enthusiast was rewarded with contributions of some fifty-thousand marks (12,500 dollars). Undoubtedly, Count Zeppelin was sincere in his noble purpose and was com-pletely honest, exuding confidence and trust, although some critics thought otherwise.

Construction estimates were called for, and orders for materials for the building of a new hangar were ordered. It was to be placed on solid ground rather than on pontoons as before, and the site selected was about 150 feet from the shore. Ample space had been furnished by the city of Friedrichshafen for a nominal renting fee, and the king had allowed a suitable area for the storage of materials.

Always a strong believer in the future of airships, King Wilhelm of Württemberg allowed a state lottery for the benefit of the construction of an airship. The *Grosse Württembergische Geld Lotterie zu Gunsten von Luftschiffahrts- Zwecken* offered, at three marks per ticket, a grand prize of sixty-thousand marks. Altogether, 8,982 winning tickets were offered, with total winnings of 180,000 marks. The drawing took place in Stuttgart on 22–24 November 1904, and netted the sum of some 124,000 marks (thirty-thousand dollars) for the intended purpose.

Further, the German Chancellor Bernhard von Bülow contributed fifty-thousand marks (12,500 dollars) from his private fund, which the chancellor could use at his own discretion without formal authorization; Count Zeppelin also added some of his own fortune to the contribution.

The construction of the *LZ 2* was now assured in a suitable hangar.

7

LUFTSCHIFFE-ZEPPELINE 2, 3, AND 4

The *Luftschiff—Zeppelin 2*, or *LZ 2*, was of the same shape as its predecessor, but several significant improvements were included in its design. The two Daimler engines for this second airship were greatly superior, now developing eighty-five horsepower instead of thirty-two as formerly. The aluminum frame was also improved by the use of triangular girders, promising greater strength than the tubular ones used before.

The *Luftschiff* was completed by October 1905 after more than a year of construction work. Test flights were scheduled to begin in November, but Count Zeppelin worried about the tricky air currents that always developed with sudden fierceness over the Bodensee at that time of year. Still, the tests had to be undertaken before winter weather conditions made such trial flights even more hazardous.

Finally, on 30 November, the *LZ 2* was prepared and ready to test fly. But the water level of the lake was too low for the float to be used in launching the airship. The two engine gondolas were then placed on pontoons, and the motor launch *Württemberg* towed the airship out of the hangar into the gentle wind. During this maneuver a quick gust of wind from the stern lifted the airship above the launch, and the tow rope fouled the elevator steering mechanism, which was at that time still under the bow of the ship. Just at this critical moment the propellers started to turn,

giving the airship an added impetus to the downward motion. The Count ordered the rear release valve pulled, so that the ship would descend onto the water. During this operation the covering of the airship was damaged in places, and further attempts to launch the ship were called off. The *Buchhorn* hurried alongside and towed the slightly damaged airship back into its hangar.

The small crowd that had gathered on this cool and slightly windy day to see the second airship rise over the lake was disappointed, but seemed generally sympathetic at the failure. Count Zeppelin and his close co-workers, engineer Ludwig Dürr, and mechanics Karl Schwarz and Wilhelm Kast were understandably even more dejected.

There was no need to hurry the repairs on the damaged craft. No test flights could be undertaken during this winter weather, but when the repair work was finished and the weather seemed unusually mild during December, promising an open winter, a test flight was scheduled to take place on 17 January 1906. The new engines had been thoroughly tested by having them run continuously for twenty-four hours, and other components had undergone similar severe trials. The airship was in excellent condition for this trial flight.

Pulled out of the hangar, the *LZ 2* glided effortlessly and most gracefully into the air above the near-placid waters of the Bodensee. Then, reaching an area of some turbulence, it began to fly in an erratic manner, and at an altitude of about fifteen hundred feet the engines suddenly stopped functioning. Despite all efforts by the engineers, they refused to start again. Now powerless, the airship was driven by the southwest wind away from the lake over Friedrichshafen and, gathering considerable speed, flew over the countryside.

As the mechanic Theodor Preiss explained later, the airship had had too much buoyancy and its weight distribution was out of balance. The ship flew at an inclined angle and was violently pitching up and down. This erratic behavior first caused the forward and then the aft engine to stall, both being flooded with fuel and then cut off completely. Then the airship drifted as a free balloon. The wind carried it toward the mountainous area of the Allgäu. When the order to lower the drag anchor was given, it was thrown into solidly frozen ground, and then, when the anchor finally grabbed, the chain broke. At an altitude of about 325 feet the airship drifted toward a farm. A girl was hanging out the washing, and seeing this huge monster approach, shouted angrily to it, "Let me hang my washing!" The airship grazed some birch trees lightly and then set down on a swampy pasture at the village of Fischersreut, near Sommersried. Farmers assisted in mooring the airship, and heavy boulders and earth were used to hold the cables. Count Zeppelin returned to Friedrichshafen by train, and members of the crew stood alternate watch over the stricken ship.

A possible disaster had luckily been averted. The airship seemed safe. But that night a violent storm broke over the Kisslegg area to buffet the huge airship unmercifully and tried to tear it from its heavy strands of twisted wire cables. Happily the lines held. The small group of men endeavored to keep the nose headed into the wind and protect the spacious sides of the hull from the constant terrible pounding of the storm, but especially from the fierce sharp gusts, which actually tore large holes in the covering material.

When Count Zeppelin returned the next morning, he concurred with the others that the airship was damaged beyond repair. The expensive engines and other valuable parts were in fairly good condition and could be salvaged and used again as new. But the remains of this once proud *LZ 2* were to be broken up and shipped back to Manzell by rail. The new disaster was, once again, a fearful misfortune.

But the sixty-seven-year-old Count Zeppelin seemed to take it in his usual stoic fashion. The following day, back at home, he discussed with his chief construction engineer the plans for the building of an improved airship.

A few days later the Count sat down to write this detailed account of the fateful flight:

A light wind was blowing from the south when we unfastened the ropes which tied the airship to the raft, a few miles south of Manzell. For several reasons the ship rose more rapidly than we had meant it to rise until eventually it was about fifteen hundred feet above the lake. However, when the propellers were set in motion, the ship turned quickly against the wind. I steered southeast to reach the wide, upper part of the lake. This meant that we were sailing against the movement of the air. I believed that the air current was relatively slight, and so I thought it would be quite safe to devote my attention momentarily to the fore and aft unsteadiness of the ship. We had not yet learned how to overcome these fluctuations. But soon I noticed that we were already too close to Friedrichshafen to land on the lake.

It had escaped my attention that we were entering into a very strong southwestern air current at this altitude. Again I steered toward the lake, but because the airship was navigating against the strong wind, it remained almost immovably suspended over the very same spot of ground. I have not had enough experience to stop the airship entirely, and so it oscillated constantly. Had we still been over the lake, I would have descended to where the air current was less strong and where I could have steered it. But being over land I dared not descend, because I have not had enough experience so far in stopping the descent at any given time before striking the ground.

While I was feeling my way along, some minor mechanical malfunctions occurred, causing the temporary stoppage of first one engine and then the other. The steering gear, too, ceased functioning altogether. Under these circumstances I was forced to land, and this landing — again because of my inexperience — had to be performed while none of the machinery was operating.

Although the anchor of the ship did not hold properly because of the frozen ground, the landing was perfectly smooth and entirely without danger to the airship. I had always predicted an on-land landing would be that way. Had we been able to land on a place where the ship could have been safely harbored, it would not have been as seriously damaged as it was during the storm which then followed.[1]

Plans were formulated for a new airship, and the problem of financing that venture was again attacked. Several months after the disaster, Count Zeppelin wrote to the minister of war at Berlin asking for financial assistance to build another airship. He suggested that a national lottery be held, similar to the one in Württemberg, but he hoped that such a lottery would yield a half million marks. In addition he petitioned the Kaiser himself for a contribution of one-hundred-thousand marks.

Count Zeppelin also approached his unfailing supporter, King Wilhelm of Württemberg, to allow another state lottery. As expected, the king complied, and the Count was pleased that his exalted friend had not failed to assist him in securing the necessary financial support the project so desperately needed just then. With these initial funds certain, construction of the airship *LZ 3* began.

With some of his problems now solved, Count Zeppelin was elated when the Institute for Technology at Dresden bestowed upon him a doctorate of Engineering, *honoris causa.*

The German government authorized a nationwide lottery to be held, and the Committee for the Study of Motorized Airship Navigation allowed the Count a sizable loan. Apparently these hard-necked bureaucrats felt sympathetic toward the unfortunate airship builder and did not blame the construction features of the dirigible for its latest mishap.

The *Reichstag,* the parliament, passed a bill on 15 April 1907, granting a substantial federal subsidy for airship construction. This grant was to be included in the annual budget, with the proviso that if the new dirigible airship could remain aloft continuously for twenty-four hours, a similar grant should be included annually for the construction of more airships.

The government also agreed to pay for the construction of a permanent hangar on the Bodensee, but insisted that it be built according to the specifications of its own engineers. When Count Zeppelin saw those plans, he strongly objected to the proposed heavy metal construction, suggesting that a lighter material would be preferable and more maneuverable in case of a storm. But since the government would pay for it, its representatives insisted on their own design, without compromise. The hangar was built with an iron frame covered with wooden boards, resting on thirty-eight immense pontoons. It was five-hundred feet long, about eighty-two feet wide, and seventy-five feet high, making it the largest such structure in Germany.

The new airship, the *Luftschiff-Zeppelin 3,* was scheduled to make its maiden flight late in September 1907. It was similar to the previous one in construction, but had damping fins with flat stabilization surfaces at the stern for improved steering and for maintaining an even flight.

Many high-government officials from Berlin were present to observe the dirigible and to evaluate their huge portion of funds invested in it. The weather was most favorable that day, and the airship rose gracefully into the air and flew magnificently. Count Zeppelin was exceedingly pleased with the test flight and found little to criticize after landing the airship near its hangar. Still, he was certain that only by building more and continuously improved airships would he ever find the perfect dirigible he desired. He had no faith whatever in theories, and little faith in tests of small models of the real object.

Other and longer test flights followed the initial one, all without incident. During the month of October alone, the Count was actually aloft for a longer time than in all of the previous years together. On one of the flights, on 30 September 1907, the *LZ 3* was kept in the air for eight hours, flying overland toward Ravensburg, a distance of some twelve miles from the lake.

Now, with the assurance of successful flights of the airship, a number of prominent persons came to be taken up and to feel the exhilaration of being suspended in the air high above the ground. The King and Queen of Württemberg and the Austrian Archduke Franz Salvator, among others, went for short flights with Count Zeppelin.

Count Zeppelin now enjoyed the adulations from high officials and important people, many of whom had either been noncommittal or openly hostile, expressing only ridicule for his invention before. But more than the praise, the Count welcomed their urging him to undertake even more-extensive flights. This would afford a needed opportunity to train the crew in the intricacies of

Graf Zeppelin and his daughter in the gondola of the *LZ 3*. (Courtesy, Luftschiffbau Zeppelin).

actual air navigation, which constantly reminded them that studied theories were only educated guesses at probabilities, not actualities.

Still, not everyone was an enthuiastic supporter of Count Zeppelin. One of his strongest antagonists was the (now) Major Hans Gross. As official representative of the government and expert in aeronautics, Gross had been on most of the committees that had to decide on the feasibility of the Zeppelin airship design, and advise the German federal government on the probable future of the airship, especially for use by the military. Gross had been in favor of the semirigid type, and with his engineer Nikolas Basenach had even built his own version of such an airship, based on the design of the French *Patric.* He was convinced of the superiority of that type, although it proved to have a relatively short cruising range and was severely limited in its payload-carrying capacity. When other government officials seemed to lean toward

the design by Count Zeppelin, the major became openly hostile. Major August von Parseval, another military aeronautical officer, also designed his own version of an airship and, after leaving the military service, became a severe critic of the Count.

With another opponent, Count Zeppelin had better luck. When an initial article had appeared in the *Frankfurter Zeitung,* reporting his first airship's test flight as a failure and terrible disappointment, the Count paid only little attention to the story. However, subsequent articles, reporting on other test flights, were as critical and scornful as the first, and Count Zeppelin became quite annoyed by them. As was his practice, he felt that, given an opportunity to discuss the whole matter with the clever reporter who seemingly knew something about the subject, he might be able to convert the writer to his views, or at least ease the severity of the criticism. He invited Hugo Eckener for a talk.

The young reporter had suggested that the various maneuvers of movements were actually unintentional and were caused by faulty designs, and that the airship would never become a good means of transportation. He believed that it was unsafe and that any expenditure was not at all warranted for the meager results achieved thus far. A visit to the yards and inspection of all of the facilities, showing the fabrication of various items and the assembly of parts to construct the airship, had a most fortunate result, inasmuch as Eckener became deeply interested in navigational problems. For a postgraduate student of economics it was quite a departure from his chosen field.

Hugo Eckener had written a book on economics and was then in the process of writing another, *Arbeitsmangel und Geldknappheit* (Work-deficiency and Money-scarcity), which was to aid him in securing a teaching position. When eventually a call came from a Hamburg college offering him a position as a docent, he refused it, since by then he had gotten "into the claws of airship travel," as he said. He believed that the "physic of the atmosphere is for the airshipman what anatomy is for the medical man." Subsequently, he studied meteorology and became the truly outstanding navigational expert in the history of airships. In fact, in later years, Eckener earned from his fellow officers the sobriquet *Papst,* or Pope, because he was infallible in his weather predictions.

The successful flights of the latest airship had been widely publicized in the daily newspapers and

The *LZ 3* landing near Constance in 1909. (Courtesy, Luftschiffbau Zeppelin).

periodicals, especially at the time of the Count's sixty-ninth birthday that July. In fact, the people reacted to the airship and its creator with such fervor that a "Zeppelin Craze" swept like a whirlwind over the entire country. The confectioners sold cleverly made marzipan airships, and a brand of cigarettes was named after the Count. White Zeppelin yacht caps, leather coats, and rubber-soled cloth shoes, just like those the Count wore, were sold by department stores, and it was the height of fashion to wear them. Gardeners named their prize flowers after him, and custom jewelers created elegant medallions with his picture. The fact that Count Zeppelin had graduated just fifty years ago from the military academy gave added impetus to this tremendous public acclaim, and the retired general was truly in his glory as the most popular man in Germany.

The Kaiser, never failing to congratulate his illustrious subjects at anniversary occasions, wrote:

It is with a very special pleasure that we send you sincere and heartfull congratulations for the twenty-first of October, the fiftieth anniversary of the day on which you began your military career, so filled with work and achievement.

We recall with great gratitude all you have accomplished in times of war and peace during your fine military career upon which you can look back with warranted satisfaction. We also recall the tireless, persistent, and self-sacrificing work you have expended on the brilliant creation of an airship, now so successfully completed, despite the immense difficulties and obstacles you encountered. We hope that this airship may become a useful asset and a blessing to the army and the German fatherland. We wish to indicate recognition of your achievement by forwarding the Military Cross.

66

May you be blessed with many years of youthful vigor and good health so that you can see and enjoy the progress of your distinguished work. This is our wish and you have the assurance of our gracious sentiment toward you, my dear General, Wilhelm II, I.R.[2]

To take advantage of the great outpouring of felicitations, Count Zeppelin wrote to the German chancellor, suggesting that it be appropriate to begin construction of the next airship, so that an entire fleet of lighter-than-air crafts could be created. Carried along by the enthusiasm of the population, the cabinet fully agreed with the Count and appropriated four-hundred-thousand marks (one-hundred thousand dollars) for the construction of a new airship, scheduled to begin at once.

Count Zeppelin also believed that the time was opportune to ask the government to reimburse his own spent fortune for the construction of the previous airships. Startled by such an unorthodox request, the cabinet nevertheless agreed and authorized the payment to Count Zeppelin of a half million marks (about 125,000 dollars) as "retroactive salary." This action pleased the Count considerably, believing that he was still entitled to live as he had been accustomed to had he not contributed his private funds to the building of his aircraft.

The conclusion of the year was on a high joyous plane, and the fact that the floatable hangar at Friedrichshafen sank that December took nothing from the enjoyable holiday of the Zeppelin family. But the holidays were short. Count Zeppelin was more anxious to be at Manzell with his workers rather than at the Stuttgart residence with his family.

The new *Luftschiff Zeppelin 4* promised to be a greatly improved model over all predecessors, and the Count did not wish to miss any of the excitement of the construction. The airship was to be 446 feet long, forty-two feet in diameter, and would have a 519,000-cubic-foot gas capacity. Two engines, also larger than those previously used, would develop 104 horsepower each. In appearance, the airship was to be considerably more slender than the others, a change that later proved to be a decided disadvantage. This new pencillike shape was unable to resist the air pressures as well as could the broader type of airship hull-construc-

The *LZ 4* over the Manzell hangar in 1908 with the King of Württemburg aboard. (Courtesy, Luftschiffbau Zeppelin).

tion design. Another innovation for the *LZ 4* was a small platform in the very nose of the airship, primarily used for weather observation, but also employable in wartime for spotting targets. This platform was to be connected with the front gondola by a crude stairway.

The maiden flight of the *LZ 4* was scheduled for 20 June 1908. As usual, Count Zeppelin appeared at five o'clock in the morning to supervise all activities in the preparation for this eventful test. The weather was superbly suited for a successful flight, and the ascent, cruising, and descent were perfect. Another flight followed on 23 June with the airship remaining in the air for over two hours. A third flight was made on the 29th, as the ship flew for six hours before returning to the base.

While these series of flights were entirely successful in every way, the whole affair was not without incident. The minister of war, Karl Wilhelm von Einem, had, along with other high-government officials, attended the initial launching of the airship. But when at the appointed time, a small leak was discovered in the exhaust system, the flight was postponed until the damaged part was repaired. The minister was duly notified of this delay; however, because he had other more important matters to attend, or because he was just irritated at this unexpected delay, he left the area greatly annoyed. The flight took place an hour later.

The satirical periodical *Simplicissimus* observed in a subsequent issue that since the war minister was not present at the launching, it should be presumed that officially the flight did not take place at all. Another humorist suggested that because of this conflict, one talked freely about both men, the Count and the minister, but that later on the talk would be only of one, and that would be the Count. (In German, von Einem means "of one," and it was a clever play on words.)

Again, the Count was asked to give a talk to a group of scientists, and he went to Dresden. Earlier that year, on 25 January, he had gone to Berlin to speak on "The Conquest of the Air" *(Die Eroberung der Luft)*. In his talk in the huge *Saale der Sing—Akademie* the Count had pointed out that three basic design features in dirigible airships were necessary to ensure safety. First, at least two independent power units were needed, so that in the event one failed, sufficient maneuverability would still be provided. Second, rigidity of form was required to ensure steerability. Third, the size had to be large enough to allow space for an ample supply of fuel to ensure power in the event the flight had to be extended because of unforeseen circumstances, such as storms.

The Count suggested that speed was not as important as safety, and that safety would be increased by improved navigational aids during cloudy and foggy weather and during the night. By means of utilizing the small platform in the nose of the airship, it was now possible to navigate by celestial bodies, a feature feasible only in such a rigid airship. While adequate passenger space was already provided in the current type of airship, this would be increased in future designs. Airships would travel at a speed of sixty kilometers per hour, covering about three-thousand kilometers in two days, or at slower cruising speeds covering as many as six-thousand kilometers in four and a half days.

Count Zeppelin stated that hangars would not have to be built movable against the wind any more, and he calculated that for one-million marks, regular service between Berlin and Copenhagen could be provided. Such an undertaking would leave ten percent profit, sufficient to pay off the interest on the capital and initial investment.

As a military man, the Count pointed out that his airships would prove to be invaluable to any general or admiral in time of war because the ships could scout enemy positions from a safe altitude, day and night. Not only could they be used as commercial and military vehicles, but could also be employed on exploration expeditions to the arctic regions or to far-off colonial countries.

Count Zeppelin spoke briefly of the legal questions of overflying political boundaries. It would be impossible to close such borders to overflying airships, but he suggested that arrangements could be made in peacetime to allow such flights. Traffic rules could be drawn up, as they would be made for travel on ground. He concluded his speech with the statement that airship construction was his life's work and that he would carry it further as long as he lived and would leave it as his legacy to the German people.

In a speech before the 49th National Convention of the Society of German Engineers at Dresden on 29 June 1908, Count Zeppelin spoke on "Experiences when Building Airships" *(Erfahrungen beim Bau von Luftschiffen),* stating that he "was happy to have lived to see the success of the airship, because I had found independently thinking men who had spent their lives creating the airships."

In an article in the *Pester Journal* of June 1908, the claim was made that Count Zeppelin had not originated the airship at all and that the Austrian David Schwarz had invented it. In the reply, published in the *Neuen Wiener Tagblatt,* the Count stated:

> After having formulated the basis in my mind in 1873, I began its construction drawings in 1892, and in 1894 presented my completed work to a committee of experts. It was only because the necessary means for the building were impossible to secure that I began in 1899 the actual construction of an airship and in 1900 the first test flight. I had not known of the airship of Schwarz when I began work in 1892. My work was not a continuation of those ideas or a development of them, but an entirely independent idea. I used an entirely different concept, seventeen individual gas cells, while Schwarz used only one large container for gas.[3]

Greatly encouraged by the series of successful flights of the *LZ 4,* Count Zeppelin entertained the idea of undertaking a twenty-four-hour flight, which would assure the final stamp of approval by the government of his *Luftschiff* project. Still, the Count did not want to rush into this all-important test, so he decided to stay aloft first for twelve hours.

The *LZ 4* over the Bodensee, powered by two 105-horse-power engines. (Courtesy, Daimler-Benz).

One of the historic milestones in early airship travel was this famed *Schweizerfahrt,* the flight over Switzerland. Professor Hugo Hergesell, who represented the German minister of the interior on that flight, wrote that July 1, 1908 was a truly memorable day in the history of aeronautics. With magnificent weather the party left the floating hangar in the little motor launch *Württemberg* for the airship which was made ready for the ascent. The passengers quickly found their places in the front gondola, where members of the ground crew had been waiting until they embarked, in order that the airship would maintain the proper balance. Besides Professor Hergesell, there were Count Zeppelin, chief engineer Ludwig Dürr, two steering engineers, and six other engineers who took part in the flight. The so-called salon, actually a small cabin located between the two gondolas, had been turned over to the writer Emil Sandt, whom the Count had invited to participate in the flight.

Seven minutes after the passengers had boarded the airship, it rose and sailed toward Konstanz.

The diligently selected route took the airship over many towns and villages, so that as many people as possible could see the *Luftschiff.* When bad weather was threatening in the Wallensee region, the Count changed course to Winterthur and over Thurgau. The *LZ 4* flew at a speed of almost forty miles per hour and reached an altitude of about 2,400 feet over the mountainous terrain. It performed most satisfactorily over the difficult areas that had erratic air currents. The airship flew over Konstanz, Schaffhausen, then along the Rhine and Aar Rivers to Lucerne, Zug, Zürich, Winterthur, and returned by way of Frauenfeld, Romanshorn, Rorschach, Bregenz, and Lindau to Friedrichshafen. The ship had been in the air just over twelve hours when it landed that evening at Manzell. A huge crowd had gathered for an enthusiastic welcome when the *Luftschiff-Zeppelin 4* touched its home ground.

In the towns and countryside along the way,

69

people had excitedly awaited the long dirigible balloon, usually calling to neighbors that *"der Zeppelin kommt,"* rather than that the *Luftschiff* approached. And thus this appellation became synonymous with the dirigible balloon. The *Luftschiff—Zeppelin* simply became the *Zeppelin* to nearly all people.

Enthusiasm over the triumphant flight again reached monumental proportions. Newspapers carried the story, similar to that which appeared in the *Thüringer Zeitung* the next day:

> Whenever the airship flew over a village, or whenever it flew even over a lonely field where a few farmers were working, a really tremendous shout of glee rose into the air toward Count Zeppelin's miracle ship which, in the imagination of all those who saw it, suggested some supernatural creation. This powerful impression was mixed with a feeling of human joy at the thought that this tenacious and courageous white-haired man up there in the sky was truly rejoicing, for after decades of hard work and stubborn persistence he had overcome all obstacles. He also had surmounted the distrust and prejudices of many scientists and the disinterested attitude he had encountered for so long in government circles.[4]

Years later, Count Zeppelin often said, "The *Schweizerfahrt* was the nicest trip I ever made in my life."

To compliment the Count on the completion of the twelve-hour flight over Switzerland, the German crown prince sent a telegram saying, *"Halte Ihnen nach wie vor die Stange. Wilhelm."* ("I hold, as before, the rod for you": the German saying for, "I keep my fingers crossed for you.") Count Zeppelin, thinking that this congratulatory telegram came from Kaiser Wilhelm, promptly wired his thanks for the message. Upon this, the Kaiser, never at a loss for a clever retort, wired his son: "In the future, please hold your tongue and not the rod." A satirical periodical published a long verse with the line: "The rod, which your people hold, is a rod of gold."

An even greater jubilant mood than brought by previous flights engulfed the German people when the newspapers heralded the story of this latest exploit of the Zeppelin airship. Sales of Zeppelin items were greater than before, and the adoration fever gripped officials as much as the staid townsmen in their cities. The city fathers of Berlin named a square *Zeppelin Platz,* and Frankfurt am Main named a lengthy park area between two broad avenues the *Zeppelin Anlagen.* Donaueschingen was the first German town to name a street, *Zeppelin-strasse.*

The successful Swiss flight also instilled such confidence in the safety of the airship travel that many prominent persons came to Manzell to go aloft with the Count. Among others, the loyal supporter, the King of Württemberg, went with his Queen on a trip over the Swabian lake region on 3 July.

The sad news of a disaster to the airship of Gross and Basenach, which was completely wrecked near Berlin at about that time, did not seem to affect the assurance that the Zeppelin-type airship was of a safer design. However, the authorities remained quite unconvinced of that judgment.

With all this adulation now heaped upon his epochal flight, Count Zeppelin believed it wise to strike while the iron was hot. So he made preparations for the twenty-four-hour flight for the middle of July. However, because he had never paid too much attention to birthdays and other anniversaries, his plans went awry.

The seventieth birthday of Count Zeppelin was on 8 July 1908. Several days before, he went to his estate at Girsberg expecting to celebrate the day in the quiet presence of his immediate family. But as soon as he arrived there, he fully realized that he could expect precious little privacy. He had become public property.

The evening before his birthday a festive dinner had been arranged at the Inselhotel at Konstanz with many dignitaries attending. After many congratulatory speeches, the dinner was concluded with a torchlight parade in front of the hotel to honor the septuagenarian. Representatives from all conceivable groups from all over Germany appeared then and the following day to bring greetings and best wishes. None wanted to be left out of the celebrations. At Girsberg, a vast reservoir of enthusiastic supporters, including officials of the federal government, the separate states, from a multitude of military organizations, various trade and craft unions of numerous areas, civic groups, and of course the many specially selected representatives of school children, had come to bring the best wishes and hopes for continuing good fortune. Over a thousand congratulatory telegrams were received.

The cities of Konstanz, Friedrichshafen, Stuttgart, and Lindau sent delegations to inform the Count that he had been given the freedom of their cities and had been made an *Ehrenbürger:* an honorable citizen.

A special envoy came from the king of Württemberg to bring best wishes and a message:

> I feel a particularly strong impulse today to send you my most sincere and heartfelt good wishes. I know that these good wishes are shared by our whole country. We all look upon you with pride and admiration. At a time of life when most men retire, you are just beginning to reap the fruits of your great work. You are still at the height of your power. I wish you many, many happy years to come.
>
> I am giving myself the pleasure of presenting you today the Gold Medal for Arts and Sciences as an outward token of my deep regard for you. I have also presented Herrn Ernst Uhland, your General Manager, with the Friedrichsorden First Class and hope that by honoring him I have honored you as well.[5]

Various universities of Germany sent delegates. The count's old alma mater, Tübingen, presented a certificate of doctor of engineering, *honoris causa.* The Society of Engineers presented him with the *Grashof-Medaille,* their highest honor. While these representatives offered formally their congratulations, a choral group serenaded the "birthday child."

Count Zeppelin thanked in brief responses the several delegations and representatives, but during all of these celebrations he made only one lengthy speech, and that to the Tübingen delegation. He expressed his sincere, heartfelt thanks to the University of Tübingen for the extraordinary manner in which the delegation had honored him. He was a doctor "who had taken his degree ninety-nine terms after entering the university."

His joy at seeing the delegation was so great that he had overcome the depression which at first overcame him because he felt that the honors bestowed were exaggerating his real achievements. He explained that the work "I have done is based solely on exact science and did not require from me any great imaginative powers or philosophical speculations." He went on to say that he never felt it necessary to fight for self-confidence and faith for the simple reason that mathematics, logic, and practical experiments gave him proof after proof and showed him that he was right. "When a man has that certainty and knows that he will reach his goal, it is not a virtue for him to find the way," Count Zeppelin told his audience.

Therefore, he reasoned, that the honors the university, as well as the people from other parts of Germany, were showing him were not based on exaggeration of his personal achievements, but on the contrary, were directed toward him merely because he was the man who happened to carry out an invention that the whole world had needed for a long time. He was indeed filled with hope and gratitude because he was confident that the invention, which a kind Providence permitted him to carry out, would become a real blessing and an asset to the German Reich. He believed that mathematicians would take an interest in the airship; engineers would perfect the technical equipment; physicists would clarify the laws which would govern air navigation; and geologists and ethnologists would make good use of it. Economists, he said, would show how German capital could best benefit by investing quickly in the construction of airships so that the country would become the first nation to build them for general use. Lawyers would, in turn, the Count suggested, formulate international laws and regulations governing the navigation of the air.

The Count was fully convinced that international laws would some day control airship travel between all the people of the world, and he felt confident that the undertaking that he had begun would develop into a great boon and a valuable treasure for all. His confidence was justified, the Count felt, by the enthusiasm of the scientific world—of masters and scholars, professors and students. He appreciated that the representatives of the Tübingen University had been the leaders in this enthusiastic welcome of his invention. Therefore, Count Zeppelin asked them to join in a vote of thanks and to cheer with him, *"Tübingen lebe hoch!"*

The student delegation joined the Count and responded with a hearty *"Hoch soll er leben . . . ."* And, by a prearranged signal, the day was finally closed with the hissing and booming noise of fireworks, furnished by the Emmishofen firm of electrical supplies.

When Count Zeppelin later told his sister Eugenie that he was hardly worthy of such great honors, she replied that he "should just assume that God has sent all these honors. He will also see that you have enough humiliations to compensate for them."

8

TRAGEDY AND TRIUMPH

After the expansive birthday celebration, Count Zeppelin returned to Manzell anxious to resume his preparatory work for the critical twenty-four-hour flight, scheduled for 14 July 1908.

All was in good order, but when the new launch *Weller* pulled the airship out of the hangar, the tow rope snapped before the ship was entirely clear of the hangar. The airship bumped against the walls, damaging a propeller and the elevator rudder, and puncturing two gas cells. The steamer *Königin Charlotte* helped return the striken airship to the safety of its hangar for repairs.

The *LZ 4* was taken out the next day, but again the hull lightly touched a hangar wall. This slight damage caused postponement of the flight once more. Eventually, on the early morning of 4 August, the airship rose according to plan and everything seemed to function properly for the long flight ahead.

The route, again carefully selected by Count Zeppelin for maximum exposure to the people in the cities, was to take them over the Schaffhausen Falls and down the Rhine. The thin, long *Zeppelin—Luftschiff* was admired at 9:30 that morning by the Basel citizenry, and by 12:30 P.M. the dirigible balloon flew at a fairly high altitude over the single-spired cathedral of Strassburg. City officials had placed themselves on top of the one flat tower of the cathedral, and "all roofs were black with people," a passenger reported.

It was three o'clock when the Speyer Dom appeared below, and Darmstadt was visible at 4:30 to the aeronauts. But soon after the airship had flown over Darmstadt, the oil pressure of the forward engine dropped alarmingly, causing it to overheat. (Some said that a cog wheel slipped off the engine.) Rather than take an unnecessary chance with the damaged engine, the Count decided to land for repairs. He always believed that "prudence was the better part of valor." The *Luftschiff* landed at Nierstein near Oppenheim on the Rhine. The emergency landing was executed without incident, and a crowd gathered quickly to see the airship and its illustrious inventor. The needed repairs were duly made and the flight was resumed.

Because of the unexpected delay it was midnight when the airship reached Mainz. Only a few anxious and determined citizens stayed up to see the dirigible balloon above, gliding majestically like a supernatural apparition.

The course was now set toward the south, with more than half of the projected journey completed. But over Mannheim the same engine acted up again. A connecting-rod bearing had burned out. Landing at night was a particularly hazardous maneuver, and at a strange place with untrained ground personnel it was out of the question to the cautious captain. Count Zeppelin ordered the other engine slowed, and eventually the airship reached Stuttgart, some seventy-five miles farther away.

Even with the reduced engine power available, the landing at sunrise was perfectly executed at Echterdingen. Count Zeppelin noted that the day, 5 August 1908, promised to be again a rather warm one, not at all unusual for Stuttgart during August; he was thus concerned over the loss of gas, caused by the unusually hot weather during the previous day.

Word that the airship had landed spread quickly among the inhabitants, and a large crowd gathered rapidly for a close look at the *Luftschiff*. The police chief was forced to ask for a company of soldiers from Stuttgart to assist in guarding the airship and to keep the estimated fifty-thousand eager spectators behind the ropes so the mechanics could do the repair work properly and undisturbed.

Count Zeppelin went to an inn, the *Hirsch*, for breakfast. Some close friends stopped by later to visit and to have lunch with him there. From time to time the Count checked on the work in progress and ascertained the safety of his airship. There was a slight wind blowing, and occasional gusts caused some concern, but soldiers were holding the *Luftschiff* down, and it appeared to be securely tied and perfectly safe. The repair work proceeded satisfactorily and the return trip was expected to resume early that afternoon.

All hopes for the twenty-four-hour journey had been ruined by the two unscheduled stops. The endurance flight could be undertaken later. Count Zeppelin told his friends that much had been learned on the trip thus far, so not all work was wasted, and it was really impossible to feel bad about the misfortunes.

Suddenly a terrific explosion shook the building of the inn to its foundation. The guests jumped up from their chairs and ran to the door. Screams and agonizing cries from the crowd shocked the ears of Count Zeppelin, and the horrible sight of one huge sea of solid flame rising into the air stunned him completely. His *Luftschiff* had exploded and was afire. The tight cloth covering of the airship frame had gone up like a sheet of flame. The Count ran toward the flames.

An eyewitness to the tragic catastrophe wrote:

The ship, pointing to the south, was lying in an exact north to south position. Two non-commissioned officers and twenty-five men (sent from Stuttgart) were holding on to the front gondola; another non-commissioned officer and twelve men were holding on to the ropes. An equal number of men were holding the back gondola, but before the storm actually broke, another twelve men were stationed at the back gondola as well.

About ten minutes to three a terrific squall suddenly swept down from the west, striking the airship broadside. The back part of the ship was raised with a jerk, the force of which lifted the men from the ground. The men holding on to the front gondola were soon lifted from the ground, and all of them jumped, even though the ship had already reached a considerable height of about five hundred feet when she dropped a bit and floated south for about half a mile. Then the front caught in some trees and she went up in flames.[1]

Count Zeppelin stood aghast in the field where the twisted skeleton of his once proud *Luftschiff* smoldered. Flames had subsided into small individual fires, crackling here and there. The crowd around him was shocked into deathly silence. Ambulance wagons came to care for the injured men, and shouts of commands by military officers were heard over the noises made by the collapse of the aluminum-frame skeleton. The gondolas were charred completely. The *Luftschiff—Zeppelin 4* was a total loss.

The actual cause of the catastrophe was never really determined, but probably the flammable hydrogen gas ignited when the airship suddenly left the ground, causing some atmospheric discharges of electricity. The greatest calamity to Count Zeppelin was, however, the loss of lives in connection with his creation. Standing there and surveying the chaotic scene before him, he suddenly looked years older than his former youthful appearance, his friends felt.

This same storm had also brought devastation to a large area. To the south it caused a terrible fire at Donaueschingen, destroying nearly the entire town and damaging extensively the residence of the Fürst zu Fürstenberg, one of the Count's early strong supporters.

Rather than remain in Stuttgart after the horrible tragedy, Count Zeppelin returned to Friedrichshafen by train. The streets of the city had been decorated with gay flags fluttering from almost every window in its streets. A parade had been scheduled and military bands had congregated for the traditional outdoor concerts: the beloved *Platzkonzerte,* so popular in the cities of Germany where military units were stationed. The king had ordered the König Karl Uhlanen Regiment into the city as a special honor to its former commanding officer, to lead the *Fackelzug,* or torchlight parade, that night. But this parade, as all other joyful festivities, had been canceled hurriedly when word of the terrible disaster had been received.

The festive reception planned for Count Zeppelin and his crew turned into a silent tribute of mourning, as the Count and the few men walked with him from the railroad depot to the hotel *Deutsches Haus* where he usually stayed. His daughter Hella, had come to walk the few blocks silently with her father in his grief.

Count Zeppelin believed that further construction of airships was definitely stopped now. Still, he had wanted to come to Manzell to collect his thoughts, rather than to sit thinking of the uncertain future in the privacy of his comfortable home at Girsberg. Having experienced many disappointing setbacks in the development of his project, he believed that this last one was surely unsurmountable, and he went exhausted to bed.

The next day was phenomenal. After the initial shock of the devastating loss of the *Luftschiff,* toward which many had contributed, the people obviously realized that the Count was also crushed by this monumental calamity. Millions of ardent admirers rose as a well-organized mass to do their best to ease the terrible grief they knew Count Zeppelin had to feel. German stubbornness not to admit defeat despite overwhelming proof came alive in almost every citizen in the fatherland.

Friends and entirely unknown individuals and delegations came to the hotel to see Count Zeppelin and to offer not only their condolences but also financial assistance. The King of Württemberg himself traveled to Friedrichshafen personally to express his sympathy.

Delegates from a bowling club in Baden came and brought 150 marks from their members. A manufacturer, Carl Lanz, of Mannheim, dispatched fifty-thousand marks (12,500 dollars) to the hotel, and an officer of the pleasure steamer *Königin Charlotte,* which cruised the Bodensee that afternoon, brought a donation of six-hundred marks that had been collected by the passengers for the cause of Count Zeppelin.

The *Deutsche Flottenverein,* the German Navy League, sent a contribution, and the *Deutsche Luftfahrverband,* the Association of Aviators, issued a public proclamation. It read:

Count Zeppelin, who is an honorary member of our association, of August 4th and 5th gave an epoch-making demonstration of the achievements which can be accomplished with his type of airship.

The two landings, which were completely successful, contributed greatly to our experience in emergency landings and it was not the fault of the invention—made by our veteran, sorely tried pioneer in aeronautics— that the airship was destroyed by the elements at Echterdingen.

We call upon all those, who, with us, feel the national gratitude we owe Count Zeppelin, to contribute to a national fund for the construction of Zeppelin airships and for the continuation of Count Zeppelin's personal experiments in aeronautics.[2]

The *LZ 4* had made five flights and had covered a total of 1,313 kilometers on those journeys.

The *Schwäbischer Merkur,* a Stuttgart newspaper, advocated a national contribution campaign and backed it with an initial donation of twenty-thousand marks (five-thousand dollars). Now the newspaper and the aviator's association both joined in the nationwide appeal for contributions. Other newspapers soon presented the appeal to their readers.

To bring all of these separate efforts together, a *"Reichskomitee zur Aufbringung des nationalen Luftschiffbau—Fonds für Graf Zeppelin,"* a federal committee to raise the National Airshipbuilding Fund, was established. The German crown prince was named president, and other prominent members included the Duke of Mecklenburg, Reichskanzler von Bülow, and the ministers von Bethmann-Hollweg and von Einem.

The kaiser contributed eleven-thousand marks to the fund, and the crown prince gave five-thousand marks. The city council of Berlin voted to donate thirty-three-thousand marks; Stuttgart bestowed twenty-thousand marks; Friedrichshafen, five-thousand marks; while many other city governments made substantial contributions.

The school children, the most passionate idolizers of the likable Count Zeppelin—and probably all proudly wearing their white Zeppelin caps—did their utmost to help in this time of desolation and despair. Hundreds of letters arrived with small coins or bringing promises of financial assistance.

One little girl enclosed her entire savings of seven *Pfenning,* so that the Count could build another *Luftschiff.* A small boy cautiously wrote that he would be happy to send his twenty *Pfenning* should it prove helpful. Another girl, a rather promising practical psychologist, sent to her dearly beloved a hilarious juvenile picture-and-verse book, *Struwelpeter,* "to comfort you, because your nice airship has burned up." Children were always dear to the Count, and these many messages of loyalty touched him deeply. He and his daughter answered them all.

The government permitted the *Motorluftschiff Studiengesellschaft,* the airship study group, to issue a special airship postage stamp to aid in the money-raising effort, with the proceeds going to the fund. Caught up in this tremendous movement, government leaders now decided to pay the promised two million marks, although the agreed condition, to remain aloft for twenty-four hours with the airship, had not been fulfilled.

Money gifts came from people in many foreign places, among them Johannesburg, Sofia, San Sebastian, Smyrna, Montevideo, and from Egypt, Turkey, Java, Brazil, East Africa, Holland, and other countries, wherever Germans had read of the airship disaster.

In fact, the wide response to the catastrophe, especially by so many individuals, overjoyed Count Zeppelin. It was far beyond expectations, and it immensely exceeded the multitude of honors, tributes, and decorations he had received on his last birthday celebration.

Although apparently everyone endorsed the activities of the count, occasionally a lone dissenting voice was heard; such a severe critic was Maximilian Harden, then writing in the *Zukunft,* or *Future.* This first adverse criticism was made soon after the Echterdingen catastrophe. While Count Zeppelin ignored such hostile articles completely, Alfred Colsman answered this one in an article published in the *Zukunft* in October 1909.

Later during the immense popularity of Count Zeppelin and his airships, Harden again wrote in derision of the "costly shaped gasbladders." He went on to say that even short-sighted men should realize that the future does not belong to the airships but to the flying machines, and that actually bringing such a "mammoth-ship" into the air, while indeed an interesting and most laudable achievement, was still a completely unnecessary one.

Early in 1914, the eminent Professor Müller-Breslau published a very favorable article on the airships of Count Zeppelin, having been convinced that the Count had the right answer to the problems of transportation for long distances over obstacles such as mountains or oceans. In scientific circles, this article made a great impression and stilled any latent criticism of these airships.

Later, Count Zeppelin referred to the Echterdingen disaster as his *glücklichste Unglücksfahrt,* his luckiest bad-luck trip. It signified an eventful turning point in airship history.

It seemed clear that the people of Germany loved the Count equally as much as he liked his countrymen. He was, unintentionally perhaps, a unifying national symbol, signifying "One Country."

Through newspapers, Count Zeppelin made public his letter of thanks:

Besides my own firm belief in my idea, nothing has helped me more to overcome my grief over this catastrophe and urged me more to resume my work quickly than the knowledge that the entire German people, to whom my work has been dedicated from the very beginning, stood behind me. The people have proved their faith in me by their unique loyalty and sacrifices which have led them to contribute so generously that I can build a new airship. It will be better than the last one because we have gained more experience.

With deep emotion I express my thanks to all the German people. I hold it my most sacred duty to prove myself worthy of the faith which the people have shown in me, and I consider this splendid national demonstration of confidence a command from my fellow countrymen to continue my work. I am well aware that this implies a serious responsibility, but the desire of the German people to send forth airships built on my system to span the world will give me courage and the strength to continue my project.[3]

The gifts had totaled over 6.25 million marks (over 1.5 million dollars).

9
CONTINUING PROGRESS

It became evident that an expanded organization was needed, and consequently the *Zeppelin-Stiftung* (Foundation) as the financial branch was created, with Ernst Uhland as director. The *Luftschiffbau-Zeppelin,* Zeppelin Airship Construction Company, was founded with a capital of four million marks (about one-million dollars) to be responsible for the actual airship building. This company was placed under the direction of Alfred Colsman, an industrialist from Werdohl, Westphalia, and son-in-law of Karl Berg of Eveking.

Count Zeppelin was the chairman of the whole organization, for he was the undisputed aeronautical expert of the country and the chief organizer of the enterprise. He had brought airship construction from its infancy to this now-expanded state.

The Count had selected his early associates most carefully. They were all experts now; certainly none of them were at the beginning, but eventually by experience in this unknown field of endeavor they had become as knowledgeable as any group of men anywhere.

When the first engineer Kober was forced to have his life-insurance policy lapse, he refused to go along on test flights and the maiden flight of the first airship. This annoyed the Count greatly, and the relationship between the two men was never quite the same. Soon after the episode, the engineer resigned and emigrated from Germany to Argentina. Occasionally he forwarded some suggestions on engineering problems of the airship, but Count Zeppelin refused to consider the propositions. Another man, Eugen Wolf, who was on the maiden flight of the first airship, left the staff when other airships crashed, and publicly stated that he hoped for the Count to abandon his dream. Wolf was quickly abandoned by Count Zeppelin, and became an explorer in Africa.

When going by motor launch from Friedrichshafen to Manzell usually with the workers on the *Württemberg,* Count Zeppelin would ask them to sing for him *"Wohlauf, die Luft geht frisch und rein,"* ("Awake, the air is fresh and pure"). One night, after drinking the new wine decorated with grape leaves, a group of workers sang the favorite as a serenade in their best *Sängerbund* manner, under the window of the room of the Count. After that, the gay celebrants appropriated the motor launch for a quick trip to Switzerland and more of the heady May wine.

But, with the sun rising over the Allgäu on the return trip, first engine trouble and then the futile search for an oar, which had been carelessly discarded into the lake, delayed the carousers, so that when they eventually reached the German shore, the Count, the boatman Ludwig Marx, and some abstaining workers awaited the launch. Each of the revelers was promptly fined five marks for stealing the boat.

The group sang no more on future trips to and

from work. When a few days after this escapade, the Count asked them to sing something, the men just grumbled obstinately and could not think of a song at all.

"Well, *meine Herren,*" replied Count Zeppelin, "then sing the song you sang on your way to Switzerland." The workmen knew that now all was forgiven, and they happily burst into harmony with their popular *"Wohlauf...."* The Count just smiled. Schlosser Preiss, the toolmaker, who had been working with the Count since the beginning, added, as he recalled the incident, "The general always appreciated a good joke."

His "gentlemen" were devoted to Count Zeppelin. Many of the few co-workers of the early years stayed with him and became heads of departments. Ludwig Marx, who began as helmsman of the first motor launch, later was in charge of the small fleet of motor launches. He remembered the old general as a real man, a true nobleman. And not because he was a count, a general, a chamberlain, or even his excellency, but because he was simply a fine person, strong of character, full of kindness, conscious of his worth, yet modest. He was religious, saying a silent prayer before every trip, and after the journey he gave thanks.

Marx was impressed when, after the first naval airship had taken off and people congratulated the Count, he removed his cap, as if in prayer, and said softly, "How little I had to do with that."

At the beginning, the group of workers was pitifully small; and even after the first triumphs the entire personnel was not more than ninety men. Count Zeppelin hired a steamer on their weekly day off and went on a picnic with them all. At one time when the elected speaker, who was to thank the Count for the outing, got stuck in his speech, Count Zeppelin kindly asked to finish it, saying, "You men and officers do not owe me your thanks. On the contrary, I am indebted to you. For while this great work was my idea, it was you, my trusted workers and employees, who completed it. Therefore, I thank you from the bottom of my heart, and drink to your health."

Count Zeppelin was proud of his men and showed a genuine interest and deep concern for their problems, and they in turn were loyal to him. Anyone who showed no confidence in the Count, who was a severe disciplinarian, was dismissed from his service and from his mind. The Count was a most benevolent autocrat who ruled his domain with a velvet-gloved iron hand.

The Count was always terribly annoyed when one of his engineers, in reply to a question on a technical subject, said that such a thing was impossible to do. To the Count nothing was impossible until it was proven irrefutably to be so; but not before that. "I cannot stand such a reply from one of my gentlemen," he said emphatically.

With the enlarged construction program, more ground space was needed, and Count Zeppelin approached the city of Friedrichshafen about the matter. Meeting with members of the city council in September, he explained the new project and expressed his desire to remain in their vicinity on the lake shore. "I am too old to move away from here," he said.

Eventually, when the city made possible the purchase of extensive acreage, Count Zeppelin had architects in a national contest submit plans and bids for the building of a large hangar. Sixty-eight plans were submitted, and the bridge-construction company, *Brückenbau Flender* of Benrath, was awarded the contract. Allowing space for two airships, this hangar was to be 603 feet long, 151 feet wide, and seventy-five feet high.

Count Zeppelin visualized three separate construction units working together: one for passenger airships, another for military craft, and a third for naval airships. Although officially this latter branch of service had shown no interest whatever in his airships, the Count believed that it could play a leading role in naval maneuvers.

While construction of a new airship was under way, Count Zeppelin had the *LZ 3* renovated, which had been damaged when the hangar sank with it into the shallow lake shore. He took the ship up on several demonstration flights, mainly to keep the intemperate public interest from dropping suddenly because of any inactivity.

During the fall of 1908, the German Crown Prince Wilhelm, Prince Heinrich (brother of the Kaiser and himself an avid automobile enthusiast), Duke Albrecht and Duchess Wera of Württemberg, and other illustrious personages went on short flights with the Count. The Kaiser himself came to Manzell on 10 November to see the *Luftschiff* rise into the air, but he and Fürst von Fürstenberg remained on the small motor launch, cruising on the lake. The emperor explained that he had expressly promised his *Kaiserin* that he would not go aloft, although his brother had convinced him that he would have enjoyed the exhilarating experience. When the airship landed, the Kaiser went into the hangar and in a short ceremony presented to Count Zeppelin the *Schwarzen Adlerorden,* the Order of the Black Eagle. Placing the wide yellow band around the neck of the count, he called him "the greatest German of the twentieth century." He thanked God that he had considered the German nation worthy to include Count Zeppelin in its midst.

This fine tribute made the old Count forget all of the disappointments and frustrations of the many early years, and tears ran down his cheeks onto the newly placed medal on his chest. He was deeply moved by this display of recognition from a fellow Swabian, whose ancestors had once resided in the lofty castle as the Zollern before they became the Hohenzollern and then kings of Prussia.

Most of the people in southern Germany had seen one of the *Luftschiffe,* but Berliners still awaited the first visit of one. Count Zeppelin planned to make a flight to the nation's capital in the early summer of 1909. The impatient Berliners would then finally be given the opportunity to see their first zeppelin. But in July the Count was suddenly taken ill, and it was not until August that the flight to Berlin was undertaken. For the *Luftschiff* to fly to Berlin without the Count was unthinkable.

His health had always been excellent, and as he said, he was "just too busy to be sick and so was feeling as healthy as an ox." This being too busy, however, had caused his troubles. He had a carbuncle on his neck and, neglecting to have it treated properly, it developed blood poisoning, which caused the serious concern of his attending doctor. Since he was not well enough to travel all the way from Manzell to Berlin by airship, Count Zeppelin took the train to Bittenfeld (near Stuttgart), where he joined his airship.

The welcome in Berlin at the huge parade ground, the *Tempelhofer Feld,* where the airship landed safely after a leisurely low cruise over the capital, was a tremendous triumph. Berlin citizens, always known for the monomaniacal enthusiasm with which they greet their honored guests, outdid themselves. At the head of his colorful entourage, the Kaiser welcomed the Count personally. After the official greeting, both men rode in the back of

the imperial Mercedes automobile. The Kaiser allowed Count Zeppelin to enter first and seated him on his right side—both signal honors but seldom bestowed by the monarch—for the slow triumphal parade drive through the gaily decorated streets of the capital to the royal palace on the spacious *Schlossplatz* crowded with wildly cheering people. An estimated three million persons saw the Count and his airship.

Paul von Szepanski wrote in the *Berliner Tageblatt* the next day:

> Count Zeppelin always keeps his promises; in fact, he more than keeps them. He promised us to come to Berlin and to give Berliners an opportunity to see his *Luftschiff* but we had certainly not expected that we would be able to see the zeppelin right from our own windows.[1]

The seventy-one-year-old Count was elated at this reception by the multitude in the festive city and by the gaiety that prevailed wherever he appeared in Berlin. It was one of his more joyful experiences, he told his friends.

The Count returned by train to Friedrichshafen, using the luxurious private car that the Kaiser had placed at his disposal for that journey.

On 29 March 1909, twenty-five persons were carried aloft on one flight. On 6 April, the airship flew continuously for twelve hours and twenty-seven minutes on a longer flight, a *Dauerfahrt.*

Many of the following flights of the *LZ 3,* however, were made under the command of Major Sperling, who had been stationed with his aeronautical detachment at Friedrichshafen since February. His company, consisting of four officers, including Major Gross, and 120 men, had undergone intensive training for several weeks before making actual flights in the airship. During March and April, seventeen training flights had been made by the military, all of which were completed successfully and were without incidents of any kind. But occasionally, Count Zeppelin took over the command, and when on one such trip his *Luftschiff* had to fly through heavy snowfall for an extended period, the Count was especially happy for this new experience and the proven sturdiness of his ship. The airship had then made forty-five trips, covering 4,398 kilometers.

Major Sperling took over the *LZ 3* officially for the military on 29 June 1909, and now as the *Z 1* the airship was ordered to be stationed on the western border of the country to watch over heavily fortified Metz. The major proceeded to his new post, but on the way ran into heavy rain. Prudently he ordered that the craft be landed at Mittelbiberach to stay over night. But the deluge kept on for another full day, and consequently the airship was completely drenched, dangerously increasing its weight. Two days later, however, the airship had sufficiently dried out, and the major continued without further incidents to his appointed base.

The army did not acquire other airships until 1911, and this first purely military zeppelin was stationed at Köln. Another ship was delivered to the armed forces in 1913 to be stationed at Baden-Oos. Her commander, Captain Gluud, during a heavy storm lost his way, having either damaged his compass or misread its directional indication, and landed on a likely appearing landing field. "Any port in a storm" seemed a necessity, but when it turned out to be the drill ground of a French regiment at Lunéville, the captain was dumbfounded. Terribly embarrassed, he realized that with the extremely strong tail wind he had overflown Baden-Oos.

When in 1909 the *Erste Internationale Luftschiffahrts-Ausstellung,* the first international Air Travel Exposition, was opened, thousands of anxious spectators crowded the halls to see these exhibits of the so-called "Ila." Count Zeppelin went to that fair and made a speech in which he gave credit for his success to the earlier pioneers of the airships, and reaped the vast applause of all who heard this modest man.

Subsequently, on 19 November 1909, the *Deutsche Luftschiffahrts-Aktiengesellschaft,* the German Airship Travel Corporation, or *"Delag"* for short, was established to organize regular airship travel in the country. Hugo Eckener was named its managing director. Caught up in the enthusiasm, a journalist named Josef Brucker founded a company to promote the crossing of the Atlantic in an airship. The steerable balloon was duly launched by Prince Heinrich and sponsored by the famed chocolate company Suchard, but the project never reached the edge of the ocean it was to conquer.

The *Delag,* actually a subsidiary of the *Luftschiffbau-Zeppelin,* the Zeppelin Airship Construction Company, was incorporated as a limited stock company with a capital of three million marks (about 750,000 dollars), one-half million of which was invested by the *Zeppelin-Stiftung.* The purpose of the new corporation was not only to promote airship travel, but also to order these airships from the construction company. Two zeppelins for passenger service between several selected cities were duly ordered, and arrangements were made to have suitable airship landing fields constructed.

To ensure the manufacture of the various specialized components for airship contruction, the construction company founded several daughter companies. The manufacture of special airship engines was entrusted to Karl Maybach, son of the chief engineer of the Daimler Motor Company, which furnished the earliest engines, and himself an able designer. The father, Wilhelm Maybach, soon after the Echterdingen disaster, had called attention to the work of his son, then residing in Paris, to Count Zeppelin. The newly designed engine, which used a specially developed cooling system that saved weight and utilized a new and safer carburetor, was described by the elder Maybach. "The arrangement and the construction of the cylinders enable a rather meager weight with sturdiness." This new six-cylinder engine was to develop 150 horsepower instead of the former 85 and 105 of the previously used engines. Thus, on 23 March 1909, the *Luftfahrzeug-Motorenbau G.m.b.H.* was created with manufacturing facilities to be built in Bissingen an der Enz. Later named the *Maybach-Motorenbau,* the company was led successfully by Karl Maybach until his death in 1960.

Other companies were subsequently founded to supply the special needs. When it was discovered that the rubberized cotton fabric used for the skin caused friction when rubbed together, and that these sparks could ignite the entire cover when the airship came to rest on the ground and collapsed, the problem was to replace the material with *Goldschlägerhaut,* or goldbeater's skin. The factory that produced this material, the *B.G. Textile Werke, G.m.b.H.,* Berlin-Tempelhof, was bought in 1912 and named the *Ballonhüllen-Gesellschaft.*

In 1913, the *Zeppelin-Hallenbau G.m.b.H.* of Berlin was founded to construct the several hangars in the country. The same year the *Zeppelin-Wasserstoff und Sauerstoffwerke, A.G.* of Staaken (called *Zewas* for short) took over the manufacture of hydrogen gas for the airships. After that factory had been destroyed by an explosion, the scientist Dr. Messerschmidt developed a new process, which promised to be safer.

When the Swiss engineer Max Naag developed a method of machining precise cogwheels, the *Zahnradfabrik, A. G.,* was founded in 1915 in Friedrichshafen. Failure of these cogwheels, used to transfer power from the engines to the propellers, had caused great concern to the airship engineers.

It was felt that an assured and responsible availability of these special items would be ascertained only by closely controlled companies within the same corporate structure. As the immensely increased construction of a fleet of commercial airships was projected, and the hope rose for zeppelins to be employed in military services, a network of suppliers seemed absolutely necessary.

A long-cherished dream of Count Zeppelin was to use his airships for explorations. He had read of the first attempts by the Swedish Andrée and the Austrian Wellmann to drift over the pole in a balloon in June 1896. Nearly a year later, on 11 July 1897, Salomon August Andrée and two companions tried it again. Starting from Danes Island, Spitsbergen, they intended to drift over the pole to America, but disappeared. Thirty-three years later, in August 1930, the Norwegian explorer Gunnar Horn found the frozen bodies of the men on White Island, 82° 56′north, 29° 52′east.

The *Deutsche Arktische Zeppelin Expedition* left Kiel in June 1910 on the North German Lloyd steamer *Mainz* to investigate the feasibility of arctic exploration by airship. At Tromsö, the party, which included Count Zeppelin, the scientists Hugo Hergesell and A. Miethe, and its sponsor Prince Heinrich of Prussia, took the smaller arctic steamer *Fönix* to sail for Virgo Bay, the area from which the three balloonists had made their fatal ascent years earlier.

Several ascents were made with a balloon, which had been carried along for that purpose. The Count, as active as the others of the group, ascended to observe the territory, and also rode several miles on a dog sled to locate a suitable site for a proposed hangar for the *Luftschiff.*

While no actual airship arctic expedition was undertaken at the time, after gathering much data, a large, profusely illustrated volume *"Mit Zeppelin nach Spitzbergen"* ("With Zeppelin to Spitsbergen") by A. Miethe and H. Hergesell was published on this possibility. In connection with this publication, Count Zeppelin wrote that people "do not seem to realize that my airships will be the safest means of transportation over distant seas . . . . It was again necessary to convince them with actions."

The book enjoyed wide circulation and came to the attention of naval officials, who ordered an airship built in 1912.

But when the expected orders for additional military airships did not materialize, the *Luftschiffbau-Zeppelin* concentrated on passenger craft. City councils were approached and told that an adequate landing field and hangar in their immediate areas would make them a regular stop on the projected zeppelin transportation network, linking the important cities of Germany. Many of the more aggressive and forward-looking councils sent representatives to discuss this proposition with Count Zeppelin, and after some conferences agreed to furnish landing facilities for the proposed route. Consequently, suitable landing fields were constructed in Baden-Baden (Oos), Berlin (Johannisthal), Frankfurt am Main, Dresden, Gotha, Potsdam, Hamburg, Düsseldorf, and Leipzig. The *Hamburg-Amerika Linie* was appointed general agent to sell tickets for the trips.

During the first year of the *Delag,* forty-one passenger flights, lasting a total of eighty-six hours, were made. By 1912, nearly five-hundred flights had been undertaken, and during 1913 a total of 773 flights were made, lasting more than 1,100 hours.

Trips were made between cities, first from

The *LZ 7* — the *Deutschland* (1910) — on her maiden flight. (Courtesy, Luftschiffbau Zeppelin).

The *LZ 7 Deutschland's* intricate rudder assembly, 1910.
(Courtesy, Luftschiffbau Zeppelin).

Hamburg to Schleswig-Holstein, and from Düsseldorf to Baden-Baden by way of Frankfurt. Others quickly followed as soon as landing facilities were completed. The airships were naturally no match to the speedier railroad trains, but for leisurely trips across the country they proved a most popular transportation medium. The fares were considerably higher than those charged for first-class-passenger train service with its more luxurious accommodations, but a large number of people took rides in these zeppelins to feel the exhilaration of soaring seemingly unsupported high in the air and to marvel at the spectacular sights spread below them. (The round-trip fare from Hamburg to Schleswig-Holstein was two-hundred marks, about fifty dollars.)

Safety was foremost in the minds of the managers of the *Delag,* and whenever a conflict of weather or safety arose, the decision was against the unfavorable weather, and flights were either canceled or terminated.

Each subsequently built airship generally incorporated some improvement over its predecessor. Names for the zeppelins now replaced the earlier numbering system. The *LZ 7,* for instance, was known as the *Deutschland,* and others were the *Sachsen, Hansa, Schwaben,* and *Viktoria Luise* (named for the *Kaiserin).*

Still, the safety record of these zeppelins was far from perfect. In 1910 the *Deutschland* was forced to make an emergency landing during a severe storm in the Teutoburger Wald, the historical forest region where Hermann had defeated the invading Romans in 9 A.D. The zeppelin was destroyed on the ground, but fortunately without the loss of lives. This mishap allowed the pun to circulate that not only was the Teutoburger Wald in Deutschland, but also was the *Deutschland* in the Teutoburger Wald.

On 31 May 1909 enroute to Berlin, where a large crowd including the Kaiser and his party had assembled to welcome the *LZ 5,* the zeppelin flew into a tree near Göppingen. The airship had been aloft for thirty-eight continuous hours. The

The *LZ 7 Deutschland,* built in 1910, had a capacity of only 19,300 cubic meters. (Courtesy, Goodyear).

The *LZ 10* – the *Schwaben* (1911) – on her maiden flight. (Courtesy, Luftschiffbau Zeppelin).

exhausted captain Ludwig Dürr and his crew stretched out under his ship on the ground, and after a much needed rest returned it safely to its hangar. The severely damaged stem of the airship did not appear to effect its airworthiness. The captain had ordered the damaged portion of the aluminum skeleton cut off and the remaining part of the cloth wrapped around the open area and tied together. The front gas cell was destroyed, but this did not harm its buoyancy. Again, the rigid form had proved itself, for a semirigid airship would not have been able to continue because its entire lifting-gas supply would have been lost.

The tenth zeppelin, the *Schwaben,* after carrying a total of 1,553 passengers in 218 flights without incident, on 28 June 1912, at Düsseldorf, had an explosion, and fire raged through the airship, which took the lives of thirty-nine passengers and crew.

Occasionally, Count Zeppelin himself commanded one of his *Luftschiffe,* but longer trips were now just too strenuous for him. On one occasion, in 1910, he had found special delight in circling low over Wörth, where forty years before he had seen action during the war, and he hovered with his airship over the celebrated Scheuerlenhof,

Graf Zeppelin and Hugo Eckener in the gondola of the
Schwaben. (Courtesy, Luftschiffbau Zeppelin).

from where he had so narrowly escaped while on
the reconnaisance raid into then enemy territory.

When the trusty patron of the Count, King
Wilhelm of Württemberg, celebrated his twenty-
fifth wedding anniversary on 7 April 1911, Count
Zeppelin cruised low over Stuttgart and, from a
height of some hundred feet, dropped a large
bouquet of red carnations on a white silk
parachute into the formal garden of the royal
palace, missing by only few meters the balcony on
which the celebrants stood.

This enchanting interlude made the life of the
aged Count Zeppelin agreeably satisfying, and it
reminded him of some of the more-exciting daredevil escapades of former years.

Count Zeppelin was terribly disappointed in the
negative attitude of the military authorities toward
the use of his airships. But he felt even more
slighted when all of the different systems of
construction were grouped together by the mili-

tary. Unsuccessfully he had repeatedly pointed out
that each one of the types—rigid, semirigid, and
nonrigid—reacted quite differently to a given
situation.

Still, a competitive group, the *Luftfahrzeugbau
Schütte-Lanz* of Mannheim-Rheinau, also built
rigid airships. Designed by Dr. Franz Schütte of
Danzig, these airships, first built in 1911, were
more slender and more streamlined than the
zeppelins and had a capacity of seven-hundred-
thousand cubic feet. The control surfaces of the
420-foot-long and fifty-nine-foot-diameter airships
were attached directly to the trailing edges of the
fixed fins, instead of using the boxlike features of
the zeppelin's steering apparatus. The framework
of the earlier Schütte-Lanz airships consisted of
triangular wooden girders, which were later replaced
by a longitudinal and traverse arrangement. The
engines drove the propellers directly, thus
eliminating the elaborately conceived and often
troublesome system of cogwheels and shafts. Later,
the propellers were even attached to the sides of

83

The Shütte-Lanz airship, *SL 1,* at the base in 1911.
(Courtesy, Daimler-Benz).

The *Viktoria Luise* (1913) landing at her home field.
(Courtesy, Luftschiffbau Zeppelin).

the engine gondolas. The keel of the airship was placed inside the hull instead of outside, as was done on the zeppelins. During the nine years of its existence, the Schütte-Lanz company produced twenty-two airships.

When in 1913 the nineteen-year-old Prince of Wales visited the King of Württemberg, he also came to Friedrichshafen to witness the test flight of a newly built airship. The enterprising young prince showed keen interest in the zeppelin and wanted to go aloft for the initial flight, but permission was not granted by his father. The sovereign had similarly objected, just a short time before when the prince asked for permission to descend in a submarine at Cherbourg. Apparently it was believed that it would be wiser to wait and have the British Prince of Wales ride in British vessels, rather than French submarine and a German airship. Both of these trips would also have been rather hazardous, and it was probably merely an understandably cautious attitude of the royal parent to withold approval of the voyages.

Compared to the elaborate festivities of five years before, Count Zeppelin in 1913 celebrated his seventy-fifth birthday in relative quietness. He stayed at Friedrichshafen and, as he said, kept working.

Before breakfast, he was awakened by a concert in front of his hotel, then he went to the manufacturing plant, where he boarded the new *LZ 20* for a test flight and acted as commander of the airship. He had a dinner at noon at the Kurhotel, with high-ranking government officials and military officers attending. That afternoon, all of the employees and workers of the plant went on two chartered steamers for a picnic to the Waldhaus Jakob near Konstanz. Ater returning to Friedrichshafen, these six hundred celebrants were given a dinner at the Buchhorner Hof.

At the Kurhotel, the Count had another dinner with some 150 invited guests, after which a torchlight parade, led by his uhlans from Ulm, passed by the birthday party. Standing on the terrace of the hotel, Count Zeppelin said, "I just

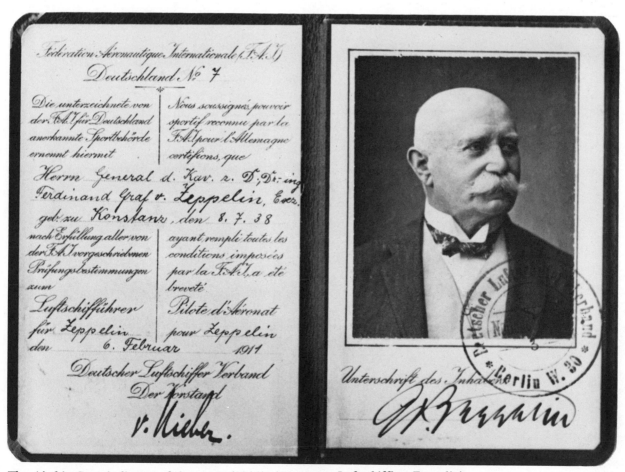

The Airship Captain license of the count (1911). (Courtesy, Luftschiffbau Zeppelin).

do not know why they are making so much of this, especially since I have promised to be here for my eightieth birthday. "

After the closing of the celebrations there, the Count went to the hotel where his workers had their festive dinner and, long after midnight, these happy celebrants in their enthusiasm actually pushed and pulled to his own hotel the automobile in which their beloved employer sat. It had been another glorious day for the Count.

Count Zeppelin had long been a well-known figure in the country. His picture had appeared in nearly every newspaper and periodical, and there was hardly a city he had not visited, either sailing smoothly above it in one of his own zeppelins or appearing in person at some occasion.

His unique attire never seemed to vary. He still wore the familiar blue suit, stiff wing collar, a tie to match the color of his suit, and, of course, the white naval cap. One time, while riding in an automobile through a city on a cold day, he said that he was indeed lucky not to have any hair on his head, because it would have frozen off with his cap in his hand instead of on his cold bald head.

Oskar Wilcke tells that in 1913 the seventy-five-year-old inveterate traveler had two busy days. In the morning of the first day he observed at the Eckernförder Bucht, the bay north of Kiel, some deep-water bomb tests to ascertain the effective-ness of proximity bombing from an airship on a submarine. The Count left Kiel that evening at seven o'clock by train, escorted by Prince Heinrich, and arrived at Berlin by 2:30 the next morning.

An automobile furnished by the military authorities picked him up at the Kaiserhof Hotel at eight o'clock and took him to the Biersdorfer Zeppelin hangar. Here the Count boarded an airship to determine from it the visibility of ground action while huge smoke machines belched out clouds of obstructing cover. The results were disappointing to him. Climbing out of the gondola, Count Zeppelin entered the automobile for a ride of some seventy-five miles to the firing range at Kummersdorf to observe the effects of bombs dropped from an airship. This demonstration lasted until three o'clock in the afternoon, and was followed by a detailed inspection of the modern fort replica, specially built to determine the damage inflicted from the famed forty-two-centimeter cannon.

At four o'clock the Count dined with the officers of the *Schiesschule,* the firing college, in their clubhouse, then took the automobile back the fifty miles to Berlin, where he arrived at about seven o'clock. He had invited a group of ladies and gentlemen friends to his hotel for eight o'clock and there he entertained them until shortly after midnight, playing the amiable and attentive host as usual.

10

THE ARMY AIRSHIPS

By July 1914, the commercial zeppelins of the *Delag* had carried a total of 34,038 passengers on 1,582 flights, and the airships had flown 182,525 kilometers (about 110,062 miles) in 3,175 hours.

The *Deutschland I* and *II,* and the *Schwaben* had been retired, and three airships – the *Viktoria Luise,* the *Hansa,* and the *Sachsen* – were still in service. Landing fields were in operation in Baden-Oos, Frankfurt am Main, Potsdam, Düsseldorf, Hamburg, Dresden, and Leipzig.

The *Sachsen,* built in 1913, was, like the sister ships, 470 feet long, had a maximum diameter of forty-seven feet, and a capacity of 19,550 cubic meters of hydrogen, enabling the zeppelin to lift 18,040 pounds. The forms of these airships were spread out nearly evenly and cylindrically. Their frames were constructed of aluminum, and the gas cells were of rubberized cotton. The zeppelins had two gondolas, the front one being the *Führergondel* (or control car) and engine room, and the rear one, the engine room only. Both gondolas were connected by a walkway, attached to the body of the airship like a keel. The propellers were fastened high on the body by means of outriggers, driven by three Maybach engines totaling 540 horsepower and giving the zeppelin a top speed of forty-five miles per hour.

With the declaration of the war in August 1914, the army took over the three commercial ships. The conversion was rather simple. The wicker furniture of the passenger cabin was discarded and the center walkway was used for bomb storage and its primitive bombing aiming device. A partition was built to make a booth for the wireless operator. The fore gondola as well as the platform on the rear was armed with a machine gun. The designation Z, with a roman numeral following, replaced the names of the zeppelins. The *LZ 22* became the *Z VII,* the *LZ 23* the *Z VIII,* and the *LZ 25* the *Z IX.* Already in 1909 the army had received the *LZ 3* as *Z I* and the *LZ 5* as *Z II.* In 1911, the *LZ 9* became the second *Z II,* and in 1912 the *LZ 12* became the *Z III* army airship. In 1913, five other airships were acquired by the army: the *LZ 15* became the second *Z I,* the *LZ 16* the *Z IV,* the *LZ 19* became the third *Z I,* the *LZ 20* the *Z V,* and the *LZ 21* the *Z VI.* When more zeppelins were lost, no replacement numbers were used anymore.

Basically, of course, these zeppelins remained the same commercial airships, designed and built to carry mail and passengers. But now each airship had a commander, three officers, and fifteen men as crew, bringing them into conformity with the other three zeppelins already in service by the military. The actual military zeppelins were slightly larger than the commercial craft, having a volume of 22,000 cubic meters. There was also one airship of the Schütte-Lanz type, stationed on the Eastern front, along with two zeppelins. Three airships were stationed near the western front.

The *LZ 8 Deutschland II* in 1911. (Courtesy, Luftschiffbau Zeppelin).

The first military mission assigned to the airships was to drop bombs on strategic bridges and military objectives and to report troop movements. But the airships were slow, cruised at low altitudes, and could not carry a sufficient bomb load to accomplish much actual damage to the enemy installations. Three zeppelins were lost almost at once.

The *Z VI* was ordered to support the attack on Lutetia to aid in the important battle against Liège in Belgium during August 1914. After dropping the three one-hundred-pound bombs over the fort, the zeppelin was forced to fly at a very low altitude. Struck repeatedly by small-arms fire, the airship kept aloft, but her captain was compelled to order it abandoned in a forest clearing near Bonn on his flight to the home base at Köln.

The *Z VII* was sent to search out the French army, which had apparently been withdrawn from Elsass, since German troops had completely lost contact with the forces. Flying at an altitude of about five-thousand feet from Baden-Oos toward the Vosges, the zeppelin was in constant danger during the night of running into the mountains, which average about three-thousand feet, except for Sulzer Belchen, which rose to 4,667 feet. But in the morning the crew discovered an encampment and dropped small bombs on it. Some short distance further they discovered large troop concentrations. For better identification, the zeppelin descended to 2,700 feet, but almost at once the air was filled with exploding shrapnel. The whole complement of infantry seemed to be trying to hit the huge hovering zeppelin. Turning it away proved an exceedingly slow maneuver and thus the long wide bulk made an excellent target. With many gas cells badly punctured, the damaged airship limped away slowly, only to be wrecked near St. Quirin in Lothringen.

The *Z VIII* had taken off also that same day from Trier. Flying over German troops, the exuberant infantrymen happily greeted their own zeppelin with rifle fire, thus inaugurating the angry crew of what was to be their fate later. When the

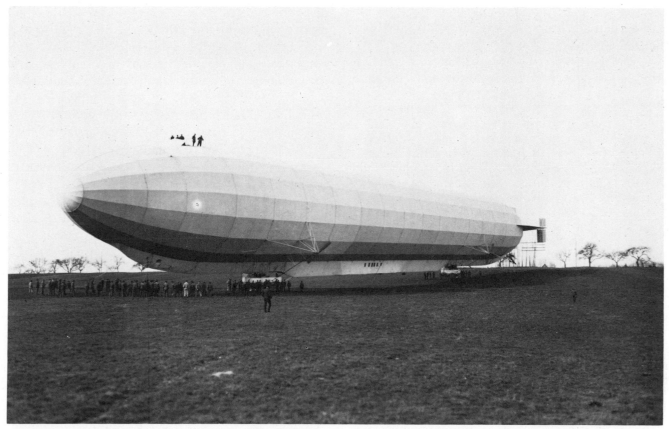

The *LZ 23*, the army dirigible *Z VIII*, in 1914. (Courtesy, Luftschiffbau Zeppelin).

airship was flying but a few hundred feet high, not having had an opportunity yet to drop the bomb load, an enemy force unexpectedly appeared below. Some bombs were hastily dropped and shots were fired by the enraged crew of the zeppelin, but this skirmish turned in favor of the enemy, being advantageously on solid ground and having better aim.

The controls were shot off the airship, untold bullet holes punctured the cells, and now the craft hovered defenselessly over the sharpshooters. Eventually, the zeppelin drifted away, only to get hung up in the trees of a forest at Badonviller. The crew made a last valiant rear-guard stand against an advancing enemy cavalry unit. Being hopelessly disadvantaged, the commander ordered the stricken zeppelin burned, but the great loss of hydrogen earlier now made it impossible to ignite the damaged ship. With French cavalry approaching the Germans scattered into the woods to see the charging *chasseurs* hacking away with their sabers at the deflated skin of the zeppelin.

After a hike of eleven hours through forests and over fields, the group of airshipmen arrived at the German lines, surprising a large patrol at rest. On hearing of the nearness of the enemy, the captain ordered his men at once to make contact with the troops that the zeppelin crew had located for him.

Shaken by this sudden loss of three zeppelins, the German High Command, for some time, did not issue any orders at all for other airships. Eventually, the *Sachsen,* which had replaced the lost *Z VI* at Köln, was ordered to bomb Antwerp. According to newspaper reports, the sight of an enemy airship had a far greater devastating effect on the inhabitants of that port city than did the actual damage done, although several houses were hit and badly damaged.

But the high command did not seem to understand the limitations and capabilities of its zeppelins, as an order later to the *Z IX* indicated: "Bombing attacks will be made on Antwerp, Zeebrügge, Dunkirk, and Calais. Return via Lille: also bombing attack there." By that time, the bomb load had been increased to about ten bombs, but these five named objectives seemed to be a few too many. Still, the mere appearance of an enemy zeppelin over the cities was terrifying enough and such a twelve-hour-long flight accomplished perhaps more than had the actual dropping of a few bombs.

Duty on these zeppelins was far from pleasant, although nearly as glamorous as that of other aviators. As Ernst Lehmann wrote:

We experienced great difficulty . . . . I remember that we tried to make a raid on Nancy, the French fortress in Lorraine, on an exceptionally cold day in February. Our ship succeeded without particular effort in reaching the hereto unusual altitude of eleven thousand feet. There the thermometer dropped past ten below zero; how much I cannot say because our instrument dials were not made to indicate lower temperatures.

There was no way of heating the control car in which we had to stand to operate the ship. The men stationed throughout the hull fared as badly, and I feared that the engine crews would freeze their fingers working on the moters. The situation became serious, when one of our engines stopped. While we were trying to get it started, another went dead. The oil had frozen into solid blocks inside the tanks. With only one engine it would have been suicidal to risk flying over Nancy, so I turned around to come back, when I found we would be lucky indeed if we were to reach the hangar. Finally, we had to rip apart the oil tanks, pick out the chunks of oil, break them into small chips and feed them almost directly into the engine through the small oil-cleaner tank. In a similar manner we got another engine started and dragged ourselves back home.[1]

One of the newly completed zeppelins was stationed at Düsseldorf, and it was there that the first enemy attack on an airship in its hangar was made, on 27 September 1914. An English aviator, Lieutenant R.L. Marix, surprised the Germans completely by suddenly appearing over the field and dropping a bomb on the hangar.

Since no planes could fly that far nonstop from an English base, it surely indicated that he must have started in Belgium and then crossed neutral Holland on his way to the city on the Rhine. Thus warned, the Germans placed machine guns on top of the hangar as defense against further raids.

These raids came indeed sooner than expected, when Marix returned on 8 October, making a steep dive from high above, released his single bomb right over the target, killing one man on the roof and setting fire to the Z IX, thereby destroying it completely. While the hangar was only slightly damaged, the only salvageable items of the airship were the engines. The unfused bombs of the zeppelin had fallen harmlessly to the ground.

Seemingly encouraged by this singular success, British aeroplanes later made two other raids on airship facilities. An attack on the Friedrichshafen installations by three aircraft from Belfort, France, accomplished nothing, except to violate the neutrality of Switzerland. A few months later, however, two successful raids by aeroplanes were accomplished on the same day. Eventually, the LZ 37 was destroyed by a plane in the air near Ghent, and the LZ 38 was bombed in its hangar near Brussels.

Construction of airships was greatly accelerated and showed a decisive increase during the first six months after the beginning of the war. Despite the dismal initial reverses, the military services were convinced of the importance of this promising aerial weapon, especially in reconnaissance work.

A new factory was erected at Potsdam, and at the Friedrichshafen yards some 1,600 technicians and eventually twelve-thousand workers were working around the clock to build zeppelins. Plans called for the completion of twenty-six airships for the army and navy by 1915. The two manufacturing facilities actually produced a new zeppelin every fifteen days.

Each new airship constituted an advancement over the previous one. The early Z XII had a gas volume of twenty-five-thousand cubic meters and achieved a speed of about sixty miles per hour, a noticeable improvement over the airships of the prewar period. The formerly open gondola cars were then enclosed, and the walkway was at least partially removed into the hull of the zeppelin. The overall shape was still rather thin and even in diameter throughout the ship, so that the skeleton rings could be mass-produced and exchanged easily for replacement in the event of severe damage. These zeppelins were able to reach considerably higher altitudes than the aeroplanes used by the enemy. Especially after dropping their bomb load, they could climb quickly into the safety of the higher skies.

After numerous reconnaissance flights by zeppelins over the coastal areas and bombing mis-

The *LZ 25* became the army dirigible *Z IX* in 1914.
(Courtesy, Luftschiffbau Zeppelin).

sions when about ten-thousand pounds of explosives were dropped on Antwerp and Ostende, the high command decided on raids on London and Paris.

The *Z XII* was selected to make the first raid on London. The zeppelin took off during the night of 17 March 1915, under the command of Captain Ernst Lehmann. After reaching the coast of the North Sea, navigation was by lighthouse on the shore across the Channel Sea. Only a slight portion of the coast was visible through the thick fog. The zeppelin cruised for several hours about the coastal area, hoping that the Thames would appear below, since the fog usually dissipated over a river. But nothing could be recognized as a landmark, and even with lowered observation basket, the fog blanket could not be penetrated. There was nothing else for the airship commander to do, but to order his ship to return.

Fog closed in again over Calais, and with engines throttled down, the zeppelin flew silently over the French city. The observer in the lowered basket, at some 2,500 feet, directed the fog-hidden airship to

the fortifications, and the bombs were dropped with considerable accuracy. The zeppelin remained for almost forty-five minutes in that area, dropping the bombs carefully for maximum damage, and then flying at an altitude of five-thousand feet returned to the base.

With fog also obscuring the landing field, the zeppelin glided in by means of its altimeter and compass. However, the barometer had fallen more than ten millimeters in the past twelve hours, so the airship instead landed mistakenly on an adjoining railroad track. The crew was sent out with lanterns to wave down any approaching train, and the next morning the zeppelin was moved to its nearby hangar for repairs, which took about two weeks to complete.

The second raid by the *Z XII* was no more successful. Extremely heavy rains were encountered over the channel, and the airship had to return. On the coast of France, the bombs were dropped over the military installations at Dunkirk, but since there were no fog clouds in which to hide, the huge zeppelin made an easy target for the soldiers in the fort. Small-arms fire damaged the airship, and a propeller was shot clear away. But

91

the stricken zeppelin eventually reached its home base.

The third attempt was still no more successful than the previous ones. The zeppelin reached the British coast at Harwich, where the bombs were dropped, and then returned to the base in Germany without ever having reached the intended target of London itself.

Early raids by army airships on continental cities were more successful. Unlike London, the "City of Lights" was never entirely darkened, and thus Paris was relatively easy to locate. The weather was also generally much better, and fogs were seldom encountered over the French capital.

The *Z X, LZ 35,* and *SL II* received orders to bomb Paris on 21 March 1915. By blinking their code names, the ground searchlights at Douai, Cambrai, Noyon, and other places on the route acted as directional beacons. Paris was easily located. But the *SL II* had been hit by shrapnel fire while over the trenches and was forced to return to its hangar, but not before dropping all of the bombs on the enemy headquarters at Compiègne.

The *Z X,* under Captain Horn, flew over Paris at an altitude of eight-thousand feet, out of reach of the batteries, which were clearly identifiable to the crew whenever a shot left their muzzles. The zeppelin cruised over the city for half an hour, selecting the targets meticulously. A power plant was destroyed, and a factory was badly damaged.

The *LZ 35,* under the command of Captain Masius, was also successful in dropping the bombs on some selected targets, but had been caught by several units of motorized antiaircraft guns using searchlights. These units followed the zeppelin on its way home, but eventually were lost when the zeppelin, by clever maneuvering, reached the safety of a forest. Again being fired upon near the frontier, the airship reached its home base in fair condition.

On her return flight, the *Z X* was awaited at Noyon by the French forces. While she was cruising at an altitude of ten-thousand feet, two salvos of antiaircraft fire severely damaged five of her gas cells. Losing altitude at the rate of about five feet per second, the zeppelin escaped over the border. By throwing overboard such items as the machine guns, gasoline tanks, reserve oil cannisters, tools, equipment, shoes, and extra clothing, the airship gained altitude at four-thousand feet and

became buoyant enough finally to accomplish an emergency landing near St. Quentin.

Three airships were stationed at the Eastern front at the beginning of the war. The *SL II,* which supported the army in the Austro-Hungarian campaign near Cholm and Lublin and stayed aloft once for sixty hours, was soon transferred to the Western front.

Field Marshall Paul von Hindenburg liked zeppelins to assist in observation as well as bombing missions, so badly needed on his wide front. Having defeated the Russian armies decisively at Tannenberg, he forthwith tried to crush them completely. But the two additional divisions that he insisted on to accomplish that final blow were never sent to him by the general staff, and so the war on the Eastern front dragged on.

The *Z IV,* under the command of Captain Quast, bombarded such important objectives as Warsaw and other railroad junctions, and on one flight of only a few-hundred-foot altitude behind the Russian lines received over three hundred bullet holes in her gas cells. After that escapade the zeppelin was withdrawn from active combat service and used for training purposes only. Its buoyancy and balance were adjudged to be permanently impaired.

The *Z V,* commanded by Captain Grüner, distinguished itself when reporting the assembly of troops at Novo Georgievsk, thus immensely assisting the high command. On one mission, while attacking the railroad yards at Mlava on 28 August, at an altitude of 3,500 feet, the zeppelin was badly hit by Russian artillery shells and crashed. The crew was captured. Three years later, in 1917, one of the men escaped safely from the Siberian prisoner-of-war camp, but some of his companions, dressed as peasants, were captured and shot by border patrols when trying to get into China.

The *Z XI* and the *LZ 34* replaced these two lost pioneer zeppelins. After raiding Warsaw, Grodno, and Kovno, as well as other strategic railroad points, these two airships were also destroyed. The *Z XI* was dashed to pieces by a squall at her hangar, and on the same day in May the *LZ 34* was lost to enemy action. The *Z XII* and the *LZ 39* replaced them. Later, the *LZ 79* and the *LZ 85* were added to them to assist mainly in bombing railroad yards.

From a base at Libau, Latvia, on the Baltic Sea,

such important railroad centers as Vilijka, east of Vilma, were repeatedly attacked, and troop concentrations at the fortified town of Dvinsk as well as the rail points at Minsk were heavily bombed.

Several of the airships of the army had been ordered in 1915 to the Eastern front from the Western section, where zeppelins had come under more severe attacks by the French troops, and losses had been far greater. Eventually, however, after some of the zeppelins had been lost in Russia, the Balkans, and the Mediterranean areas, the army decided to turn their remaining airships over to the navy.

Airship hangars were located in several scattered areas near the Eastern front, and this author remembers well the zeppelin hangar at the edge of the *Kreisstadt* in the Province Posen, where he lived as a boy. The zeppelin landing field was located a determined long-hour's walk — without distracting interruptions along the way — in a wide, open field.

Having been driven away by the threat of the plundering Russian armies and especially the marauding savage Cossack hordes at the beginning of hostilities, I returned when the invaders were stopped and spent the war years there.

A massive concrete hangar sheltered a zeppelin nearly all of the time. Occasionally, a new one came to replace the older one, which had flown away to the front, or had been transferred elsewhere, or was lost in battle. (First, the *LZ 39* was stationed there, to be followed by the *LZ 101* and *LZ 111.*)

Moving slowly in the air above the city, our zeppelin was an impressive sight to us all — all except the young and gay officers stationed at the huge airfield on the opposite side of the town, who never seemed to have anything to do with the more-staid airshipmen. Their tiny and fragile *Rumpler Tauben* or *Fokker* monoplanes and *Pfalz* biplanes were nimble and maneuverable and flew tricky patterns that were a lot of fun to watch, while the awkward, yet majestic zeppelin rose slowly into the air and then just glided along or hovered stationary over a specially marked area on the ground, when not out on patrol duty at the fighting front.

By February 1916 the army had seven newer-type airships. The *LZ 90* and her sister ships had a capacity of 32,000 cubic-meters gas volume and were constructed in a streamlined form with tapered stern and more-efficient controls. Armed with eight machine guns, each ship carried two in each gondola car, one on the upper platform, and one on the stern. The engines developed a total of 960 horsepower. Flying at an altitude of ten-thousand feet, this type of zeppelin could carry almost seven-thousand pounds of bombs. Without the bomb load, the airship could reach an altitude of twelve-thousand feet.

With increased altitudes and improved navigation, however, there also came newer and more-effective counterweapons. For the first time, the airships encountered incendiary shells fired at them. Only one hit sufficed then to ignite the zeppelin and send it to its doom. The *LZ 77* was the first victim of this advanced method.

Aeroplanes also were constantly improved. The advantage of altitude by the airships was erased, and aeroplanes were able to reach almost the same altitudes previously achieved only by lighter-than-air craft.

Land and sea defenses were also improved by floating balloons attached to strong cables and by more accurate and further firing of light cannon. Against these methods, an ingenious procedure was developed. A basket was lowered from the gondola of the zeppelin into the cloudless air, while the airship hovered in the safety of a thick cloud above. At first, a simple butter tub was attached to a long steel cable and lowered about five hundred feet below the airship. The observer was connected with the command car by telephone. However, the wild swaying tub made observation extremely confusing to the motion-sick observer below. Later, a wicker basket was used, equipped with a card table, wicker chair, telephone, compass, and lightning rod.

By early 1917 aeroplanes had advanced to carry heavy bomb loads, and antiaircraft defenses were so effective that the zeppelins were not important military weapons any more. The *LZ 107* made its last raid on Boulogne on 16 February 1917. The existing army airships were ordered to be dismantled, except four, which were turned over to the navy for patrol duty over the Baltic Sea and stationed at Seerappen, near Königsberg, as their home base.

The army had had at its command a total of thirty-three zeppelins during the 1914-1918 war period, and these had made 232 military flights.

By their reconnaissance work, particularly over the Eastern front, they had contributed immensely to the formulation of a victorious strategy by the high command. And in 111 raids, they had dropped 132,700 pounds of explosives over Russia, 98,300 over France, and 80,500 over England; with other bombing raids, they released a total of 311,500 pounds of bombs.

Of the fifty army airships, seventeen were destroyed by enemy action, two by stationary antiaircraft guns, and eight were wrecked, mainly because of adverse weather conditions. The remaining airships (fourteen of which were zeppelins, eleven of which were of other construction types) had become obsolete and were dismantled. Fifteen officers and fifty enlisted airshipmen were killed in action.

11

THE NAVY AIRSHIPS

The German Navy received its first *Luftschiff* in 1912. The *LZ 14,* called the *L 1,* this first airship was slightly larger than the army craft and specially constructed to resist stronger wind velocities. Since the navy had no hangar of its own at that time, the regular open harbor at Hamburg served as temporary mooring place.

Count Zeppelin had taken command of the *L 1* in October for its long delivery flight from Friedrichshafen to Berlin. First he cruised over the North Sea, touched Denmark, and then headed for Berlin. Navy officials were exceedingly satisfied with the fine demonstration flight, which had covered a distance of over one thousand miles and lasted thirty-one hours. They were exalted with their acquisition. But after only six months in service, this proud naval lighter-than-air vessel found an early watery grave. Caught off Helgoland in a fierce storm on 9 September 1913, the *L 1* was completely wrecked. It crashed into the turbulent sea, and only six members of the crew were saved. Twenty-six men perished.

Despite this appalling loss, the navy ordered another airship built immediately. The *L 2 (LZ 18)* was to be stronger and considerably larger — 518 feet long and 55 feet in diameter, containing 29,000 cubic meters (953,100 cubic feet) of gas. Each of its two Maybach engines developed 360 horsepower. A third gondola car, used only as a bridge by the commander, was added. For extra

protection against the elements this gondola was enclosed with a type of celluloid material, and all three gondolas were connected by an inside corridor. This construction feature became quite controversial, because the protective shield did not allow sufficient ventilation, thus possibly permitting the inside passage to be filled with highly explosive gases. Still, the new feature was incorporated into the zeppelin.

On the transfer flight to Berlin on 17 October 1913, the *L 2* performed in a most satisfactory manner, but at the subsequent takeoff under official naval command from the Johannisthal

The *LZ 14,* the first naval dirigible *L 1,* 1912. (Courtesy, Luftschiffbau Zeppelin).

95

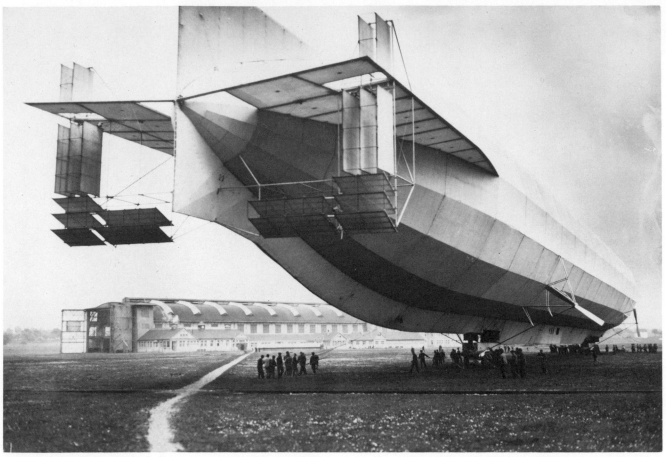

The *LZ 24,* the naval dirigible *L 3,* in 1914. (Courtesy, Luftschiffbau Zeppelin).

field, the airship suddenly burst into flames, killing the entire crew. Apparently a spark had ignited the accumulated gases, just as some of the construction engineers had feared. The ensuing horrescent explosion destroyed the craft.

In May 1914 the *L 3* was placed in service. Actually the *LZ 24,* the *Hansa,* was taken over from the *Delag,* and, with a complement of naval personnel, the *L 3* was sent to Dresden.

When the King of Saxony came to inspect the zeppelin and met Hugo Eckener, he asked what sort of doctor he was. "Political economy," Dr. Eckener replied. "Then," King Friedrich August said, "you surely know nothing of aeronautics."

Other airships were constructed in haste, and by the end of the year, the navy had two more zeppelins in service, one being used as training ship.

The *L 3* made a total of 141 reconnaissance flights over the North Sea, including one that lasted thirty-four hours. Soon after war was declared, the *L 4* and *L 5* were acquired, and by the end of that year one had flown fifty scouting missions over the Baltic Sea. The navy added another three zeppelins, the *L 6, L 7,* and *L 8.*

But when the *L 6* was delivered, there were no more trained crews. A junior lieutenant, Freiherr Horst Treusch von Buttlar-Brandenfels, was given command of the airship. The other ships were similarily staffed.

These early zeppelins, converted from commercial passenger airships, could only carry three one-hundred pound bombs placed in what was formerly the passenger cabin in the center of the catwalk. When the zeppelin was over the intended target, the gunnery officer would take out his pocketknife and cut the ropes that held the bomb in place. Aim was by estimate only, and direct hits were solely accidental, although some improvement in aim was noticed in experienced officers. However, on the first patrol over the North Sea, the *L 6* was hit by small-arms fire from the crew on the deck of a mine-laying vessel and sustained some six hundred holes in the gas bags, causing difficulties in properly maneuvering the heavy zeppelin.

Difficult to understand by lay persons, the hydrogen gas did not ignite from simple bullet holes, which usually entered the hull from below and often traveled the entire width to leave the hull on the top side. They only caused some gas to escape.

Since the altimeter employed by the officers was actually a sensitive barometer, the accuracy of the indicated altitude was not always certain. On occasions, when the weather changed suddenly and the barometric pressure fell an eighth to a quarter of an inch during an afternoon, the airship commander found that his ship was appreciably lower than he believed it to be. During a dark night, when the visibility was zero, he flew into a solid forest of tall pine trees, thinking that he was still several hundred feet above the ground.

Once the L 6 was met by a formation of enemy planes flying directly toward the airship. This zeppelin was not equipped with machine guns — the two-centimeter Becker guns came later — but, since the British had no phosphorous bullets at that time, the greatest damage the planes could possibly do would be to pepper the gas bags with holes. This would make the airship heavier and complicate the return flight considerably; however, the aeroplane pilots were almost as uncertain about their strange target as the zeppelin commander was about taking evasive action. Each stubbornly kept to his course, apparently headed for certain collision. Then, just before the collision seemed imminent, the planes turned, as did the airship. Not even pistols were fired in anger at each other, and this first confrontation proved absolutely nothing.

Money rewards totaling 4,250 pounds were offered to the pilot who would be the first to shoot down a zeppelin over Britain. Military decorations, perhaps the Victoria Cross, bestowed personally by the king, would surely await that fortunate aviator, and the admiration of a thankful populace was assured him.

When a raid by a flight of zeppelins over England was announced to the alerted defending squadron of British aeroplanes, the small group of valiant aviators quickly took off in search of the invading airships. But generally bad weather and solid fog made it impossible to locate the cruising raiders, and the planes scattered about in search of the zeppelins.

One of the flyers, frustrated because of the utter lack of effective and decisive attack by an aeroplane, had decided that a definite way to attack and destroy an airship was to land on the expansive top of it, then drop his bomb while at the same time taking off, so as to be safely away when the gas in the zeppelin would ignite and unquestionably explode.

Seeing a bare outline of a bulky hull ahead of him in the fog, the daredevil British airman actually landed atop of the airship. But he noticed that the wheels of his small plane pressed unusually deep into the seemingly soft hull. He suspected another one of those many ensnaring strategies of the ingenious German airshipmen. Then, just before actually releasing his bomb, a narrow clearing in the sky revealed several similar hulls at some distances. The flyer suddenly realized that they constituted the defense line of barrage balloons, utilized as an air barricade against the zeppelins. The chagrined airman took off the soft balloon top and soon landed at his aerodrome, disappointed that he could not put his clever theory into practice. He had not even seen an enemy zeppelin on this assignment.

Later, a gasoline bomb was developed, to be dropped onto the hull of a zeppelin from an aeroplane flying above. An electrical contact would ignite the fuse when the pilot released the bomb through the floor of his cockpit. A cluster of large fishhooks attached to the bomb supposedly would catch in the covering material of the zeppelin to hold the explosive. No record exists to show that this contraption ever functioned properly. However, since several flyers lost their lives in attacking zeppelins, it can be assumed that they became victims of their own exploding fire bombs. Contrarily, the causes of some of the losses of airships were not definitely established either.

The first actual contact with enemy naval forces was made when, on 15 December 1914, British warships were reported near Helgoland. Two airships, the L 5 and the L 6 were ordered out to reconnoiter the situation. The zeppelins sighted several British flying boats, seemingly on a raid to the Nordholz base. Because of their faster speed, the enemy planes escaped the airships, which tried to give chase. The L 5 headed for the mothership of the planes and found that two of its flying boats had landed near the vessel. The airship destroyed them there, using machine-gun fire and small bombs to do so. The other airship, the L 6, sighted twenty mine layers on the return flight, but its sending apparatus failed, and thus no assistance from surface vessels could be summoned to give battle to the mine layers. The fleeing mine layers were soon joined by their two protecting cruisers, the *Undaunted* and the *Arethusa,* and some destroyers. Small-arms fire greeted the zeppelin flying above the warships. Machine-gun fire from the zeppelin rapidly cleared the decks of the warships, and the airship maneuvered into bombing position. Then, suddenly, a German flying boat appeared and dropped two bombs on the enemy warship below; but both missed. The last bomb dropped by the zeppelin also fell short, but the airship kept up the harassment, flying over the squadron of British ships for about two hours and giving the impression that it might drop other bombs. The slower-traveling warships took evasive action, fully expecting other bombs to be dropped on them, but no damage was inflicted on either side. On its return flight, the *L 6* flew low over the German cruiser *Moltke* to drop a written report on its mission.

During 1915 the naval airships flew a total of 389 long-distance reconnaissance missions and participated in thirty raids on England.

The German general staff disagreed with the Kaiser on these air raids according to Captain Ernst Lehmann, who wrote:

From the first days of the war the Kaiser had been strongly opposed to raids of any sort against England; and when in the face of constant pressure from his admirals and generals he finally approved and authorized the first sporadic raids, it was with the understanding that only objectives of real military importance should be bombed. He made these reservations much plainer than that. He actually stipulated that such places as Buckingham Palace, Westminster Abbey, St. Paul's Cathedral, and the residential sections should not be bombed, even by accident!
... We were to attack the inner city of London, all docks and railroad stations, and so on, but by no means were we to risk hitting the residence of England's King, Westminster, or St. Paul's.[1]

Also mentioned by Lehmann was

the Kaiser's interest in protecting royalty among his enemies. On April 13, 1915, the Zeppelin *LZ 35* was ready to set out on a raid over supply centers behind the British lines, Cassel, St. Omer, and Hazelbrouck. Just before departing, the commander, Captain Masius, was handed a telegram in code. The reason was soon made known. Headquarters had received word that the Allied leaders were to hold a secret meeting at St. Omer and the kings of both Belgium and England were to be present. By direct order of the Kaiser, the attack on St. Omer was forbidden and Poperinghe substituted. The town council house at St. Omer stands isolated in the middle of a large open square and it would have been a simple matter to hit it with one of my two dozen bombs.[2]

But the Allies did not reciprocate. Their aviators delighted in bombing Charleville and Stenay, where the Kaiser and the crown prince frequently stayed.

After the first several months of using airships in various ways, all zeppelin raids on England followed a definite strategy; only the number of airships utilized varied. The first participating zeppelin always left its base at high noon, even if later there were five, nine, or seventeen zeppelins taking part. As soon as the leader had cleared the airfield, the trained ground crew took on the next airship, and so on, until the several hangars were empty and all of the zeppelins designated were on their westerly course.

Flying only a few-hundred feet over the Helgoland *Bucht,* or bay, the airships exchanged signals with short-range aeroplanes. Here, zeppelins from the Tondern base, and the Alhorn, the Wittmundhaven, and the Hage bases, rendezvoused with the Nordholz airships and exchanged coded signals. Yet, each airship flew independently, and the fleet was never in any sort of formation. The inexperienced commanders usually showed a tendency to stay close to zeppelins piloted by seasoned *Luftschiffmänner,* airshipmen, but each commander tried to discover an unmanned coastal point to fly unobserved over the enemy island. The first airship often had the dubious honor of getting the fiercest welcome from the alert coastal batteries.

Comprehensive tests had been made to determine the visibility of a high-flying airship during moonlit nights. Flights were scheduled only during dark nights, when a zeppelin could not be seen from the ground. But with increasingly higher altitudes it was believed that an airship could not be seen from the ground, despite the brightness of the moon. Tests showed this assumption to be correct, but in actuality this proved false. The tests had been carried out in the vicinity of industrialized cities, and the inherent dust particles from such activities created quite different atmospheric conditions than did pure air in the open country. This was discovered only after some airship losses, and flights during the full of the moon were then abandoned. Thus the advantage of moonlit ground targets was lost.

At dusk, zeppelins, flying at an altitude of about twelve-thousand feet to fifteen-thousand feet were still plainly visible in the light of the setting sun. Their wireless apparatus was only used to signal important messages, such as abandonment of the mission because of engine trouble or some other mishap. Each electric discharge could of course be picked up by the ground equipment of the enemy, and repeated sending would indicate the chosen approach route. Later an improved communications system was employed. The bases at Tondern and Cleve sent coded bearings every half hour, and these directional transmissions could easily be tuned in by the cruising airships without betraying their own positions.

Cold nights were preferable for raids. A difference of three degrees meant either approximately one percent difference in weight-carrying ability of the airship, or an increase of three-hundred feet in altitude. All available buoyancy sometimes meant the difference between being a reachable target for the antiaircraft batteries, or flying safely above the exploding shells. With alcohol added to the fuel for high-altitude flying, stoppages of engines seldom occurred; but once the engines stopped, they would hardly ever start again, and thus the Maybach engines were allowed to idle slowly if need be, and were never ordered to stop entirely.

There was no protection from the biting cold wind. The gondola cars were open and offered practically no shelter, and there were naturally no heating units of any sort on board an airship. Fur-lined coats and heavy fur-lined boots were the only protection against the elements, and the exposure in higher altitudes was especially disagreeable.

At first the crew members were issued individual bottles of compressed oxygen, and when a certain elevation was reached, each man inhaled the oxygen by opening the valve in his bottle. Later,

however, a form of liquid air was developed. Carried in large cylinders, this air had a better taste than the musky oxygen. The effect was also quite different. After putting this individual pipe-end into his mouth and thus partaking from the large container of liquid air, the recipient felt an extraordinary sensation. Unlike a Turkish-hookah addict, the liquid-air consumer felt like a superman, ready to take on any antagonist twice his own size in any sort of combat.

An ingenious light mine was developed as a defensive weapon for the zeppelins. Attached to a parachute, the bright light could be timed to dazzle at a certain altitude, to light up the ground below, and to illuminate the darkened targets. Attached to a long cord, this blinding magnesium flare could light up the sky below the airship and above the firing land batteries, so that the target ship was safely hidden by the brilliant illumination, which functioned on the principle of a powerful searchlight used for covering a torpedo attack in surface naval warfare.

A raid on the coast of England was planned for 18 January 1915. Four naval airships took part in that action, the L 3, L 4, L 5, and L 6, but only two of the zeppelins reached their destinations. The L 3, commanded by Captain Fritz, and the L 4, under Captain Platen, were the first zeppelins to reach the coast of England.

Navigation was complicated because of the existing blackout of all landmarks on the English coast. But the beams of the lighthouse at Ostende and Steenbrugge formed an imaginary line pointing directly to the mouth of the Thames river, whose shining water reflection led to London.

The other ships experienced troubles of various kinds and were forced to return to their bases at Nordholz. Another attack was made, with favorable weather assisting, in April. But by then the L 3 and the L 4 had been lost in a storm. The crew of one had been able to save themselves after landing their damaged airship on Danish soil and then letting the zeppelin rise and drift over the sea to a certain crash. But the men of the other were lost at sea with their crippled craft.

That year the British developed a new strategy, using Curtis flying boats to lie in wait for the approaching zeppelins. These flying boats positioned themselves on a line north of the Dutch island Schiermonnikoog, and upon seeing a German airship silhouetted in the sky by the rising sun, would take off to attack the slower-flying zeppelin from the rear. The Germans quickly developed a "small cannon" to keep the pilots at a safe distance, and this ploy worked quite effectively for a while, until the flyers realized that the cannons were merely cleverly disguised firecrackers.

All German airships were strictly forbidden ever to fly over Dutch territory, because it was neutral, but also perhaps because the Dutch were accurate sharpshooters who never hesitated to use their weapons on any wayward zeppelin over their territory. However, occasionally their neutrality worked in favor of the Germans. Once, when a disabled zeppelin flew slowly to its home base, a British warship noticed it and gave chase, firing at and pursuing the enemy above. The airship commander then managed to reach the Dutch coast, where he hovered just three miles off the neutral coastal line. Shells fired from the British ship would have fallen on Dutch territory, and thus none were fired. By nightfall, when the warship gave up the pursuit, the zeppelin limped safely home across the water.

The Nordholz base was soon enlarged to accommodate more airships and larger crews. Other airships were added to the fleet, but because of serious losses, the total number of zeppelins in actual service increased but slowly. Four of them became quick casualties.

The L 8 was lost in March 1915, on returning from a raid on the English coast. Her gas bags punctured by artillery shells, the disabled ship failed to make her home base in foul weather, and was forced to land in Belgium, where she was destroyed by a storm on the ground. Soon thereafter the L 7 encountered this problem: After a raid the airship passed unexpectedly at only four-thousand feet over an enemy flotilla; she luckily escaped, but unfortunately found herself almost at once over an even-larger group of warships. After being hit, the airship was now forced to land at sea near Horns Reef on the Danish coast. Here an enemy submarine rose suddenly to attack the floating zeppelin, killing all but eight men of the crew who escaped by swimming.

And the L 6, after having dropped her bombs, made a low run over some British destroyers to attack them with machine guns. However, the airship received a great number of hits from the defending sailors below and was forced to withdraw from the attack and try to reach Nordholz, only to be destroyed by fire when landing at the base. The L 9 also burned, while inflating at the base.

The L 9 was actually the first of a larger type of zeppelin, and under Captain Heinrich Mathy had been successful in sinking a submarine off Terschelling on 3 May. But the naval airships really did their best service in scouting. In that they were superb.

On one return flight from a raid, the L 19 spotted three British warships carrying planes for an attack on the mainland, perhaps in retaliation to the London raids. From a secure altitude the zeppelin dropped a bomb on the vessel, which had already lowered one flying boat into the sea, and by wireless had alerted German naval vessels in the vicinity, thus foiling the planned air raid on Germany.

Generally, mine fields were spotted by cruising airships, and their locations were reported to the minesweepers. Occasionally, with a high-ranking officer from the sweeper command on board, the zeppelin would fly low and slow over the newly laid mine field, then return the officer to his own vessel from where he would then direct the operation of clearing the area.

The L 10 was struck by lightning on takeoff above the base while letting off gas, and was completely destroyed. Only two weeks before, the similar L 11 had successfully battled the elements for some three hours when caught in a raging storm, but the crew had its share of scare and excitement when men and machines were constantly lighted up in the weird St. Elmo's fires.

Airships often encountered extremely stormy weather over the North Sea on their flights to England. The fight against the elements was always dangerous, but Hans von Schiller found that storms also had exhilarating moments.

On one occasion his ship headed toward a solid bank of clouds, but when they changed course to avoid it, they encountered strong head winds, which became stronger and stronger and stopped them completely. Still, the storm increased in fury, the thunder claps came closer, and lightning struck horizontally over the ship. The wireless apparatus became useless. Coming from all directions, the storm dashed the vessel from side to side. The walkway swayed dangerously, and the crew held on to the girders and supporters so as not to be tossed out. The Captain ordered men inside the ship except those on duty, either at the navigational instruments in the control car or the engine car at the engines.

The lookout on the upper platform reported that it was raining in buckets. The pitching airship was unable to rise above the mountainous clouds before it, and with its nose down dived into the darkness. Lightning strokes flashed at short intervals, hailstones rattled on the dripping outer skin, and the airship shuddered in agony. Often it was tossed a hundred yards high only to drop suddenly two or three hundred yards before steadying itself. A terrific bolt crashed by the airship, filling the inside with a blinding light. The man on the upper lookout post reported that the muzzle of his machine gun was spitting sparks, and when he spread his hand, small flames spurted out of his fingertips.

Von Schiller recalled seeing the platform brightly illuminated and in the center of a luminous circle sat the lookout, wet through to the skin, a veritable halo around his head. This extraordinary phenomenon, St. Elmo's fire, is not unknown to mountain climbers and to sailors. The duraluminum frame of the airship became charged with electricity and sent forth sparks at all connecting points. Looking from the control car, von Schiller could see sparks coming from all protruding objects. Wires and cables glowed in a bluish violet light. St. Elmo's fire was truly a spectacular sight, but with lightning flashes close by every minute or so, the lives of the airshipmen were dependent upon the absolute containment of the hydrogen gas. Any escaping lifting gas from the cells would be disastrous, should lightning strike.

It seems unbelievable to the uninitiated that an airship filled with highly flammable hydrogen gas is not destroyed when struck by lightning, but lightning obeys the laws of nature: it is only distributed on the enormous surface of the metallic frame, which protectively encloses the gas cells. As long as no gas escaped into the spaces between the cells and the outer frame, lightning was no danger to the airship; but a slightly punctured hull, caused by shrapnel or bullets, usually proved fatal in a lightning storm for the airshipmen and their zeppelin.

The machine gunner stationed on the platform was, of course, never allowed to use his weapon without explicit orders. When reporting an attacking aeroplane even in the sights of his gun, he was ordered to fire only when the airship was not climbing and automatically releasing highly explosive hydrogen gas. Otherwise the burst of his machine gun fire might have set the zeppelin afire.

Generally, when the weather had been favorable for a raid on England, it was miserable over Helgoland, and solid ground fog covered the home bases. Then, a yellow captive balloon, or *gelber Fesselballon,* would hover at three-hundred feet above the home landing field. The latest weather information was telephoned to the incoming airship by the observer in the basket of the balloon. Also, the experienced zeppelin commanders could always tell when they got close to the ground by the darker color of the mist, and with forward engines shut off completely, listened for the shouts of the *Boden-Seiltänzer,* the ground acrobats, who were ready to grab the handling ropes and the handlebars on the gondola cars to guide the airship into its hangar, and quickly get ready for the next returning zeppelin.

For really effective bombing of England, the earliest types of zeppelins were too small and too slow and their bomb load capacity insufficient. The 20 and 30 types were better suited for that purpose, but by then the British defenses were also considerably improved. It was a constant, tremendous effort by both sides to stay ahead of the other in that respect.

The actual physical bomb damage in London and other target cities was always officially reported as being negligible; still, according to a published account, one raid had caused damage of more than 7.5 million dollars.

Zeppelin raids terrified the people, but perhaps the use of the high-powered, penetrating searchlights and multitude of firing antiaircraft batteries was more responsible for the terror than the few zeppelins flying silently high above this tumult and dropping their few small bombs.

But more than having a dreadfully frightening effect on the inhabitants, the constant raids kept an amazingly large amount of war material and fighting men tied up on home defenses and thus kept them from being utilized at another front. A total of 162 small-pressure balloons of the Pont Blimp, Coastal, and North Sea types were employed by the British to defend their coast. To the higher-flying zeppelins attacking, these stationary balloons often acted as identification markers outlining the actual borders of the coastal areas. Having passed over them, the commanders knew that their airships were over the solid-ground territory of the enemy.

That beauty could be seen in this adversity was suggested by this paradoxical story from London, carried by the *Frankfurter Zeitung* of 17 May 1915:

> It was necessary for the German airships to come to London so that her true beauty could be fully realized and appreciated. The beauty is the great spectacle of darkness, which descends upon this city on the Thames. So that no ray of light may lure the enemy, the city puts on her garment of black velvet.[3]

Commander Heinrich Mathy also found beauty. The grayish outline of the zeppelins silently gliding through wavering ribbons of light and tufts of shrapnel, which hung thick, was a beautiful, impressive, but fleeting picture to him. But his eyes and mind had no time to contemplate this sight, they were concentrated on the task before him, realizing that at any moment his airship might plunge down, a shapeless mass of wreckage and human bodies, shattered beyond recognition.

Another lighter side to these raids was the report that many of the fashionable stores displayed "Robes for Raids" or "Zepp Nighties," as the nightdresses and dressing robes were advertised.

But the Princess Blücher, in *An English Wife in Berlin,* wrote that a friend, who had just returned from London in November 1915, told her that the zeppelin raids over London had aroused England's anger tremendously. The English would never show fear of any kind, the friend suggested, "but their faith in the impossibility of any enemy reaching London has been shaken, and a certain tradition has been broken, and every Englishman is aroused."

Undoubtedly, the zeppelin attacks were demoralizing, for they proved that the island, ("their fortress built by nature for them") offered no more isolation from enemy attacks on her inhabitants, despite the powerful fleet of naval warships patrolling her shores.

In his book on *Propaganda Technique in the World War,* H.D. Laswell wrote, "It may be unreliable, but there is a story with a flash of insight which tells of the German aviator who objected to dropping any more bombs on London because he had not entered the war to be a recruiting officer for the British army."

However, Edwin J. Kirschner, a plans analyst for the United States Air Force and a man with extensive experience in air transportation and maintenance, stated that "in World War I the zeppelin raids over the British Isles were as great a threat as the airplane raids of World War II."

Considered in the light of the fervor with which the Allies were to carry out similar but thousand-fold more devastating air raids on German cities in the next war, it would appear that they must have been quite effective in destroying civilian morale, despite all vehement official denials of the effectiveness of these zeppelin bombing raids on Britain. Strangely, however, in World War II the industrial production in obviously devastated German areas was hardly affected by the saturation bombing, perhaps because the newly made homeless workers had no place to go except to their less damaged factories.

When the *L 15* received several hits during a raid in April 1915, the airship was forced down off the coast of Kent, where a British destroyer picked up the crew of fourteen men, including the commander, Captain Breithaupt. The damaged zeppelin was taken in tow by another ship, but the hull sank before it reached the shore and could not be salvaged. The captured men were promptly interrogated by officials who called them contemptuously "zeppelin murderers, the worst of the bestial Huns." When the captain was told that "his raids had killed only women and children and hurt only civilians, but had damaged nothing worthwhile and no military targets at all," he replied calmly that "it is obvious that you are being deprived of the truth."

In August 1915, the *L 12* was so severely damaged after a raid on London that Commander Peterson was forced to land that night on the turbulent North Sea near the Belgian coast. With three of her gas bags emptied of hydrogen and still more escaping from other bullet-ridden cells, the airship was considerably out of shape but still buoyant enough to stay afloat on the sea. During the hard landing, one of the airshipmen, named Frankhänel, was lost. However, after discarding most of his clothes, the brave sailor swam after the fast-moving airship. After a long struggle he finally caught up with the floating airship and crawled aboard, to the joy of his comrades. Located the following morning by a German torpedo boat, the stricken zeppelin was towed to the Ostende harbor, where the partially deflated airship was lifted onto the pier out of the water. None of the crew were lost in this delicate maneuver, but the zeppelin caught fire during salvage operations and was completely destroyed.

On one raid, an airship commanded by Captain Buttlar-Brandenfels was hit by groundfire, which destroyed several of the center gas cells, causing the zeppelin to become unbalanced and unable to maintain its altitude. While calculating just where to land on the sea below, loud cracking noises indicated that the ship was about to break in two. Hans von Schiller, the officer second in command, who was always known by his friends for his quick wit, asked his captain if he wished to command the bow or the stern portion after the breakup, so that he himself then could take charge of the other part. But the expected break never actually occurred, because the sturdy anchor rope used to fasten the two parts together by tying the rope across the empty chambers left by the deflated gas bags held securely.

Flying now slowly at three-thousand feet, the anxious crew hoped to stay aloft until after sunrise when, with some luck, the warmth of the shining sun would cause the remaining gas to expand sufficiently to keep the crippled zeppelin long enough in the air to reach land. Sea landings generally proved disastrous and were not a pleasant prospect to the apprehensive crew. The airship reached its home base safely. For this strategem, or perhaps the preceding fifteen air raids and innumerable reconnaissance flights in five other airships, Captain Buttlar-Brandenfels was awarded the *Pour le Merite* by the Kaiser himself. The entire crew was decorated with the Iron Cross, First Class.

At the historic naval battle in May 1916 in the Skagerrak and Kattegat, the seas surrounding Jylland, several naval airships did distinguish themselves as important participants.

By bombarding Sunderland on the English east coast, Admiral Reinhard Scheer proposed to lure the British fleet out to sea and to fight. (The strategy of the enemy was to stay close to home ports and maintain the navy intact to ensure the integrity of her island territory. The German navy,

on the other hand, operated on the open seas to keep sniping away and to engage the British in smaller battles to reduce her naval strength.)

Ten zeppelins had been scheduled to take part in the battle plan. The first of the larger 55,000-cubic-meter-displacement ships had been delivered to Nordholz just a day before, but it could not take part in the engagement because no experienced crew was available to man the zeppelin. The weather had been absolutely foul for several days, and strong winds made flights too hazardous.

Admiral Scheer had to modify his plans. He stated: "For a raid against Sunderland, a far-reaching air reconnaissance was indispensable because such tactics would lead us into an area of the sea where we could not afford to accept a battle against our will." Thus, the battle area was changed to the Jylland section, where the enemy's naval bases were farther away than those of the Germans.

Only the *L 16* and *L 21* could be taken out of their movable hangars, while the other airships had to remain in their stationary hangars until the weather permitted their takeoff later on that day. When they finally took to the air, the *L 9, L14,* and *L 23* never even sighted a ship at sea. The *L 23* patrolled and observed the north perimeter of the fleet, the *L 21* was stationed at the northwest end, with the *L 9, L 14,* and *L 16* still farther west. None of these zeppelins witnessed the actual battle or sent messages of enemy fleet movement to their command ship. Even the wind was against them; they never heard the sound of the battle which was carried in the opposite direction. But their silence assured the admiral that no enemy surface-ship activity would endanger his left flank.

But the *L 11* sighted and correctly reported the main force of the approaching British fleet on the south, in square 0.33.13. The *L 24* also sighted a group of enemy warships steaming ahead. Together with the *L 13, L 17,* and *L 22,* these zeppelins had taken off as soon as feasible during the preceding afternoon and night and proceeded to their appointed stations.

Again, the *L 11* reported after five o'clock on that morning of 1 June that the remainder of the British fleet had turned. The *L 17* and the *L 13* saw no enemy vessels, because heavy clouds made any reconnoitering impossible.

Despite the adverse weather, two of the ten airships had located the principal enemy force and thus gave the German admiral a decided advantage in his major naval battle of the war.

The utilization of zeppelins was well worth the result. According to a secret report that Admiral William A. Moffett of the United States Navy revealed to Congress, the British Navy attributed decisive importance to that aerial reconnaissance. The report stated:

From the results already given of instances, it will be seen how justified is the confidence felt by the German Navy in its airships when used in their proper sphere as the eyes of the fleet. It is no small achievement for their Zeppelins to have saved the high-seas fleet at the battle of Jutland; to have saved their cruiser squadron on the Yarmouth raid, and to have been instrumental in sinking the *Nottingham* and *Falmouth*. Had the positions been reversed in the Jutland battle, and had we rigids to enable us to locate and annihilate the German high-seas fleet, can anyone deny the far-reaching effects it would have had in ending the war?[4]

(The British, under Admiral John Jellicoe, lost five major cruisers, nine destroyers, and 6,097 men. The Germans, under Admiral Reinhard Scheer, lost two major ships, nine cruisers and destroyers, and 2,545 men.)

Admiral Scheer, Chief of Naval Operations, wrote:

For us, airships were an indispensable weapon during the War, chiefly because at that time hydroplanes had not yet been highly developed. An airship can reconnoiter in a much larger area than a battleship. The Zeppelins were able to move more quickly than a battleship and they were safer from enemy attacks. For this reason airships were a great help to the Navy.[5]

On another assignment, on 18 August 1916, zeppelins also did brilliant reconnaisance work. By that time, three more of the larger 55,000-cubic-meter-type airships had been added to the fleet. With eight airships, the *L 11*, the *L 13*, the *L 21*, the *L 22*, the *L 24*, the *L 30*, the *L 31*, and the *L 33*, taking part in patrolling the English coast, each was assigned to a sixty-mile sector. For two days, when the weather was ideal, these zeppelins cruised along their appointed sections and noted all surface warship movements. Each patrolling airship reported its own position and all movements of the British fleet to their commander-in-chief of the High Sea Fleet. Admiral Scheer stated that this service was of the utmost value to him.

On the return flight, some of the zeppelins noticed a large, seemingly harmless fishing fleet of nearly a hundred vessels off the Doggerbank, a favorite fishing ground off Scotland. Flying leisurely at an altitude of only nine-hundred feet, the officers of the *L 30* were unable to identify the flags of the boats and so descended for a better look. They were suddenly fired upon from rapidly uncovered hidden guns. Quickly dropping ballast and all available excessive load, the attacked zeppelins were barely able to escape this clever ruse and send a wireless alarm. An alert naval squadron raced to the scene and subsequently sank some of the fishing boats, while the airshipmen resolved not to trust strange vessels of any kind.

By the beginning of 1916 all airships were ordered to carry parachutes so that the crew might save itself if their zeppelin was afire. But the ready usability of these parachutes by the crew in the catwalk or elsewhere, except in the gondola cars, was so problematical at best that many of the commanders refused to add this extra weight to their already heavily laden ships. For the parachute load reduced the bomb load by about one ton, and this consequent reduction resulted in a change of orders. Most crews elected not to carry parachutes.

Even so, there was an occasional case of a crew member escaping death when a zeppelin was set afire by enemy gun fire. When the *L 48* was attacked by aeroplanes after a raid near Harwich on the south coast of England on 17 June 1917, it was hit by a series of green-sparking bullets. The hydrogen in the airship was instantly ablaze. One

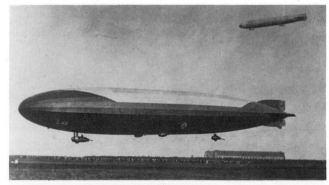

The *LZ 95*, the naval dirigible *L 48*, in 1917. (Courtesy, Luftschiffbau Zeppelin).

of the crew on the catwalk quickly climbed into the top part of the bow of the airship. The zeppelin, usually tail heavy when flying at high altitudes, fell to the ground. After the crash the man climbed out of the flaming wreck with his clothes afire but able to save himself. Even the wireless operator, with both legs broken and still in his small control car, got hung up in a tree, to be rescued after the airship had burned out. He and the badly burned airshipman were then taken prisoners—the only known men ever saved from a burning zeppelin over enemy territory during the war.

Naval airships were also used for purposes other than patrolling and raiding. When a lashing storm devastated some small islands off the coast, the *L 16* took a load of provisions to the inhabitants of these North Sea islands, isolated by raging seas and ravished by the storm. Landing successfully on each of these islands, the airship brought much needed relief to the stricken people.

That same spring the *L 23* was sent out to search for a downed flying boat. The drifting plane was located and the fliers taken aboard. Only after salvaging the engine of the plane did the zeppelin fly back to its base. In April, the same airship, commanded by Captain Ludwig Bockholt, discovered an unidentified schooner in a prohibited area and went down to investigate. Dropping a small bomb in front of her bow, the vessel duly stopped her engines, and the zeppelin landed on the calm sea behind her, wisely out of reach of the guns of the crew. A small party was sent to board the schooner, discovered that the *Royal* carried contraband, and ordered the captain to sail for Cuxhaven. A tender was called by wireless to take over the war prize. For some time the zeppelin remained over the captured vessel to ascertain her altered course, but when the tender came to take over, the *L 23* headed for her own home base, proud that she had actually captured a surface merchant vessel from the air.

By September 1916 the British military authorities had vastly improved their defense system over London. They sent up large numbers of small, single-seater aeroplanes against the huge zeppelins. In the dark of night, the airships were nearly invisible, but caught in the glare of a searchlight from the ground, they could be seen for miles. Often, an aeroplane had approached a zeppelin long before the plane had been spotted by the

lookouts, and the pilot would pepper the huge target with incendiary bullets, before the machine guns of the airship could get into action.

The only effective defense against these highly maneuverable planes was the ability of the zeppelins to climb to greater heights. Altitudes of 13,500 feet usually left the aeroplanes out of firing range. Throughout most of the war, the advantage remained with the airships, although improvements were of benefit to both. And the lighter-than-air ship had the advantage of remaining in the air considerably longer than the heavier-than-air craft, which had to rely on its engines to keep it aloft. Over London, the heavy antiaircraft fire often made it impossible for the aeroplanes to attack the zeppelins effectively, for they had to fly through their friendly hail of fire while the zepplins rose to the safety above the bursting flack.

Dark nights were generally neither cloudless nor foggy. Planes would try to maneuver the invading zeppelins into the glares of the ground searchlights, which obstructed the targets and caused the airships to lose their bearings. The ideal situation of scattered clouds for a zeppelin to hide from searchlights, antiaircraft batteries, and pursuing aeroplanes was exceedingly rare.

To lessen easy detection from the ground by searchlights, or in the bright moonlight, extensive tests were conducted using a zeppelin covered entirely with a new camouflage paint. The *L 18* was flown under various conditions resembling those over England. The nearby Isle of Sylt had been chosen to resemble best the actual circumstances found over the British Isles. However, before any definite conclusions were reached on the camouflaging of airships, the *L 18* was destroyed in the hangar at the Tondern base, and the project was quietly dropped.

When during one of the night attacks on England the zeppelin air fleet was caught in abominable weather and finally a thick fog, the *L 34* was shot down over Hartlepool, the *L 21* was shot down near the coast at Yarmouth, and the *L 36* crashed near her home base. The *L 39*, on the return from England, was driven over the French headquarters at Compiègne, where heavily concentrated antiaircraft fire destroyed the zeppelin. The *L 22* and the *L 43* were lost over the North Sea, and the *L 48* was shot down over England. It had been a disastrous raid for the seven participating airships.

According to an English account of the period, toward the end of 1916, the British military authorities were forced to keep twelve air squadrons, comprising 2,200 officers and men and 110 aeroplanes, and 17,340 officers and men in the antiaircraft service, on duty as home defense against the raiding zeppelins. This very considerable number was only the nucleus and did not include the numerous workers needed to supply the material. This military personnel and materiel was urgently needed at the battlefields of the continent to aid the Allied cause, but the Lord of the Admiralty, Winston Churchill, had stated before the House of Commons when the German airships appeared able to make raids on England, "Swarms of hornets would be ready to meet any zeppelins which dared to come over Britain."

On 2 September 1916, thirteen airships took off for a raid on London. The *SL 11,* a Schütte-Lanz type airship, was soon shot down in flames. It crashed, a ball of fire, at Cuffley near Enfield, where the wooden hull burned for more than an hour. After that, the German High Command decided that all airships should fly at an altitude of at least fifteen-thousand feet—and up to seventeen-thousand feet—over the heavily fortified British capital. Since none of the zeppelins then in service could reach that safe altitude, no further attacks on London were ordered until such a time.

A major attack on England was planned for 19 October 1917. Thirteen airships were to take part in a raid on Sheffield, Manchester, and Liverpool, but the *L 42* and the *L 51* were unable to leave their Alhorn base because of strong cross winds. The eleven airships which started were the *L 41, 44, 45, 46, 47, 49, 50, 52, 53, 54,* and *L 55*. When the weather deteriorated even more than expected earlier, some of the zeppelin commanders, recognizing this added hazard, flew further north than originally charted, but others of the participating airships reached the south coast of England.

One of the zeppelins drifted so far south that

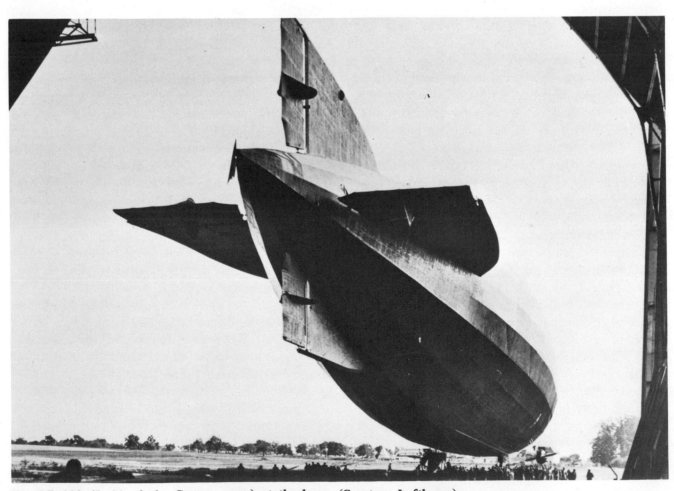

The *LZ 100 (L 53* of the German navy) at the base. (Courtesy, Lufthansa).

instead of flying over Sheffield, the commander discovered that he was actually over London, about 250 miles off course.

At the designated altitude of 16,500 feet, the tempestuous storm and cloud cover made it so difficult that some of the airships were forced to climb to twenty-one-thousand feet, their maximum altitude. After several hours suffering in this icy, thin air, they tried to reach the coast of the continent closest to them. If they could only reach the relative safety of Belgium or France, they expected no problems in reaching their home bases.

However, disaster awaited them. Four of the zeppelins drifted over France, unable to escape the strong winds, and were shot down over hostile territory when they were forced down to a lower altitude, thus becoming easy targets for small-caliber firing.

The *L 44* was brought down near Lunéville. The other three were over enemy territory, when their fuel supply became exhausted. The *L 45* descended into the valley of the Durance, and the crew set the ship afire. The crew of the *L 49* was also taken prisoner of war when their airship landed.

The *L 50* landed safely. The crew began to disembark, but before all men were off, the ship rose without warning into the air and was carried by the strong wind into the higher mountains of Switzerland. Here, the rest of the crew got safely out of the airship, leaving their zeppelin to rest on the high plateau. Then the airship rose again into the air, only to disappear completely forever, apparently falling into the sea. But the men perished on the lone mountain. Their frozen bodies were found later.

A fifth zeppelin, the *L 55*, was attacked by aeroplanes while over France, but climbed by throwing off all unnecessary ballast and some precious fuel to escape the lower-flying aeroplanes. At an altitude of 7,600 meters (25,300 feet) — a new record — blood ran from the nose, mouth, and ears of the men. Vertigo attacked one man after another. The valuable water turned into ice, and the cooling water for the engines, despite the alcohol content, also froze. The zeppelin was unable to reach its base at Alhorn and was forced to land at Tiefenrot on the Werra River. There it was dismantled, since no transportation was available for the damaged craft.

This October attack had resulted in the calami-tous loss of five new zeppelins. It was one of the major disasters of the war.

When the chief surgeon of the German Colonial Troops, Colonel Zupitza, who had been captured in Togo (also called Togoland), but was later exchanged in 1916, reported that the remaining German forces in Africa were in dire need of medical supplies, the doctor also suggested to the colonial minister at Berlin that a zeppelin be sent to aid the isolated troops of the illustrious General Paul von Lettow-Vorbeck, the brilliant defender of German East Africa against superior Allied strength.

Count Zeppelin received word of this daring scheme and with his usual ebullient enthusiasm predicted a successful conclusion of the venture-some project.

Encouraged by the recent provisioning of storm-and-icebound North Sea islands by their *L 16*, and especially the endurance flight over the Baltic by the *L 120* on 31 July 1917, the navy agreed to the African expedition, and ordered the *L 57* to be prepared for it.

On its endurance test, the *LZ 120* had carried 2,640 pounds of bombs, 6,160 pounds of arms, provisions, and spare parts, and about 7,700 pounds of water ballast. The crew of thirty men including Captain Lehmann, weighed about 5,500 pounds, thus allowing 37,000 pounds for gasoline and oil, calculated to be sufficient to operate the zeppelin at moderate speed for a hundred hours. The airship cruised over the Baltic Sea for four days and returned, without incident of any kind, to the Seerappen base on 31 July, accomplishing its goal and using 34,750 pounds of fuel and oil for the flight of over 101 hours.

The *L 57* was outfitted for the trip and properly loaded at the Jüterbog base. But on the test flight the zeppelin was caught in a severe storm and had to return to its base, where the strong winds made moving into the hangar impossible. The zeppelin was badly damaged, and to keep the expedition secret, it was decided to destroy the wrecked airship on the ground by burning it.

Meanwhile at the Staaken yards an improved type of zeppelin was about completed. This air-ship, actually the *LZ 104*, renamed *L 59* by the navy, was cut in two. With two compartments added it was enlarged to a 68,500-cubic-meter displacement, and stretched to 750 feet with a diameter of eighty feet. Uniquely constructed for

The LZ 104 became the *L 59*, the *Afrika-schiff*, in 1917. (Courtesy, Luftschiffbau Zeppelin).

maximum usage of the component materials by the colonial troops, the airship's covering was of cotton to be remade into tents and tropical uniforms. The gas-cell material could be used for waterproof sleeping bags, and the linen partitions were usable for shirts. The duraluminum girders and struts could be converted into skeletons for portable, collapsible barracks and wireless towers. The five Maybach engines were to serve as power-plants for the dynamos. Even the walkway was reusable, made of shoe leather, and the antenna that consisted of three sturdy wires, each 400 feet long, was adaptable for several purposes.

With the crew of twenty-two men and the cargo, the airship weighed 175,000 pounds. Besides the requirements of 48,000 pounds of fuel, 3,350 pounds of oil, 20,150 pounds of water ballast, 950 pounds of drinking water, and 1,550 pounds of provisions, the special items for the troops consisted of 311,900 boxes of ammunition, 230 machine-gun belts with 13,500 cartridges, sixty-one sacks of bandages and medical supplies, two hand-operated sewing machines, three sacks of

sewing equipment, mail, telescopes, spare gun locks, bush knives, and spare parts for the wireless apparatus. To save weight and gain space, the bomb-release mechanism had been discarded.

The entire project had been kept secret and the crew was under the impression that they would fly to do service on the Balkan front. (On 3 November the *L 59* left its base and arrived at Yamboli twenty-eight hours later.)

Since no officials en route had been advised of this flight, the appearance of a strange zeppelin seriously alarmed the military posts over which it flew. The port officials at Burgas, Bulgaria, sent up a German flier who recognized the insignia just before firing on the airship. The Turks, however, were not that cautious, and fired wherever it proved feasible. Five rounds actually penetrated the gas cells. When night came, the enemy was the elements, and over Aka Hisser the zeppelin, with leaking gas cells, began to lose altitude. Captain Ludwig Bockholt was forced to order the ship to return, by way of Constantinople, to its base at Yamboli, Bulgaria, for repairs. After a thirty-two-hour flight covering nine-hundred miles, the landing was successfully accomplished.

It was not until five o'clock in the morning of 21 November 1917, when the airship again took off for Africa. The thermometer read 32° Fahrenheit and the barometer 30 inches. It was ideal for the takeoff for the heavily loaded airship on this daring and courageous expedition over three continents, and Hugo Eckener advised the commander of the airship that the weather reports were as favorable as could be hoped for.

The *L 59* flew over Adrianople, and the Sea of Marmora, ever alert for air or sea planes lying off the coast of Chios. Turkish authorities now had been forewarned, and this time there was no wild firing on the zeppelin. The airship left Asia Minor near Millet and flew over Crete. Then it ran into a severe storm.

The cry, "Ship afire," by the lookout luckily proved a false alarm and was only St. Elmo's fire. With an aureole, like a brilliantly lighted wreath around the hull, the zeppelin flew that night over the Mediterranean.

Africa was sighted the next morning. The men saw the Gulf of Solum, and the first land of the dark continent. Over the Libyan desert the air temperature rose to 68° Fahrenheit, and with gas escaping through the valves, the airship had to drop a ton of water ballast to equalize that loss. In the afternoon, after frightening some camel caravans traveling in the desert below, the zeppelin flew over the oasis town of Dechel. When the airship approached the Nile, a huge cloud of flamingos rose, and darkness came when the zeppelin crossed the river at the second cataract. That night, Khartum was widely circled, so as not to alert the British garrison there.

The temperature rose to 95° Fahrenheit. The wireless operator experienced difficulties with his antenna and could receive nothing. When he was finally able to contact the naval base at Nauen, he received a coded message, "Abandon undertaking and return. Enemy has occupied part of Makonde highland and is at Kilaugari."

Shocked by this report and the order, Captain Bockholt decided that there was nothing to do but to obey the orders of headquarters, although more than two-thirds of the distance had then been successfully covered. The airship had reached a point of 16° 30' north latitude and 30° 0' east longitude.

The German naval commander had believed the situation of General von Lettow-Vorbeck to be hopeless and thus ordered the zeppelin to return. But, as proved later, he had based his conclusion on an intercepted but highly exaggerated report by the British at Malta. The true facts were otherwise, but this was, of course, not known to the Germans at that crucial time. Actually, the troops of the Colonial General, who became a legend in his own life time, were then forcing their way across the Rowuma River, and on 25 November, with a small group of black Askaris, the German troops stormed the fortified camp of the Portugese, killing more than two hundred, capturing the surrendering men, and letting about three hundred men escape.

Turning homewards, the zeppelin was forced by strong winds to fly low, and being considerably slowed by head winds, at times the ship trailed its long antenna on the ground. The captain ordered some eleven-thousand pounds of ballast and cargo dropped overboard. A crate of wine and cognac, especially carried to be emptied with the general himself at the conclusion of the journey, was jettisoned. The dropped ammunition exploded when it struck a rock below.

Due to this extra effort, when the morale of the crew reached its lowest possible point because of the wasting of the precious beverages, the airship rose to clear the mountains, and the temperature now fell to 23° Fahrenheit from the previous 90° F.

Sunrise of 24 November brought a clear blue sky overhead and the island of Crete below. Constantinople was reached at night, and at three o'clock in the morning of 25 November 1917, the *L 59* landed again at Yamboli.

The zeppelin had covered 6,845 kilometers (4,225 miles) in ninety-five hours of flight at an average speed of forty-five miles per hour. Sufficient fuel for another 3,750 miles remained aboard. The covered distance was equal to that from Friedrichshafen to Chicago. With no weather reports en route, mainly over hostile territory, and such extremes in encountered temperatures, the Africa flight was a truly remarkable feat indeed.

After a complete overhaul, the *L 59* was again stationed at Yamboli, and, as part of the Balkanfront war effort, from that base made raids on Naples, a flight of some twenty-six hours. One planned raid on Port Said did not succeed, however, for only three miles from her target the zeppelin had to return to escape destruction by storm. On a subsequent bombing mission to Malta on 7 April 1918, the zeppelin apparently ran into some trouble. A friendly submarine, the *U 53,* while cruising off Brindisi, reported seeing a large fireball in the air, then watched it sink onto the waters to remain for about twenty minutes before disappearing altogether.

The submarine sped the fifty-five miles to the suspected area, but an extensive search proved fruitless. The true reason for the disaster was never learned, but an explosion aboard was believed to have caused the destruction of the *L 59.*

The airship base at Alhorn consisted of six hangars when in January 1918 the *L 51* caught fire from some undetermined cause in hangar number one. The fire spread with amazing rapidity to the other four zeppelins, the *L 46, L 47, L 58,* and *SL 20,* near it. All were destroyed. Exhaustive investigations were made as to the cause of this mysterious holocaust. However, while nothing definite was ever proven, sabotage was strongly suspected by the navy's board of inquiry.

In the spring of 1918 the British had devised a new way of launching attacks by aeroplanes from the sea. Speedy cruisers were built with a large flat deck, which was used as a take-off apron by the lighter land planes.

On occasions, the airships were engaged in running harassments with such British warships, thus preventing whole squadrons of aeroplanes from being launched at sea to make their mass attacks against industrial centers in Germany.

But with those specially equipped warships stationed at strategic points, the range of the British aeroplanes launched in that manner was appreciably greater than that of the heavier, flying boats. And altitudes of nearly twenty-thousand feet were often reached. Consequently, the defensive tactics of rising above the altitude limits of the pursuing aeroplanes was now of no value to the zeppelins.

Some air bases in Germany were bombed successfully by marauding British aircraft. The airship base at Tondern was attacked in July 1918, resulting in the destruction of the *L 54* and the *L 60,* berthed in their hangars.

What was to be the last raid on England was carried out on 9 August 1918 by five of the "70" type zeppelins, with Frigatten-Käpitan Peter Strasser personally leading the mission. The *Führer*

der Luftschiffe, or chief of the airships, who had first been active on the old *Sachsen,* now seldom had an opportunity to ascend, and the chance of trying out the newest and most advanced type zeppelin was just too good to pass up.

Each of these class zeppelins had a gas capacity of 62,000 cubic meters—the *L 71* actually had 68,500—larger than the previous types, and was powered by seven supercharged Maybach engines. One of the high-compression engines was placed in the front gondola car, two in the aft car, and one each in the four lateral gondola cars, giving the zeppelin an average speed of about eighty miles per hour. These airships could also climb to an altitude of 25,300 feet, higher than others before, and thus regained the superiority over the existing enemy aeroplanes.

Whole new series of zeppelins were to be under construction soon, airships of 75,000-cubic-meters capacity and flying at ninety miles per hour. The planned *LZ 100* was to be even larger than others and was to have a protective cover against incendiary bullets. But the last of the eighty-eight zeppelins produced for the military services, the *LZ 113,* was the last of the special *Kriegsluftschiffe,* the war airships. It signified a tremendous advance over the earliest type. The size had increased from 18,700 cubic meters to 68,500; the engines had boosted their power from 510 horsepower to 2,030, providing a speed from forty miles per hour to eighty; the carrying ability had increased from 6,500 kilograms to 52,000; and the obtainable altitudes from 2,000 meters to over 8,000. Flying distances had also been extended to the 6,845 kilometers (over 4,200 miles) flown by the *LZ 104* in 1917.

Captain Strasser, perhaps in the knowledge that time had run out on further raids by zeppelins, which he had commanded for such a long time now, was anxious to complete his illustrious career with this auspicious event and was on board the *L 70,* commanded by Captain von Lossnitzer.

But even before reaching the coast of England the *L 70* was shot down with incendiary bullets by a DH 4 pursuit plane. The extreme temperature encountered did not allow the zeppelin to rise above 17,300 feet, not a sufficiently safe altitude. The once-proud airship crashed aflame into the sea, and all men were lost.

During the war, the German Navy had seventy-eight airships under its command. Of these, nine were of the Schütte-Lanz rigid type, three were nonrigid balloons of the Parseval design, one was an "M" type semirigid balloon, built by the Prussian Military Commission according to the Gross-Basenach concept, and the remaining sixty-five were zeppelins. Six airships were used solely for training purposes.

Although a total of fifty-two naval airships were lost during the war period, their contribution to the war effort was really tremendous. Unlike the army airships, which were used primarily to devastate main railroad-junction points and disrupt major troop movements, the naval airships were primarily utilized for reconnaissance work, a task for which they were superbly suited.

The naval airships made a total of 3,055 flights (although Dürr stated 4,488) in 19,929 hours covering 1,290,143 kilometers (about 80,118 miles). The main purpose was that of *Küstenschutz* and *Aufklärung,* coastal patrols and scouting missions, and 1,148 of these were flown, with only about two-hundred raids, mainly on England. Eighty-five of these missions were flown by army airships under the overall command of the navy.

Twenty-six airships were lost during the war due to enemy action, fourteen because of bad weather, and twelve through fire or explosions. Of these, nineteen airships crashed and their entire crews were lost, while twenty-four other crashes destroyed the airships only, without loss of life. In six cases the crew was captured and taken prisoner, while in three situations the crew was interned on neutral territory. But a total of forty officers and 396 enlisted men lost their lives in the naval airship service during the war.

By the end of the war, seventeen airships had been deactivated as obsolete, and nine airships were left at Armistice Day, still in commission. They were, with other naval vessels, to be turned over to the victorious Allies.

The Allies also used lighter-than-air craft during the war, but in rather modest numbers and types.

The French military employed a pressure-type balloon, built at the Aeronautique Militaire, the Nieuport-Astra, and the Zodiac factories. These airships had a limited radius of action and quite insignificant lifting capacity, which made them unsuitable for any major operations. They were used primarily for observation purposes.

The Italians built a few nonrigid dirigible balloons of from 4,700- to 12,000-cubic-meter capacity. During the battle of the Piave, one airship actually dropped eighteen bombs on the Kaiser's Highest Command Headquarters in Portogruaro. On 5 August 1915, the *Citta di Jesi* was shot down over Pola and its crew of six men was taken prisoner. There was no other significant activity of airships reported on that front during the hostilities.

12

THE COUNT AND THE WORLD WAR

When in 1914 war broke out, zeppelins were expected to be decisive war weapons. It had then been suggested that one large bomb dropped from a cruising airship upon an impregnable fortress or important city would cause immediate capitulation. And significant military objectives, too distant for infantry soldiers, could easily be reached by these dirigibles, an impossible feat of the free-flowing balloons utilized by the French forces during the Franco-Prussian war.

Count Zeppelin believed that *"der schärfste Krieg ist der mildeste Krieg,"* "the fiercest war is the mildest war," and that it should be executed with all possible vigor to bring quick results. He presumed that a fleet of airships could devastate London, thus bringing England quickly to defeat. In fact, this method had been suggested by an experience of Monsieur L'Hoste when in 1866 during maneuvers he had dropped dummy torpedoes on a French battleship. His aim had been true from the unchallenged position of his balloon right above the defenseless warship.

Mainly because of this demonstration, the chief military powers of the world had outlawed that kind of warfare. As Collier's *New Encyclopedia* (of 1902) stated, "It has been suggested that dynamite might be thrown at an enemy from balloons, but the Peace Conference at The Hague in 1899 decided against the use of balloons to drop explosives from the sky to injure combatants on the ground." This original ban extended for five years, and in 1907 the Second Conference again proposed it, but not all countries ratified the prohibition.

But when the war engulfed all of Europe, none of the combatants were perturbed by this noble agreement. Germany was mainly concerned over her strangling *Einkreisung,* the encirclement, by hostile powers. Even with a completely effective barricade, zeppelins could easily take off from their safe bases, bomb the objectives in enemy territory, and then return to their hangars, deep in their own protected country. The idea was simple, but the execution of these plans was difficult because of the small number of airships available.

At the beginning of hostilities about ten zeppelins had existed. While their bomb-load-carrying capacities were limited, their *Schreckenswert,* their terror value, was believed to be enormous.

Although Count Zeppelin had considered his airships primarily to be "Special Ambassadors of Peace and Good Will," he repeatedly stressed their military value. Still, no special designs for such purposes had been developed because the military was too reluctant to recognize that fact and hesitated to cooperate on such plans. The Count had concentrated on the design of a superairship with a gas capacity of 2.5 million feet and capable of crossing the Atlantic to visit America, to be completed in 1915. As he told Karl H. von Wiegand in January 1915, "I have always hoped to be the first to pilot an airship across the Atlantic. To do so would be the crowning effort of my career."

But whenever he appeared in public, Count Zeppelin heard the song, *"Zeppelin flieg, hilf uns im Krieg. . ."* (Zeppelin fly, help us in war. . .).

Sitting in the relative quietness of his Stuttgart residence or the bustling manufacturing activity at the Friedrichshafen yards had no particular appeal to Count Zeppelin. His idea of winning a war was to be fighting battles although perhaps not quite as daring as his former thrilling adventures. Still, he requested active service with his regiment.

But the military officials did not allow the aged general to join his regiment, even at a reduced rank. They stated that he was needed in Friedrichshafen to direct the construction of airships, speeded up to maximum productivity. When he suggested that he be made an admiral of a fleet of zeppelins, that suggestion also was turned down.

The restless Count traveled extensively, visiting his old regiment at the front, or spending some time with the Kaiser at the Highest Command Headquarters. He inspected the new airship-hangar facilities near the North Sea. After such trips Count Zeppelin would stay at Friedrichshafen for a time to supervise the construction of airships.

The Count spent the traditional Christmas holidays that first war year with his beloved regiment at the front. Wearing his general's uniform with a smattering of medals pinned on his tunic, he was seated at the head table during the *Weihnachtsessen,* the Christmas dinner, after which he thanked his fellow officers for the "realization of an old soldier to spend Christmas at the front." Then he returned to Friedrichshafen and the zeppelins.

Ernst Lehmann wrote:

Count Zeppelin's living quarters in the Kurgarten Hotel at Friedrichshafen occupied an entire wing of the building. It was there that he preferred to spend most of his time when not at the factory. Occasionally he would visit his country estate, Ober-Gunzberg (sic), only a few miles distant, but practically all his attention was devoted to the mammoth creatures of the air which he had created. When not traveling, he divided his hours about equally between the study in the hotel and the workshop in the great plant, which was growing constantly.

To find him, one had to search the building. If he could not be found in one of the hangars, he might be in the workshops; if not there, then in the research laboratories. There was always something going on which he desired to direct or wanted to observe personally. Indeed, despite his advanced years — he was then seventy-eight — he was invariably walking about, so that it was difficult to locate him in any spot.

If one's own living room reflects his personal tastes and hobbies, then Zeppelin's can be described in a word or two. It contained simple, modern furniture. Pictures of his airships adorned the walls. A large cabinet held many of the medals, cups, decorations, and similar objects of distinction that had come to him from the government and nearly all the larger cities, universities and clubs in the country. It was rather difficult to see in this grand old man of Germany the careworn Count Zeppelin, who, in 1894, then at the age of fifty-six completed his first design for a rigid airship.[1]

After one of his many trips to Johannisthal, where he liked to talk to the airship commanders just returned from raids over England to hear of their experiences, Count Zeppelin stopped briefly in Berlin, and on 1 February 1915 granted a lengthy interview to the American correspondent Karl H. von Wiegand, who represented the United Press Newspaper Syndicate.

Until then, the Count had refused to discuss his opinion on aerial warfare with any foreign correspondent or to reply to the accusations by the English of indiscriminately dropping bombs at night from his zeppelins.

"Aerial warfare has come to stay," was Count Zeppelin's quick reply. Von Wiegand reported:

It is as potent a factor today, as is submarine warfare. In the strife of nations, war in the air will become as vital a factor as that of any other branch of the military and naval service. It may become almost as important as the undersea warfare, depending of course on the [further technical] development of warships and the new developments of submarines.

Aerial cruisers, in my opinion, largely will tend to change the face and aspects of war; and, (he added hopefully) therefore, in the future, making war less likely. Whether there will ever be great battles in the air [on the scale so luridly pictured by imaginative writers of fiction], like those which have taken place on the sea, can only be answered by the distant future. Personally, I am not inclined to think so, but who knows? This is an age of progress.[2]

As to the vehement protests by Germany's enemies that by the use of zeppelins, bombs were dropped on unfortified places, killing women and children, the Count stated—and here the voice of the old soldier and inventor carried a note of grief that was unmistakable to the interviewer—"No one regrets more than I do that noncombatants have been slain. But have not noncombatants been killed by other instruments of warfare? Why then this outcry?"

And then he answered his own question:

Let me tell you. It is because England fears the Zeppelin dirigibles. She realizes that they promised to destroy her splendid isolation; because, having failed to succeed in building something similar, she hopes to arouse the world to bring pressures to bear to prevent by Germany the use of these great weapons of modern warfare which are unavailable for her own use. Does anyone believe for a moment that England in her determination to crush Germany by every means in her power—even attempting to starve women and children—would not use zeppelins if she had them?[3]

The Count continued:

If the military effect of the Zeppelin airship tends toward shortening this terrible war by only one day, thereby saving perhaps thousands of lives; if the Zeppelins—as they now only begin their development as a new military weapon—should prove to be so effective a weapon of hostilities that wars are less likely to occur in the future; then their advent will be a benefit to humanity, quite aside from the peaceful agencies.[4]

Von Wiegand wrote that the Count concluded in a strong voice:

And now, in this most critical hour when Germany's very existence is at stake, when an effort is being made to starve our women and children, should Zeppelins add the slightest strength to the fatherland against the ring of enemies seeking her complete destruction, then my life will not have been in vain.[5]

(The veteran zeppelin commander, Captain Heinrich Mathy, took issue with Balfour who said that London was not a fortified city and that its defenses against aerial attacks were poor. Mathy knew that there were several forts and batteries around outside the city. He said, "If Balfour had stood by my side and looked into those flashing guns everywhere, he would not have said that London was not a militarily defended city and perhaps not think so poorly of its aerial defense.")

The journalist asked, "How can the killing of noncombatants be prevented?"

Count Zeppelin pointed out that:

We cannot always see an object from a great height. . . .How many noncombatants have been killed in this war by Zeppelins, as compared with other engines of war fare? Is not the killing of noncombatants also true by other weapons, especially by artillery and mortars? Do not shells often drop in undefended or nonmilitary parts of towns or cities? How can you tell, for instance, exactly where the shells from mortars or other artillery will strike? For instance, the shells from the new Krupp gun have a reported range of forty-two kilometers (about twenty-five miles). The purpose of the Zeppelins as a warcraft is not against the noncombatants, but against military forces, defended towns and cities, ships, arsenals, and docks.

The crews of the Zeppelins are exposed to greater dangers, but they are just as humane as the other branches of the service. They have no intention to kill women and children any more than the officers and gunners of the artillery, so far as [it] lies in their power to avoid.

There is a proof of this — the best proof possible. It is to be found in the unexploded bombs found in English towns. When the Zeppelins are discovered and under the heavy fire of the enemy, it may be vital to ascend quickly. So it may be necessary to throw off bombs that are used as ballast. Then, whenever it is possible to do so, the explosive contacts are disconnected so that the bombs, falling where it is feared there are noncombatants, will not explode. That is probably what occurred in those English towns, where they say unexploded bombs were discovered.[6]

When asked what would define a city or object to be bombed, the Count replied:

The rule is similar to land warfare. It is based on two fundamental unwritten laws — the law of humanity that forbids the killing of non-combatants, whenever avoidable, and the law of necessity of military exigency. A city or town occupied by military forces, or defended only by trenches, is subjected to attack, unless surrendered or evacuated. That such places often are attacked and badly shot to pieces, you've probably had occasion to see for yourself at both fronts in this war.

Therefore, it seems to be rational that a city or town having military forces that fire upon aircraft, or mount guns for that purpose, is subject to aerial attack the same as if attacking a force of infantry or artillery.[7]

Von Wiegand added that regarding attacks on London, the Count said that such a decision was up to the admiralty or the general staff.

As to actual combat between aeroplanes and zeppelins, the Count told that interviewer:

So far as I know, there has been only one. In it the Zeppelins drove off the aeroplanes. It must be remembered that the Zeppelins sail smoothly and that the aim and fire of their machine guns and quick firers, mounted on top, are much steadier and more effective than is possible from the aeroplane.[8]

Although the Count himself had been most anxious to take command of one of his zeppelins on a raid over England, the admiralty had not allowed him to do so.

I strongly desire service and am ready when ordered to take my place on the line, but so far I have had to be satisfied with personal craving. I have decided that it is merely pride and egotism and that I am of greater use elsewhere until my actual presence with my aircraft is necessary.[9]

With a twinkle in his eyes, he added: "Besides,

the Zeppelin warcraft should not have anything on board which cannot be thrown overboard as ballast." When their conversation turned to the United States, Count Zeppelin said: "I had many friends in America, but I fear that few of them have cared to live as long as I have. Perhaps none will be left when I come again—if I come in one of my airships."

When von Wiegand asked: "But not to bomb New York or Washington?" The Count replied indignantly: "Throw bombs on people who have been so kind to me while I was among them?"

He was deeply troubled over the charges of ruthlessness in the use of dirigibles in the war and the intimations that this action was beyond the limits of civilized warfare.

I want to sail on a peaceful mission when I go to America. My greatest ambition has not been to create a machine of destruction. It has been to demonstrate that Zeppelins were suited to far greater purposes than to be used as mere instruments of warfare.[10]

Count Zeppelin seemed to ponder the matter in his mind and then spoke with a deep intensity as though he were talking to himself. "I must try to live long enough, or I fear that it will not be accomplished—at least not in the near future."

When asked if he really thought that transatlantic travel would be possible or practicable, Count Zeppelin stated:

Not only possible but practicable.

This war has interfered with my plans. Designs for a suitable airship are already on the drawing boards. I know that aerial travel will become the quickest and safest method. Zeppelins in their development have, in my opinion, a great future before them. Few people know the delight and safety of travel therein. They will become great factors for quick passenger and mail service. It is absurd to talk of perfection of Zeppelins. They are only on the threshold of the ultimate possibilities . . . and have not yet reached perfection by any means. Comparatively speaking, we are only in the beginning of aerial navigation.[11]

The Count suggested that:

A flight to New York should take about three

to four days, perhaps more, perhaps less. It would depend on the wind and weather. Anyhow, it could hardly be expected that the first voyage could be made in the shortest time any more than the first steamers established the record.[12]

As to the trend in the designs of zeppelins, the Count said:

Where they are to be utilized for warcraft, a form of construction that will permit them to fly much higher than at present. For commercial purposes they must have greater carrying capacity and greater speed. As compared with the years it took to develop the railroads, my aircraft are merely beginning their careers. At present they are too much dependent on wind and weather.

With the exception of the first flight that I made I cannot conceive a more inspiring moment than when I can pilot one of my cruisers into New York and then go on to Washington.[13]

Von Wiegand observed that there was no doubt that the veteran inventor was keenly aware of the defects that had to be overcome before his airships were completely successful, and that he had no doubt that these many problems would be solved.

"Perhaps there won't be wars when the stage of perfection is reached," the Count said hopefully.

At the suggestion that a zeppelin be sent to the United States for exhibition purposes at the Panama Pacific Exposition at San Francisco, he said emphatically, "No, no, I do not wish to have an airship sent across the Atlantic in the hold of a steamer. She will make it under her own power."

Although the authorities had turned down all efforts by Count Zeppelin to get into active military service, to Karl von Wiegand he looked not over sixty, yet he was then seventy-seven years old. He was short of stature, but had a well-knit athletic figure that showed astonishing elasticity and quickness of movement. He had very clear eyes and a ruddy face with a snow-white mustache. At the time of the interview he had two black eyes, which he had received in a tumble while making some experiments in the air over Johannisthal. He did not wish to go into the details of the experiment he had conducted, but his attitude indicated that it was an important one.

After the dinner, when the interview was ended, the companion of the Count excused himself, explaining that he had promised to see a friend, a popular dancer then appearing on a Berlin stage, off at the railroad station. "Perhaps your Excellency knows her and would accompany me," he suggested. With a broad smile Count Zeppelin replied, "No, but if I were a trifle younger, I wager that I would know her."

Another observer, Rudolph Stratz, who saw Count Zeppelin frequently at about the same time at Friedrichshafen, found him to be a small, thin man with a white mustache. He wore a sports jacket. Actually he was a very old man, but seemed very lively. His eyes were strangely bright and a little moist; his nose slightly curved; and there was an intensity of expression in his eyes, suggesting the fanaticism of a discoverer of new worlds. Other than that he looked like the typical, old reckless hussar. Stratz said that he reminded him of the legendary hussar general, old Zieten! At the same time his manner denoted the perfect gentleman from head to foot, the diplomat, the general, the Count, the landowner. And surrounding him was that air of wholly unconscious assurance which appears to surround all truly great men.

As he had done on several occasions before, when the building of the *LZ 98* was completed in April 1916 and delivery to the authorities made at Hannover, Count Zeppelin rode along as a passenger on the eighteen-hour trip. On route, he asked Captain Lehmann to fly over the village of Zeppelin, the ancestral home near Bützow in Mecklenburg on the Baltic Sea, which the Count had never visited before. As he looked down on the vast areas of thick forests and rich fields, he said, "All that land you can see below once belonged to my ancestors, but they drank and gambled it all away."

Count Zeppelin fully realized that aeroplanes had made more rapid progress in technological developments than had airships, and that they, rather than his zeppelins, would dominate the air. He became greatly interested in the manufacture of such aircraft. As a subsidiary of *Delag*, the Dornier factory in Friedrichshafen was building seaplanes, and the Count spent considerable time in that manufacturing plant.

Count Zeppelin also expressed that conviction early in 1917 when he visited with Field Marshall Paul von Hindenburg at his headquarters at Pless on the Eastern front. As Hindenburg remembered in his *Reminiscences (Aus meinem Leben):*

Count Zeppelin visited us at Pless, and the simplicity of his manner touched us all and made a profound impression. He felt that his airships were already antiquated weapons in warfare and in his opinion, the aeroplane and not the airship will control the air in the future.[14]

The Count was convinced that a really large aeroplane, powered by several engines, could carry bombs weighing as much as one-thousand kilograms each. He believed that such heavy bombs would be most effective against harbor installations by severely damaging them. Count Zeppelin was also of the opinion that bombs thrown close enough to the hull of a warship would create sufficient forces to damage the sides of the vessel. Since greater force is exerted toward the least-resistant area, that is, closest to the waterline, and not equally in all directions, the Count reasoned that greater damage could be done actually if the bombs were not dropped onto the warship itself.

The *Waggonfabrik* at Gotha, Thuringia, had built an all-metal aeroplane, designed by Claude Dornier, who had joined the company in 1910. The R-model, powered by three engines with a wing spread of forty-two meters, was built soon after the war broke out, and on 6 June 1915 the three-propeller plane made its initial flight from Gotha to Friedrichshafen. Before that event, the *Dornier Metallbauten, G.m.b.H.,* had been formed in 1914 by the Zeppelin works at Friedrichshafen. The subsidiary company then became the *Abteilung Flugzeugbau-Ganzmetall.* A year later the *Grossflugzeugbau Gotha and Staaken* was also acquired as an associated enterprise of the *Luftschiffbau-Zeppelin.*

Early in February 1917, Count Zeppelin went to Munich to attend a meeting at the Deutsches Museum where the Geheimrat von Linde named him honorary member of the museum, and King Ludwig II awarded him an elaborately designed certificate.

Count Zeppelin's health seemed to be failing—he was then 78 years old—when he attended a large aeronautical exhibition in Berlin later that month. Rudolph Stratz remembered, perhaps a bit too dramatically, that "like a little old gentleman, the Count stood at the entrance gate looking for something in his pockets. Apparently he had forgotten his invitation card. Later, in the hall he appeared somewhat distressed. His eyes seemed a little veiled, and he appeared unsure of himself."

Other friends, however, commented on his vigor as they met him at this same exhibition, where a large, captured British aeroplane was one of the main attractions. The Count entertained his close friends at the Hotel Kaiserhof, where he always stayed when in Berlin, and August von Parseval recalled that:

> none of us realized that this would be the last time we would see him. He was the same as always, the real Zeppelin, the ever youthful enthusiast, despite his white hair. The modest man, the considerate host, who was carefully attending to his guests. We shall all remember him as we saw him that evening because it was this simplicity which shaped the true beauty of his character. Never did he pose as a great and important man. Always in his relationship with his friends he personified sincerity and kindness.[15]

But before Count Zeppelin returned to Friedrichshafen from that trip to Berlin, he was taken ill. At the end of February he was rushed to the Sanatorium des Westens, where his doctors diagnosed his problem as an obstruction of the intestines. An operation to ease that condition was immediately performed and declared successful, but within a few days the patient contracted pneumonia.

His daughter Hella hurried to Berlin to be with her father, but the doctors advised his wife that it was not necessary to come immediately to his bedside. So she waited until it was too late. Count Ferdinand von Zeppelin died on 8 March 1917, at the age of seventy-eight years and eight months.

"I am very tired and would like to sleep," were his last words to his daughter.

A lingering final illness, which he dreaded so much, fortunately never came to him, and his greatest wish, never to grow too old to work, had been fulfilled.

The burial took place at the Pragfriedhof in Stuttgart on 12 March and the funeral was "attended by ten thousand mourners," the *Schwäbische Merkur* reported. As the funeral procession moved past huge, black-draped, tall columns with flames burning in urns atop each of them, the casket was carried by twelve uhlans of his regiment. The procession was headed by the military band and a representative column of his beloved regiment. The clergymen, the family members, representatives of the Kaiser's family, the King and Queen of Württemberg, high military and government officials, leaders among the sciences, and other mourners followed. Bells pealed and cannons were fired in salute. Two of his airships flew slowly overhead, their keels draped with black crape. A squadron of aeroplanes flew low in a last respectful greeting.

For the brief graveside service, the pastor had selected as his text the words, "I must be active, as long as it is day."

The zeppelins hovered above and, after the casket was lowered into the grave, the airship commanders dropped flowered wreaths on the grave of the creator of their dirigible balloons.

That night, a memorial service was held in the city, with an orchestra playing Beethoven's *Eroica* and director Alfred Colsman giving the eulogy.

The words, *"Dein Glaube hast dir geholfen,"* that is, "Your faith has helped you," are chiseled into the simple tombstone over the grave in the family plot.

The *Frankfurter Zeitung* of 8 March 1917 said: We did not know that Count Ferdinand von Zeppelin was ill, and we were shocked to know of his death. All of Germany mourns his loss, and today, people the world over will be talking about the inventor of the Zeppelin airships. With his death a truly great man is gone. And even though the peoples of the world are full of hatred toward each other at the present time, Zeppelin's death and the fact that he was, certainly, a great man will not go unnoticed in the other countries of the world.[16]

13

POSTWAR ACTIVITIES

At the time of the armistice, one of the naval airships was still under construction at Friedrichshafen and in the possession of the Zeppelin Works; it was hoped that the victorious Allies would allow the company to use that zeppelin to resume its commercial flights.

Actually, under greatest secrecy, it was planned to fly this *L 72* across the Atlantic to New York to show what a zeppelin could accomplish in peacetime. Necessarily, no foreign governments were informed of the plan, but officials of the German government had indicated their approval of the scheme. The airship was to fly over the English Channel during the dark of night, or if the weather proved adverse, to fly the northern route around the British Isles; when finally the shores of North America were reached, it would ask for permission to fly over the United States and to land there.

Preparations for the flight were made in March 1919, and everything appeared to be going along satisfactorily; however, when the time came for the departure in April, the German government forbade the takeoff of the zeppelin. The *Verbot,* or prohibition, was never explained to the adventurous airshipmen, but when some eight weeks later, a British dirigible crossed the Atlantic, it became evident that the Allied Commission had issued the prohibiting order.

The six military airships remaining at the end of the war had been ordered to be turned over to the Allies as part of their reparations. The *L 61* and *LZ 120* went to Italy; the *L 64* and *L 71* to Britain; the *L 113* to France; and the *L 30* in a dismantled form to Belgium, as was the *L 37* to Japan. But their crews had destroyed others on 23 June 1919 on the ground at their respective bases, imitating the naval crews that sank their vessels after turning them over to the British at Scapa Flow. The Germans were also ordered to turn over the newly finished *L 72* as well.

Renamed the *Dixmude* by the French, the 62,000-cubic-meter airship was soon sent on a record flight over the Mediterranean area, lasting over 118 hours and covering a distance of about five-thousand miles. In December 1923, the *Dixmude,* in a heavy storm, crashed into the sea near Sicily returning from a flight over Africa, losing the entire crew of fifty-two men. The disaster was thought to have been caused by the inexperience of the flight personnel, although the French certainly were not unfamiliar with airships.

The sugar refiners Paul and Pierre Lebaudy had built in 1902 the semirigid airship *La Jaune.* Impressed with it, the ministry of war had ordered a sister ship constructed; the brothers also built other airships for other governments. The Russians ordered another airship seven years later, in 1909, and the British were also reported to have purchased a semirigid airship from the Lebaudys. In fact, during the First World War, the French built

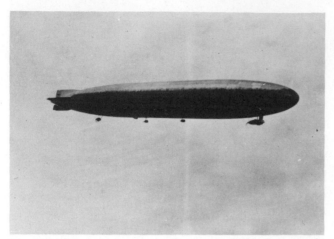

The *LZ 114,* turned over to France in 1919, became the *Dixmude.* (Courtesy, Luftschiffbau Zeppelin).

some thirty different types of airships, most of which used a cross-section initiated by the tricylindrical form built by Astra-Torres, with the gas bag divided into four compartments.

Airship opponents in Germany pointed out that about eighty dirigible airships were lost during the war by the army and navy, while the proponents proudly called attention to the fact that an amazing total of nearly five-thousand successful raids and reconnaissance flights had been made with often truly spectacular results. While the loss of the personnel was certainly lamentable, the materiel loss was merely as much of a calculated risk as the loss of a warship at sea or a cannon in ground battle.

Zeppelin Company officials did not necessarily mourn the loss of the military airships as reparation to their former enemies because these specially designed war-airships were not well suited for commercial purposes anyway. Designed to fly at unusually high altitudes at rather fast speeds, their conversion into profitable commercial airships with comfortable passenger accommodations would be a difficult and expensive task.

Anxious to get back into the commercial-flight business, the Zeppelin works built two smaller passenger airships, the *LZ 120* and *LZ 121.* A contract was negotiated with the *Svenska Luft Trafik Aktiebolaget* of Stockholm to institute regular airship flights between Stockholm and Berlin. The originally planned schedule called for two zeppelins to fly between the two capitals on a two-day rotating basis.

The *LZ 120,* the *Bodensee,* completed first, had

a capacity of only twenty-thousand cubic meters. The four engines of 260 horsepower each gave the airship a speed of eighty-three miles per hour. The zeppelin began service on 20 August and completed 103 flights in 1919 between Friedrichshafen and Berlin within ninety-eight days, carrying 2,450 passengers. The one-way fare was 575 marks (about $150) per passenger, and the flight took six hours, compared to the eighteen by express train. Actually not any larger than the earlier commercial zeppelins, this newer airship had double the carrying capacity — forty-two percent of its weight, or 9,600 kilograms — and double the speed of the previous types.

The *Nordstern,* with a capacity of 22,500 cubic meters, had just been completed when the Inter-Allied Air Commission ordered both airships to be handed over to France and Italy as reparation payments. Now, all work activity on airships at Friedrichshafen again came to a halt, but officials hoped that this suspension would be only temporary.

The *LZ 121,* the *Nordstern,* became the *Méditerranée* and served the French until 1927. The *LZ 120* was delivered to Italy and became the *Esperia,* but on her first official appearance under the Italian flag she was completely wrecked.

The Italians then constructed two semirigid airships. The *Norge* left Rome on 10 April 1926 to be outfitted at Leningrad for a polar expedition. On 9 May, under the command of Colonel Umberto Nobile and the experienced explorers Roald Amundsen and Lincoln Ellsworth, the airship started its polar flight from Spitsbergen. That same day, Richard Byrd and Floyd Bennett flew over the North Pole in their three-engined Fokker monoplane. On 12 May 1926 the *Norge* hovered above the pole, descended to plant the flags of the respective countries represented, then flew by way of Point Barrow to land at Teller, in Grandley Harbor near Nome, Alaska.

The sister ship, the *Italia,* was completed the following year, and again Colonel Nobile flew to Spitsbergen in 1928 for further explorations. On a seventy-hour flight, much new territory was mapped. On another flight over the Pole in May, the airship encountered violent storms on its return flight and crashed onto the ice some 220 miles from the supply ship *Citta di Milano.* Nine men had been thrown on the ice when the stricken airship rose suddenly and disappeared with the

The *LZ 120 Bodensee* being extensively rebuilt. (Courtesy, Luftschiffbau Zeppelin).

The *LZ 121*, the *Nordstern*, in 1920, landing. (Courtesy, Luftschiffbau Zeppelin).

remaining seven members of the crew. After a week of desperation, three men walked southward, only to be lost forever, while the remaining six were eventually rescued. Roald Amundsen, who flew a search plane, was lost in that effort.

During the war, about ten semirigid airships had been built under the supervision of Colonel Nobile at the *Stabilimento di Construzioni Aeronautiche* in Rome. Another company, *La Societa Leonardo da Vinci* of Milan, had built five such airships, primarily for bombing missions. Soon after the war, the United States Navy purchased a small, semirigid airship from Italy, and another, the *Roma*, was bought by the United States Army in 1921.

The Italian semirigid airship *N1 Norge*, which flew over the North Pole in 1921. (Courtesy, Goodyear).

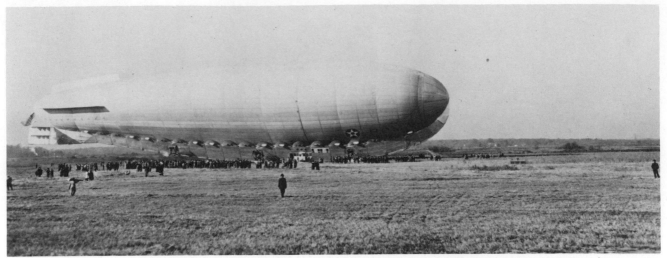

The semirigid airship *Roma*, bought from Italy by the United States Army in 1921. (Courtesy, Goodyear).

Russia had purchased two airships from France in 1909, but no activity in that field was reported until 1931, when by public subscription some fifteen million rubles were collected for an airship-building program. General Nobile had come to Russia in 1928, soon after the *Italia* disaster, to supervise airship construction of the planned semirigid type, and no doubt that event had stimulated interest in airships in Russia. The Italian general was to remain there for ten years.

Plans were announced two years later for the construction of two large-sized airships and one metal-covered airship at Dolgo Prutnaja, near Moscow. In 1936, the Dirigible Construction Trust began work on an airship for Arctic research. And a Russian airship was said to have set a new record of 130 hours and twenty-seven minutes continuous flight, but two years later this airship was destroyed when it crashed into a mountain.

Larger airships were constructed for a commercial route between Moscow and Leningrad. A semirigid airship, built in 1934 for commercial purposes, established an endurance record of 169 hours flying between Moscow and Sverdlosk, but this four-engined ship met with an accident on 6 February 1938 on a flight to Murmansk to test its suitability for arctic exploration. An expanded airship program was promptly announced by the authorities, but nothing more was heard about it. Jane's *All the World's Aircraft* of 1950 and 1951 listed two Russian passenger airships, the *Victory* and the *Patriot*, in service as civilian transports in 1946.

Although the British War Office had in 1877 established a balloon corps, no airships were built until after some demonstrations in 1907. That year, proposals made by Wilbur and Orville Wright had been rejected by the First Lord of the Admiralty. Having consulted expert advisers with regard to the suggestion as to the employment of aeroplanes, the Admiralty were of the opinion that they would not be of any practical value to the naval service.

Public opinion, however, urged the start of construction of an airship in 1909. This resulted in the *Mayfly,* an eight-hundred-thousand-cubic-foot (24,340 cubic meters) rigid dirigible. Unfortunately, this airship failed to complete even its preliminary test flight in 1911 and was wrecked at Barrow.

After becoming a part of the Royal Naval Air Service, a contract for a dirigible was let, but the war intervened and construction of the projected *R 9* was halted. With the German airships appearing over England, work on the airship was resumed. But when the completed airship was tested, the performance was so disappointing to the officials that no others were ordered built.

After the war, the British built two airships of the Schütte-Lanz type, the *R 31* and the *R 32,* and a zeppelin type, the *R 33,* copying the captured German *L 33.* Another slightly improved version of this zeppelin type, the *R 34,* made the first successful crossing of the Atlantic. That airship left Scotland on 2 July 1919, and arrived at Mineola, New York, in 108 hours flying time, on 6 July.

The British *R 100*, the first airship to cross the Atlantic, was eventually dismantled. (Courtesy, Goodyear).

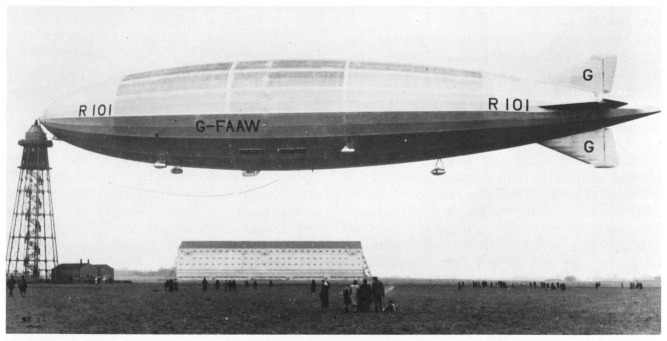

The British *R 101*, a day before she took off on her tragic flight to India. (Courtesy, Goodyear).

Leaving four days later, the R 34 arrived back at Pulham, England, on 13 July after flying for seventy-five hours.

While this successful Atlantic crossing created new interest by the British in lighter-than-air-craft activity, not much came of it. The American government ordered a rigid type airship of similar construction, built by the Royal Airship Works at Cardington. This was the R 38, an improved version of the R 34, to be designated by the United States Navy as ZR 2. The airship was 695 feet long with a maximum diameter of eighty-five feet, and a capacity of 2,740,000 cubic feet (79,280 cubic meters). Powered by engines of 2,100 horsepower, the airship had a speed of seventy miles per hour. With an American training crew aboard, but still under British command, the R 38 crashed on its fourth test flight on 24 August 1921, over the Humber River at Hull, killing all sixty-two persons aboard. Not yet officially accepted, the airship had flown only fifty-six hours. With this tragedy of the ship breaking in two, all airship construction was halted in Britain.

It was some eight years later, when encouraged by the success of the German zeppelins LZ 126 and LZ 127, that the British ordered construction of their R 100 and R 101 by the Airship Guarantee Company. Planned for service to Canada and the Far East, the R 100 was 709 feet long with a maximum diameter of 130 feet, contained some five million cubic feet (140,000 cubic meters) of gas, and was powered by Rolls Royce engines of 4,200 horsepower, which actually proved to be too heavy. The airship made a round trip across the Atlantic, but the builders were not quite satisfied with the performance of the airship.

The R 101 was, in the words of Lord Thomson, "One of the most scientific experiments that man has ever attempted." The airship was 777 feet long, had a maximum diameter of 131 feet 8 inches, and a height of 140 feet. The capacity was 5,500,000 cubic feet (141,000 cubic meters).

After the initial unsatisfactory test flights, the airship was altered by installing diesel engines and adding a midsection of eighty-four feet to increase the gas capacity and lifting power. The framework was then much stronger, but consisted of fewer steel girders with larger spaces between them. The gas bags were pressed closer together, but the motion of the airship rubbed them against each other in a strong wind, causing friction and generating static electricity. (Lord Thomson assured the House of Lords in June that "there is going to be no risk while I am in charge.")

On 4 October 1930 the reconstructed airship, after seemingly inadequate tests, took off on a long-distance flight to India. Over France the R 101 ran into a heavy rainstorm, and flying extremely low the ship became so nose heavy when some cells collapsed that it dipped toward the ground. The airship failed to recover sufficient altitude. A sudden violent gust forced the dirigible into the ground, where it exploded on impact against a hillside at Beauvais. Apparently gasoline was ignited when the airship struck, and then that fire ignited the hydrogen. The use of helium had been considered, but this safer gas was heavier and consequently had less lifting power. The cost of helium was then about twenty times higher than hydrogen, and filling the R 101 would have cost fifty-thousand pounds. Forty-seven persons aboard, including the designer and high officials, including Lord Thomson, were killed. Consequently, all interest of the British in airships ceased, and the R 100 was then dismantled.

One of the first successful airships used in the United States was one based on the Santos-Dumont models and built by Thomas S. Baldwin in 1904. Some years later the Signal Corps acquired another Baldwin airship and inaugurated an aerial squadron.

In 1910 and 1912, two airships, the America and the Akron, were built especially to fly across the Atlantic, but both were unsuccessful in that endeavor. After 1911, the Goodyear Tire and Rubber Company began experiments with nonrigid types of airships and balloons, not only for private concerns, but also for the governments of the United States, Britain, and France.

During the war, nonrigid types were tested to be used by the United States Navy in coastal patrol duties, and soon this activity was expanded to actually eight different types.

In March 1916 Admiral George Dewey, together with the general board of the Department of the Navy, recommended the development of airships, and Congress duly authorized the construction of airships, influenced, no doubt, by the spectacular success of the German zeppelins. Eventually, in 1921, the semirigid airship Roma was bought from Italy. The dirigible was a 1,240,000-cubic-foot (37,750 cubic meters) airship, had a length of 410 feet and a maximum diameter of seventy-five feet, and reached a speed of seventy miles per hour with its six engines of 400 horsepower each. After having been carefully reassembled in the United States, on a test flight in February 1922, the airship became unmanageable and crashed into high-tension wires near Langley Field, Virginia. Filled with hydrogen, the *Roma* exploded, killing thirty-four men of the crew of forty-five.

The British airship *R 38* was still undergoing tests after the purchase by the United States Navy, but it was destroyed in 1921 before delivery and officially becoming the *ZR 2*.

Meanwhile an airship was being built at the Philadelphia Naval Aircraft Factory. Based on the German *L 49* zeppelin design, the *ZR 1* (for zeppelin rigid number one) made its maiden voyage on 4 September 1923. The *Shenandoah* was 680 feet long, seventy-nine feet in maximum diameter, and had a capacity of 60,845 cubic meters (two million cubic feet) of gas. Originally designed, of course, to use hydrogen gas, it used helium exclusively and was the first airship to do so. (A thousand feet of helium gas has the lifting power of sixty-two pounds, hydrogen has sixty-eight pounds, a difference of only ten percent.)

The German *L 49* had been captured practically intact in October 1917 at Bourbonne les Bains. The crew was completely exhausted from the

The *Shenandoah* under construction in January 1924. (Courtesy, U.S. Navy).

high-altitude flying, and the engines had frozen up when their airship settled on the ground. And the *L 33* had been forced down in England in 1916, also nearly undamaged. Principal changes over these zeppelin designs were the insertion of a ten-meter section into the center of the ship, the strengthening of the bow and provision of mooring

The *ZR 1 Shenandoah* made its maiden flight in September 1923. (Courtesy, Goodyear).

The *Shenandoah* cruising over the bay. (Courtesy, U.S. Navy).

gear, the redesign of fins and rudders, the fitting of a top walkway, and the change of the power cars and power units.

The *Shenandoah* carried out various naval missions, served as a scouting airship, and made transcontinental demonstration flights, visiting most of the larger cities in the country. The "Daughter of the Stars" had made fifty-six flights covering some twenty-five-thousand miles, had several times crossed the country, had moored at the mast at Lakehurst and on the tanker *Patoka* at sea, had participated in naval maneuvers, and had done a wonderful public-relations job for the navy. On her fifty-seventh flight, the airship was to fly from Lakehurst to St. Louis, Minneapolis, Detroit, and back to the New Jersey base.

Caught in a violent storm over the Ohio valley on 3 September 1925, the *Shenandoah* was tossed wildly about. The control car was torn loose from the hull and crashed to earth at Caldwell. The main section of the airship broke into two parts and one crashed to the ground. But the stern section was carried along by the storm several miles from the

other before it was brought down, with all men in that part saved. Of the entire crew of forty-three men, twenty-nine survived, mainly because the *ZR 1* was inflated with helium.

The official report of the disaster cited the inexperience of the crew—to save the precious helium, a number of valves had been closed—and also suggested a weakness in the construction, since the airship apparently encountered aerodynamical stresses imposed on it by the vertical currents of the squall in which it had been entrapped without warning, far beyond those contemplated by the designers of the old German zeppelins after which it was modeled. The Court of Inquiry declared it an "inevitable accident."

But General Billy Mitchell, the pioneer airpower advocate, publicly blamed the War and Navy Departments for the *Shenandoah* disaster, thus initiating his own court-martial. He charged that the catastrophe was the direct result of incompetence, criminal negligence, and near-treasonable administration of national defense by the two departments, and that all planning for aviation was

126

The *Shenandoah* moored to the USS *Patoka*. (Courtesy, U.S. Navy).

The *Shenandoah* moored to the USS *Patoka*. (Courtesy, U.S. Navy).

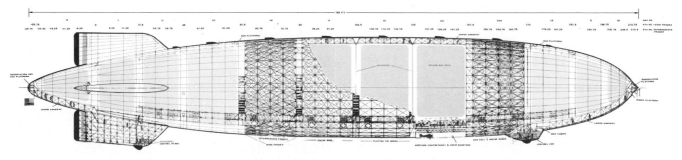

Schematic drawing of the *Akron* by the Goodyear Zeppelin Corporation, 1931. (Courtesy, Goodyear).

done by nonflying officers who knew nothing whatsoever about it. At his trial, the general also stated that the crew of the *Shenandoah* was not supplied with parachutes, "an inexcusable action by the navy."

Admiral William Moffett testified that because the original design (of 1915) was for an airship that utilized hydrogen, when helium was instead used, its efficiency dropped by about forty percent. As a strong supporter of lighter-than-air craft, the admiral urged further airship development despite this disastrous setback.

The *LZ 126* airship received under reparation agreements from Germany, designated as *ZR 3* and christened the *Los Angeles,* had arrived in the United States on 15 October 1924.

Article 198 of the Treaty of Versailles prohibited further airship construction by Germany after the war. The *Luftschiffbau-Zeppelin* at Friedrichshafen decided to manufacture kitchen utensils, but the manufacture of pots and pans held absolutely no interest for the former airship builders. Under the guidance of Hugo Eckener, a plan was contrived to convince the Allied powers, and especially the Americans, that they should take an airship instead of the demanded monetary compensation, and the specific value of three million marks (about $750,000) was agreed upon.

Having been able to get the Americans to consent to that proposal, Eckener now found an even greater obstacle to those plans in the German government. The fact that the deal was not to be considered consummated until the airship was actually delivered in the United States, the government officials were far from convinced that the airship could indeed be flown safely across the Atlantic and the delivery made. Eventually, however, the German Foreign Office officials agreed to the proposition.

Financing the construction of the airship was another problem, since the government furnished only one million marks of the needed amount. Again, the German people responded nobly, as they had so many times before, to build this zeppelin. The Zeppelin-Eckener-Spende brought in slightly over two-million marks, and when the cost of construction exceeded the available funds, the *Luftschiffbau* raised an additional eight-hundred-thousand marks to complete the project.

A minor problem was that the hangar was smaller than the proposed zeppelin, and so the airship was reduced from the originally designed two-hundred-meter length and thirty-five-meter maximum diameter. Its overall length was to be 670 feet (about twenty feet less) and the diameter, 92 feet (about twelve feet less) instead. Other specifications were maintained as planned.

This *LZ 126* was of a newly designed streamlined form with a thicker stem and a capacity of 2,470,000 cubic feet (seventy-thousand cubic meters). The duraluminum skeleton consisted of twenty-two girders for greater stability, and the large number of gas cells were placed between the girder rings. The control gondola car was actually built into the body itself, and the five-engine gondola cars were suspended on struts. Each of the Maybach engines developed 400 horsepower, giving the airship a maximum speed of seventy-nine miles per hour and a cruising speed of sixty-eight miles per hour, with a range of 12,500 kilometers, about the circumference to the earth (12,700 kilometers). The zeppelin weighed 182,600 pounds and had a carrying ability of 46,000 kilograms or fifty-six percent of its total weight.

Hugo Eckener believed that a comprehensive series of demonstration flights was absolutely necessary to convince the people of the safety of airships. The *Dixmude* and *R 38* tragedies were still fresh in the minds of most people, and Eckener insisted in proving to them the unqualified safety of zeppelin travel.

When terribly bad weather prevailed on the scheduled day for the first test flight, Eckener refused to cancel or postpone the trial, showing his complete confidence in the airworthiness of the zeppelin. After a short time aloft, the accompany-

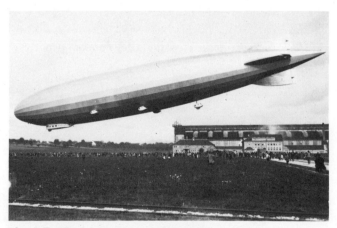

The *LZ 126* lands at Friedrichshafen in 1924. (Courtesy, Luftschiffbau Zeppelin).

ing Storch airplane was forced down because of the storm, but the zeppelin kept on flying through the disturbance.

Electrical discharges were not harmful to the airship. Only a small burned mark was left at the spot where lightning struck the hull. The charge was carried along through the metal skeleton and escaped through the antennae, usually damaging the sending apparatus. (Lightning strikes are only dangerous when gas is being let off at the very moment of the strike. The capable commander never tries to gain altitude by such a maneuver through thunder clouds. Of course, absolutely tight gas cells are mandatory, as are perfectly functioning gas valves, which close completely after every use. When these two details are not properly maintained, disastrous trouble ensues.)

To be of maximum publicity value, the trip across the Atlantic had to be made in the shortest possible time. The necessary supply of fuel created a problem. Some thirty tons of fuel could be carried, sufficient for seventy hours of flight with the five engines running at regular speed, and covering 4,650 sea miles, but without hampering, adverse winds. Operating at a slower speed, some fuel could be saved, and, since winds generally occur at that time of year over the Atlantic, this method of operation seemed advisable.

The flight to the United States was, of course, exceedingly important and was most conscientiously planned. The chosen route via the Azores was a longer one, but the weather promised to be more moderate than the weather that would have been encountered on the shorter northern route.

The carefully selected crew of twenty-eight men included five licensed airship commanders. Departure was scheduled for early 11 October but the wet fog over the Bodensee area delayed the start. This moisture would have increased the weight of the zeppelin by 4,400 pounds, and discharging that much gas would have unbalanced the airship. Consequently, the departure was set for the following morning.

Heavy fog clouds hung low over the area and the temperature was 50° Fahrenheit (10° Celsius). The *LZ 126* actually carried thirty-nine tons of fuel, including one and one-half tons of water ballast. At an altitude of 2,250 feet the zeppelin had risen above the fog, and the Alpine peaks became visible in their stark grandeur. The route led along the Rhine Valley to Basel, but then the French forts of

Belfort and Besancon had to be avoided. Weather over the Bay of Biscay was rough, true to tradition, and the airship changed course slightly to fly along the turbulent coast of Spain to Cape St. Vincent. The European continent was left behind at the mouth of the Gironde River. Weather reports as far as the Azores were favorable.

That afternoon, the *City of Boston,* a freighter out of New York, was seen below, and the startled wireless operator obviously experienced difficulties believing what he heard on his apparatus. Eventually, he responded with the correct position of his ship and proceeded to attend to more-orthodox business on the way to Port Said.

On the second day, the zeppelin rose to an altitude of five-thousand feet. The engines had used up 680 pounds of fuel per hour, and the loss of 17,600 pounds had to be equalized by releasing eight-thousand cubic meters of hydrogen gas. At noon the Azores appeared below. Two small sacks of mail were dropped at Terceira, and the cloud-hidden 13,500-foot high Pico Alto had to be avoided.

When the *Robert Dollar* steamed along below the zeppelin, the happy crew waved at the airship gliding smoothly above. Soon the cruisers U.S.S. *Detroit* and U.S.S. *Milwaukee,* ordered by the United States Navy to stand by, were contacted for weather reports, and Commander Eckener changed course to avoid the reported low-pressure area and climb above the predicted storm.

When on Thursday night, 15 October 1924, the first land of the New World was sighted the crew

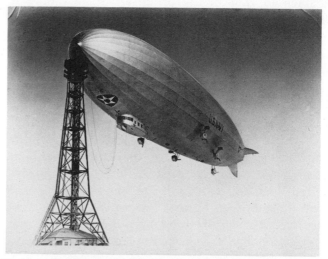

The *Los Angeles,* originally the *LZ 126,* the most successful of all United States Navy airships. (Courtesy, Goodyear).

An impressive array of four classes of U.S. Navy blimps. (Courtesy, Goodyear).

The *ZR-3* landing on the flight deck of the USS *Saratoga*. (Courtesy, U.S. Navy).

was jubilant. They had reached America at Sable Island, Nova Scotia. The actual Atlantic crossing had taken seventy hours.

The zeppelin flew over Boston and New York, circling the Statue of Liberty and returning to fly low over Broadway so that New Yorkers could get a splendid view of the proud airship. Landing at Lakehurst, the *LZ 126* had flown 5,066 miles in eighty-one hours and seventeen minutes at an average speed of sixty-two miles per hour. Congratulatory messages, including a telegram from President Calvin Coolidge, greeted the men who had brought the zeppelin across the ocean.

Nine members of the German crew remained at Lakehurst to assist the Americans in operating their newly renamed *ZR 3*, the *Los Angeles*. For several years the *Los Angeles* flew many missions in all sorts of weather. The meritorious safety record established by that airship was due in great part to the excellence of its crew, which was unquestionably the best trained and most proficient airship crew of any United States dirigible. The twenty-five men aboard at the time had a

most disconcerting experience when in the summer of 1926, while the airship was moored at the Lakehurst mast, a sudden reversal of wind caught the ship and it rose to an angle of ninety degrees to stand on its nose. None were hurt, and the ship soon attained its normal horizontal position. But most of the flights were uneventful. Trips were made to Panama, Bermuda, and Puerto Rico. The *Los Angeles* proved a very dependable and safe airship. It was finally decommissioned at Lakehurst on 30 June 1932, and eventually dismantled in 1939.

In 1926 the United States Navy ordered an airship with metal covering from the Metal-clad Corporation of Detroit. The stubby, blimplike *ZMC 2* had a skin of metal only 0.0095 of an inch thick and a capacity of merely two-hundred-thousand cubic feet, but it proved the feasibility of that type of construction. After twelve years of service the airship was decommissioned and sold for scrap.

When the Goodyear Corporation acquired the patents of the *Luftschiffbau-Zeppelin*, the navy

The *Los Angeles* in flight with the airplane attached below. (Courtesy, National Archives, Navy Dept.).

The stubby *ZMC-2,* built in 1910, had a thin cover of metal, and served the United States Navy for twelve years. (Courtesy, Goodyear).

The *ZR-3* stands on her nose at an 87-degree angle as a cold front moved across the station on 25 August 1927. (Courtesy, U.S. Navy).

The gondola of the *C*-class blimp. (Courtesy, Goodyear).

131

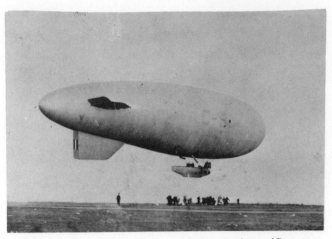

A United States Navy blimp of the *C* class. (Courtesy, Goodyear).

A United States Navy blimp of the *K* class. (Courtesy, Goodyear).

A United States Navy blimp of the *L* class. (Courtesy, Goodyear).

planned a really large-capacity rigid airship, utilizing these patents. Two airships, the *Akron* and the *Macon* were to be of a 6,500,000-cubic-foot gas capacity, with perhaps even superior aerodynamic characteristics than the "ideal" *LZ 127* built in 1926 by the Friedrichshafen works. The ratio of length to maximum diameter was six, a much preferred figure than the earlier ratios of 8.5, or even 12 to 1. The two sister airships were 785 feet long, actually ten feet longer than the German *LZ 127*.

The reversible Maybach engines were mounted in the hull, and the swivel propellers were driven by extension shafts and bevel-gear sets, capable of driving the airship in all four directions if needed—forward, backward, up, or down—and, of course, allowing a vertical takeoff or landing. The engine location reduced drag considerably and increased the accessibility for the immediate servicing of the power plants. The use of helium made this unique arrangement possible, since there was no ignition of the lifting gas possible by a spark from the engines.

The *Akron* was able to store five airplanes in its hull, and launching and stowing tests had been successfully carried out before the official commissioning of the airship on 27 October 1931. On 3 November the airship demonstrated its airlift abilities when a total of 207 men went aboard and went up on a flight, testing rapid troop-movement capabilities.

The airship flew various naval missions, and on one flight over the Caribbean area in 1932, when encountering snow and ice, the ship picked up eight tons of ice on its hull and carried it along with no difficulties whatsoever. With water running off, the *Akron* arrived safely at the West Indies.

But on 4 April 1933, the *Akron* was caught in a fierce storm off the New Jersey coast. The altimeter seemed faulty, and the radio was out of contact with the ground stations ashore. The hurricanelike winds carried the airship along at speeds around one-hundred miles per hour through fog and darkness. In a sudden downward thrust the *Akron* hit the stormy sea, lost its rudder and dropped into the ocean. Only three of the crew were saved, and seventy-three men were lost, including Admiral Moffett.

The official Court of Inquiry decided that the crash was due to the unreliability and inaccuracy of the barometric altimeter and that some safety

A United States Navy *ZPG3W* blimp. (Courtesy, Good year).

A United States Navy *ZPG2W* blimp. (Courtesy, Good.year).

The Goodyear blimp *Columbia,* a familiar sight to many Americans. (Courtesy, Goodyear)

regulations had not entirely been observed.

Despite this devastating blow to lighter-than-air craft, the navy completed the *Macon* and commissioned it in June 1933. This airship, almost a duplicate of the *Akron,* cost $2,600,000 to build, while the first model had cost $5,358,000. The *Macon* performed well, and when some minor repair work was needed early in 1935, the airship was laid up only temporarily; but before all of the work was satisfactorily completed the *Macon* was placed into service to take part in the fleet maneuvers. When the *Macon* was returning on 12 February to the hangar in a squall, the top fin of its rudder was damaged. This rather minor mishap later caused the upper fin to separate entirely from the hull, carrying along a part of the main frame structure. The rupture of some gas cells then caused the airship to lose altitude and settle on the

sea near Point Sur. The crew was taken off the stricken *Macon,* and the airship sank slowly into the Pacific. Only two of the crew of eighty-three men were lost.

The *Akron* had made a total of seventy-three flights of 1,696 hours and the *Macon* had made fifty-four flights totaling 1,798 hours in the air. Both airships represented considerable progress in airship construction over previous United States naval airships. The *Shenandoah,* for example, had a flying range, without refueling, of 2,600 miles, while the *Akron* and *Macon* could stay aloft for 10,500 miles. Useful lifting capacities were 44,100 pounds for the former and 182,000 pounds for the latter. Speeds were 57.6 miles per hour as opposed to 83.8, and the structural strength of the two models was 1.0 for the *Shenandoah* and 2.5 for the two sister ships. However, Ernst Lehmann pointed out

134

The *Akron,* aloft, taking off. (Courtesy, Goodyear).

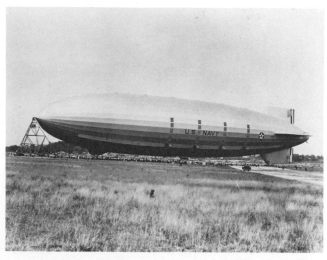

The *Akron,* commissioned in 1931, made seventy-three flights of 1,696 hours. (Courtesy, Goodyear).

The *Macon* in flight. (Courtesy, National Archives, Navy Dept.).

The *Macon,* sister ship to the *Akron,* made fifty-four flights of 1,798 hours. (Courtesy, Goodyear).

The *Macon* being hangared. (Courtesy, Goodyear).

The *Macon:* the huge airship being shown from the rear in her hangar. (Courtesy, Goodyear).

the difference between the German zeppelins and the naval airships. The reinforcements of the sterns and fins of the American dirigibles were weakened through the economizing of cable braces and especially through the total absence of the cruciform girders which in the airships designed by Ludwig Dürr supported the stabilizing and rudder surfaces. The two naval airships were thus unable to withstand excessive strain.

Several government committees urged further airship developments despite the loss of these two airships, and in 1938 Congress actually authorized the construction of an airship for the navy. Plans for an airship of a seven-million cubic-foot capacity were made, but the *Hindenburg* disaster halted all airship activities in the United States.

14

THE DREAM COMPLETED: THE *GRAF ZEPPELIN*

Airship proponents were fully convinced that longer-distance travel belonged to the airship, while shorter distances could be covered by the airplane.

The ability to reduce their flying speed to zero and hover stationary over a given spot, the ability to fly more safely through fog, snowstorm, or at night, and to fly silently and offer more pleasantly furnished and much more comfortable accommodations to passengers were believed to make the airship the ideal means of transportation. Airplanes, and especially seaplanes, had also made tremendous strides, and such advanced aircraft as the Dornier flying boat, the *DO-X,* with its powerful six double engines mounted atop the huge wings, had considerable flying range. (On 4 June 1931 the seaplane was to fly to New York, after crossing the South Atlantic.)

Still, August von Parseval believed that any distance over one-thousand kilometers (621 miles) belonged to the airships, while shorter ones were the scope of the airplanes.

Hugo Eckener was convinced that particularly the crossing of oceans was the sole domain of the airship, and soon after the delivery of the *LZ 126,* he made public a detailed study of the possibilities of airship travel from Europe to America. He stated that three elements were needed to further airship transportation: time-saving speed, unquestionable safety, and economic feasibility.

Considerable saving in time over the existing luxury ocean-liner travel was possible. The fastest time for an ocean crossing could be thirty-five hours, while the longest could conceivably be ninety hours. Eckener felt that airship navigation was principally a meteorological matter and only secondly one of seamanship. Generally, airships should need one-half of the westerly and one-third of the easterly surface ship's crossing time.

The airships had a good safety record, and if helium could be used only partly, the remaining hydrogen could be made nonflammable. Instead of gasoline-using engines, Eckener proposed that heavier diesel engines be built, which would use heavy oil as fuel, and thus practically eliminate the inherent danger from that source.

While a certain hazard prevailed when landing an airship during a storm, ocean liners were similarly handicapped by not being able to berth on very stormy occasions. Airships could have auxiliary landing sites, if storms could not be evaded, either by flying around or waiting until the turbulence had cleared. Landing masts promised easier facilities, but an almost wind-still field was necessary to accomplish a safe landing. Instead of locating airship landing fields near metropolitan cities, Eckener suggested that meteorologically suitable sites be selected. He noted that ocean liners did not discharge their passengers at such large cities as Chicago, Paris, London, or Berlin, and neither should airships be expected to do so. He did not

The *Graf Zeppelin* coming out of its hangar. (Courtesy, Lufthansa).

object to airplanes having their smaller landing fields near large cities, since they would be flying shorter distances when time would be a greater element to consider by the passengers.

Eckener calculated that a capital outlay of about thirty-five million marks would be needed to build the three zeppelins and to construct landing facilities and hangars for the basic transatlantic service contemplated. He figured that the carrying of passengers, air freight, and mail would bring in some 317,000 marks, against expenses of some two-hundred-thousand marks, for each of the proposed one hundred ocean crossings annually, or fifty round-trip flights. This was based on a rate of 2,500 marks per passenger fare. The airship was expected to carry thirty passengers and a payload of five tons. Other minor income would come from such auxiliary items as advertising and visits to hangars, leaving a total of over 117,000 marks for each flight, or 11.7 million marks per year to be

used for the financing. Eckener reckoned that his proposed plan would actually return thirty-five percent on the original investment, certainly a most attractive proposition to the bankers who were asked to finance such an undertaking. The only requirement still to be met was the international agreement of mutual cooperation between the governments of the two continents to ensure airship travel on the scale suggested by him, Eckener concluded.

Not only the airship-transportation officials, but people all over the world were startled when Captain Charles A. Lindbergh completed his solo flight from Mineola, New York, to Paris in his monoplane *Spirit of St. Louis* on 21 May 1927 in thirty-three hours and thirty minutes. Although the first non-stop Atlantic airplane flight had been made from St. John's, Newfoundland, to Clifden, Ireland, just eight years earlier by John Alcock and A.W. Brown, the feat of young Lindbergh captured the imagination of the world and made everyone realize that an airplane could actually accomplish such a long-distance flight of 3,610 miles. Less than a month later, on 6 June 1927, Clarence Chamberlain carried the first passenger, Charles Levine, from Mineola to Eisleben, Germany.

These daring pathfinders were soon followed by others who flew across the Atlantic Ocean from America, and when on 12-13 April 1928 Baron Günther von Hünefeld and his crew flew from Dublin, Ireland, to Greenly Island, Labrador, the first East-to-West airplane flight had succeeded.

Although all of these spectacular pioneering achievements proved that an airplane, even a single-engined land plane, could span this formidable water barrier between the two continents, the basic belief prevailed that, over such long distances, air-traveling passengers could only be carried safely and economically by airships.

The first airship specially designated for flights across the oceans, the *LZ 127,* was designed as a mail-carrying passenger airship. With comfortable accommodations for only twenty passengers for long-distance travel, it could also transport a huge quantity of mail or air freight.

The size of the hangar at the manufacturing facilities limited the size of the zeppelin. The necessary compromise of largest possible volume for lifting capacity with the best possible streamlined form for speed resulted in the disadvantage of the speed factor.

The *LZ 127* was christened *Graf Zeppelin* on 8 July 1928, the ninetieth anniversary of the birth of Count Zeppelin, by his daughter Hella, Countess von Brandenstein-Zeppelin. Since this airship represented the very ideal of the Count, and incorporated all advancements in the field of zeppelin construction, it seemed fitting that it was named after the idealistic inventor.

While under construction, over two-hundred-

The *Graf Zeppelin* aloft over Friedrichshafen. (Courtesy, Lufthansa).

thousand visitors had come to the Friedrichshafen plant to see the new airship being built. The *Graf Zeppelin* was 790 feet long with a maximum diameter of 102 feet and a height of 112 feet. It had a gas volume of 105,000 cubic meters and weighed 129,800 pounds. The useful lift was 132,000 pounds, under normal atmospheric conditions. Deducting the weight of fuel, crew, and other essentials from this figure, the airship could carry a total net load of fifteen tons, or twenty passengers and 26,400 pounds of mail or freight over a distance of 6,250 miles at an average speed of between sixty and seventy miles per hour.

The five twelve-cylinder Maybach engines, developing 530 horsepower each, were located in five-engine gondola cars with propellers attached as tailfins. Some of the gasoline on the earliest test flights was carried in cells for safety reserve or for additional ballast.

The gas cells were made of fine goldbeater's skin, and the covering hull was fabricated of a specially strong light-cotton mixture, protected by several coats of varnish mixed with metal powder. The final coat of this paint gave the hull the greatest possible smoothness and least possible frictional resistance. It also made the zeppelin appear as a lustrous metal object, glistening brilliantly in bright sunshine.

The skeleton was made of duraluminum, an aluminum and copper alloy with the strength of steel but only one-third of its weight. While of the same weight as that used in the *LZ 126*, this material now was actually twenty percent stronger. The airship was the size of an ocean liner, but its weight merely that of a small tug boat.

A corridor ran the entire length of the *LZ 127*, giving easy access to all areas. High above this corridor was another, an axial walkway, to serve for inspection of the gas cells and, incidentally, to contribute to the stability of the airship by reinforcing the sixteen cross-sections of the skeleton.

The *Graf Zeppelin* over a Junkers *JU 52*, workhorse of the Lufthansa. (Courtesy, Lufthansa).

The *LZ 127 Graf Zeppelin* on an early-morning flight to this country anchored to the mooring mast. (Courtesy, Goodyear).

Instead of liquid gasoline, the fuel was carried in a gaseous state. This allowed it to be carried in two-thirds of the former space, placed in gas cells, and eliminated the problem of wasting buoyant gas when making a landing. Since the gaseous fuel weighed the same as air, it made no difference if the airship was loaded with sufficient fuel for an extended journey, or if it had used up practically all of its fuel supply on board. And, of course, the strain of heavy gasoline supplies on the frame of the airship was entirely eliminated. The *LZ 126* had carried thirty tons of gasoline on its Atlantic flight, the weight equal to that of a small railroad locomotive hanging in its frame. In a bad storm, with the airship severely shaking, the lack of such great weight was a decided advantage. And the fire hazard was also immensely reduced. Actually, nonliquid gas was not a new development at all, for already in 1872 the German inventor Paul Hänlein

The *Graf Zeppelin* over the *Frauenkirche*, Munich. (Courtesy, Lufthansa).

had used gaseous fuel — illuminating gas — as fuel for the engine that powered his primitive airship.

However, representatives of the ministry, which had contributed 1.1-million marks toward the construction of the zeppelin, expressed grave concern over the use of gaseous fuel, and the airship used the regular gasoline-benzol mixture on its test flights.

Under the command of Hugo Eckener, the maiden flight on 18 September 1928 lasted three hours and fifteen minutes and proved so encouraging that the next test flight, a long-distance test, was scheduled for the following day.

The *Graf Zeppelin* took off at 7:30 in the morning and flew in the direction of Zürich, Switzerland. The small Klemm-Daimler escort plane soon fell behind and was lost. Then the cities of Basel and Freiburg came into view and disappeared. The zeppelin headed north and flew over Mannheim, Ludwigshafen, Mainz, and Frankfurt. Over Dramstadt the airship rose higher to release gas because it had used up quite a quantity of fuel.

When the *Graf Zeppelin* reached Stuttgart, the dirigible and its crew paid homage by flying slowly and low, hovering briefly and dropping a wreath over the grave of Graf Ferdinand von Zeppelin. Then the airship returned to its base at Friedrichshafen.

The third test flight was made to determine the exact turning radius of the airship and the climbing ability with either all or individual engines at full power. Evening cold decreased this rising capability considerably, while during strong sunlight the airship became lighter. (These static differences are dynamically equalized by flying the airship in an inclined position: when it is heavy, the nose is pointed up, and when the airship is light, the rear is held up.) Some navigational experiments with radio beams and with flares over a body of water were also conducted during this third test flight.

Several outstanding scientists, including the notable Oskar von Miller, as well as foreign dignitaries and airship experts, had been invited to participate in the fourth test flight. On this flight, tests using gaseous fuel were also undertaken.

For the next trial flight, Eckener had decided to fly the *Graf Zeppelin* in a northerly direction. While over Ulm and then Nürnberg, reports of stormy weather over Berlin were received, causing a change in the original flight schedule. Instead of a visit to the capital, the cities of Würzburg, Frankfurt, Köln, and Düsseldorf were visited. That night the airship flew over Rotterdam, and crossing the English Channel cruised over Lowestoft and Yarmouth before turning back to Bremen. Flensburg, the birthplace of Hugo Eckener, was visited, then Kiel, Hamburg, and finally Berlin.

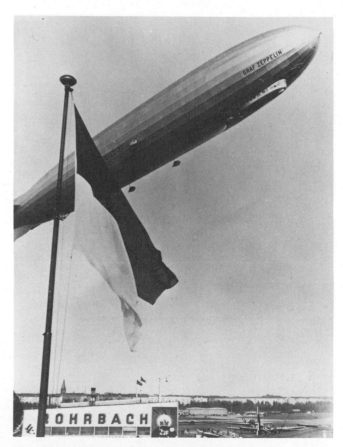

The *Graf Zeppelin* over the Berlin-Tempelhof airport. (Courtesy, Lufthansa).

The *Graf Zeppelin* lands on the Bodensee (Lake Constance). (Courtesy, Lufthansa).

The *Graf Zeppelin* landing at Tempelhof. (Courtesy, Lufthansa).

On a glorious clear forenoon the citizens of the German capital saw the *Graf Zeppelin* cruise slowly and majestically over their city. It was a truly magnificent sight and an unforgetable occasion when this silvery mammoth airship appeared over the rooftops of the houses at the Reichskanzlerplatz, where this author first saw the proud *Graf,* as Berliners referred to their new idol.

Commander Eckener dropped a small parachute with a bouquet of flowers into the garden of the palace where President Paul von Hindenburg celebrated his eighty-first birthday. On the return flight, citizens of Leipzig, Dresden, Chemnitz, and again Nürnberg saw the airship before it landed at its Friedrichshafen base after the thirty-four and a half-hour flight, which had covered 1,950 miles. The preliminaries were successfully completed.

The significant flight to New York was now to come. From the earliest reservations received for this trip, twenty passengers were chosen, each paying a fare of $3,000. The zeppelin also carried sixty-six-thousand letters and postal cards with specially issued commemorative stamps and some valuable freight. But since the expenses were more than the receipts from fares and freight charges collected, the ministry contributed a half million marks to underwrite the *Amerikafahrt.*

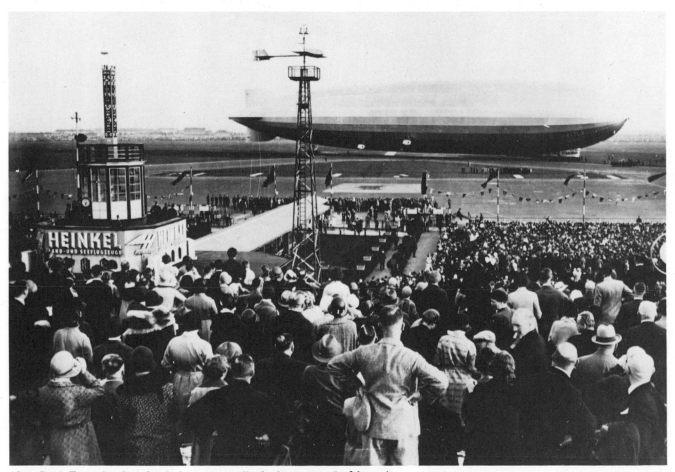

The *Graf Zeppelin* has landed at Tempelhof. (Courtesy, Lufthansa).

Reports of impending storms delayed the scheduled departure for one day. On 11 October 1928 the weather appeared favorable for the trip and the *Graf Zeppelin* left its anchorage at 7:55 that morning for the momentous voyage. The route charted was different from that of the *LZ 126* four years before. The time of year had to be taken into account.

The route led over Basel, the Rhone Valley, and Gibraltar. The islands of Madeira and the Azores were overflown, as was Bermuda after running into a storm over the ocean. Then, early on a promising morning, the coast of the United States appeared as a light brown line on the horizon.

By 12:28 the *Graf Zeppelin* flew over the capital, where high-government officials could see the airship from their offices or even their homes. At the White House, the charming Grace Coolidge had invited friends, and the first lady and her guests watched the huge silvery dirigible glide majestically overhead. Then the zeppelin headed for Baltimore, Philadelphia, and New York. That 15 October evening, at 5:38 the *Graf Zeppelin* landed at Lakehurst. It had been in the air for 111 hours and 44 minutes.

The officers of the airship attended receptions for three days. President Calvin Coolidge received Hugo Eckener and his staff at the White House, and Mayor Jimmy Walker welcomed them on the steps of the New York city hall. And even some business was transacted with financiers for possible future investment in an international airship-transportation company.

The return trip was to take the *Graf Zeppelin* home on a shorter, northerly route across the ocean. Started on 29 October with twenty-four passengers the airship encountered solid fog over Newfoundland and then a raging storm. It was the

The *Graf Zeppelin* over the *Brandenburg Tor*, Berlin. (Courtesy, Lufthansa).

The *Graf Zeppelin* over the piers of New York. (Courtesy, Lufthansa).

over the Dead Sea, the *Graf* bettered the depth submarine record. The trip lasted eighty-one and a half hours and covered about five-thousand miles.

A month later, a similar, but slightly shorter flight followed. Then, a third flight included a landing at Cairo, Egypt, and many others followed with landings at Italian or Spanish cities. These successful flights were scheduled because of their great popularity with the passengers.

But when a second trip to the United States was to be undertaken, it failed, ending in Toulon, France. Torsional vibrations had caused crankshaft cracks in one of the engines, and after governor arms had broken on two other power units the *Graf Zeppelin* made an emergency landing on French soil. The government offered the use of the hangar at Cours-Pierrefeu. New engine parts were shipped by railroad and fitted to replace the damaged ones, and then the airship returned to its base hangar at Friedrichshafen.

On 1 August the *Graf Zeppelin* flew across the Atlantic to Lakehurst to pick up several passengers for its projected "Around the World Cruise." (The greater share of the expense was underwritten by the Hearst press, which insisted that the trip start at the Statue of Liberty.)

From Friedrichshafen on 15 August 1929, with twenty passengers, two of which were reporters (the others were guests), with five-hundred kilograms of mail and freight, the airship flew over Leipzig, Berlin, Stettin, Danzig, and Königsberg, then crossed the border and flew over Russia in an almost straight line. An advantageous tail wind speeded its progress. The navigator noted that the Stanovoi mountain peaks were actually several hundred feet higher than the maps indicated, but the clear weather conditions there assisted in flying over them quite safely. When nearing Japan, the airship flew around a typhoon, utilizing the strong air currents to shorten the flight time. After 101 hours of flight and 7,030 miles, Tokyo was reached on 19 August and a landing was made at the Ksumiga-ura naval base. The trip was resumed on 23 August. Heavy fog obscured most of the Pacific Ocean below, but two days later the Golden Gate was clearly visible when the United States was reached.

The *Graf Zeppelin* turned south to Los Angeles, having flown there in seventy-nine hours. After but a short stay from morning until midnight the journey was resumed by way of Chicago, Cleve-

worst night in the memory of the airship officers, but under the skillful handling of Commander Eckener, the zeppelin came through the ordeal in good shape.

The *Graf Zeppelin* landed at Friedrichshafen on 1 November having covered the 4,560 miles in seventy-one hours and fifty-one minutes. A huge crowd welcomed the zeppelin and men home from the successful historic flight. After four days of gay celebrations at Friedrichshafen, the *Graf* flew to Berlin. The officers enjoyed a wildly enthusiastic reception by the people and a colorful ride through its decorated streets to the presidential gala reception.

During the thorough overhaul work in the winter months, a few minor alterations were made on the airship. Then, after several short flights, came a trip to the Near East on 24 March 1929. Twenty-eight passengers boarded to travel on the *Graf Zeppelin* over Marseilles, Corsica, Rome, Crete, Haifa, Jerusalem, Athens, Vienna, and returned to Friedrichshafen. Flying seventy meters

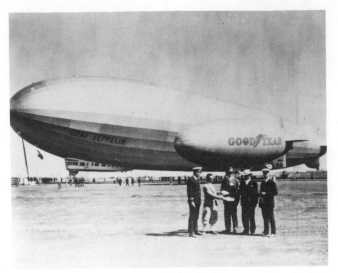

The *Graf Zeppelin* and the *NC8A Volunteer* at Los Angeles in August 1929. (Courtesy, Goodyear).

land, and Detroit to the Lakehurst naval air base, a distance of 2,995 miles, flown in fifty-two hours. Hugo Eckener stayed behind to transact some business and Ernst Lehmann took over the command of the airship across the Atlantic to its home base where it landed on 4 September 1929. The *Graf Zeppelin* had covered, in six stages, exactly 34,200 kilometers (21,238 miles), or 3,662 miles less than the distance around the earth at the equator. The ambitious world-encircling flight had been accomplished without irregularities.

(That year, on 21 October the huge Dornier DO-X flying boat carried 169 persons on a flight lasting one hour over the Bodensee. This was the largest number of persons ever transported in a single aircraft.)

(In the United States in the summer of 1929 the first transcontinental passenger air service was inaugurated. The passengers left New York by train, because the Allegheny Mountains were considered too big an obstacle to overcome safely. At Columbus, Ohio, a tri-motor Ford airplane of the Transcontinental Air Transport was boarded to fly to Waynoka, Oklahoma. Since no lighted airways and no radio navigational aids were installed along the route, passengers went by Santa Fe train from Waynoka to Clovis, New Mexico, overnight. From here, another tri-motor Ford airplane took them to Los Angeles. The first trip took forty-eight hours, but this was cut to thirty-six hours the next year when an all-air service was introduced, but with an

overnight stop at Kansas City, according to the *Encyclopedia Americana*. The first commercial passenger flight to cross an ocean was not made until ten years later when on 28 June 1939 the *Dixie Clipper* of Pan American Airways departed from Port Washington, New York, to cross the Atlantic.)

On 18 May 1930, the *Graf Zeppelin* left Friedrichshafen with twenty-two passengers on another extensive journey. The first scheduled stop was Seville, Spain, but because a strong tail wind had pushed the airship to an average speed of 125 miles per hour, the speedy zeppelin was forced to cruise over Lorocco and Tangiers and wait for the cooler evening hours to land at Seville.

On its way again, the equatorial doldrums brought cloudbursts of rain. After sixty-two hours of flight, the *Graf Zeppelin* landed at Recife de Pernambuco, Brazil, and resumed its flight at midnight. At gay Rio de Janeiro the travelers experienced an outpouring of unbounded enthusiasm by the populace, totally unknown elsewhere. The authorities were able only with the greatest

The *Graf Zeppelin* over the New Jersey countryside. (Courtesy, Lufthansa).

146

difficulty to keep the spectators from their usual display of fireworks, the exuberant expression of the carnival celebrants. Eventually, the *Graf Zeppelin* returned to Pernambuco. At the anchor mast at Giquia, a tropical downpour added 8,800 pounds to the weight of the zeppelin. Then, the flight continued by way of Natal. Adverse weather reported over Cuba caused cancellation of a scheduled stop there, and continuing, the airship landed at Lakehurst. It was 31 May.

Leaving on 3 June and, because of its weight, flying extremely low over New York City so that the top of the Woolworth building was actually only 160 feet below the airship, the *Graf Zeppelin* reached Seville, Spain, sixty-one hours later. Another bad storm over the Rhone valley caused some anxiety, but the airship landed that 6 June safely at Friedrichshafen. Its triangular distance flight was completed. The zeppelin had made 130 flights when the airship was overhauled that winter at its home base.

The *Graf Zeppelin* took off on a polar expedition flight under Hugo Eckener on 24 July 1931. That date had been most carefully selected because Count Zeppelin had believed it to be his lucky day. Consequently he had given the date to a lake in the Cross Bay region at the time of the 1910 expedition. Now, twenty-one years later, this follow-up journey to that preliminary survey trip was to be made. The scientific leader was Professor Samoilovitz, the Russian arctic expert who in 1928 with the icebreaker *Krassin* had rescued some of the men from the Nobile expedition. The noted explorer Lincoln Ellsworth was also a member of the group, which included other experts, natural scientists, biologists, and surveyors to explore the surface conditions in the arctic regions, measuring terrestrial magnetic fields, obtaining data on temperature, barometric pressure, and humidity and other scientific matter.

The airship was prepared for the journey at Leningrad. Virtually stripped of all passenger comfort, even chinaware was taken off and paper plates were to be used for dining instead. All of the saved space and weight was then used for scientific paraphernalia for arctic exploration.

The icebreaker *Malygin* with Umberto Nobile awaited the *Graf Zeppelin* off Franz Josef Land, and the Russian ship was met on 27 July in the sheltered bay at Hooker Island, when the airship descended to float on its bumper bags. North of Franz Josef Land the explorers found nothing but solidly packed ice. They noted that Gamsworth Island and Albert Edward Island were only on maps and that they did not exist at all. Farther on, toward Nicholas II Island, also called Northland, glacial peaks of up to 3,500 feet rose over the solid fog bank. Hampered by the thick cover, the zeppelin was forced to turn south toward the Taimyr Peninsula, where immense herds of reindeer fled before its menacing shadow. After crossing the Kara Sea and the stony island of Novaya Zemlya, the *Graf Zeppelin* headed for home, actually reversing its outward route. Landing at Berlin, the zeppelin had covered 8,265 miles in 145½ hours of flight on this polar flight.

Although the *Graf Zeppelin* made several special trips, such as the African, Near Eastern, and Arctic journeys, the flights to America were really its main purpose. Three flights to South America were

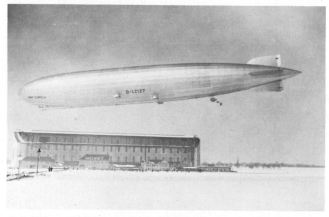

The *Graf Zeppelin* begins a winter flight in February 1929. (Courtesy, Luftschiffbau Zeppelin).

The *Graf Zeppelin* over the Bürgenstock Mountains. (Courtesy, Luftschiffbau Zeppelin).

made in 1931; in 1932 there were nine. The South American route, especially, was favored by trade winds, while weather conditions over the north Atlantic were generally unpredictable. Thunderstorms, squalls, and fogs caused either long delays or lengthy detours for the airship and thoroughly disrupted any regular schedule.

On all flights the passengers were pampered. Accommodations were arranged in the elongated control gondola car, which reached into the hull of the airship. The public rooms had slanting glass windows, so that the passengers could view the scene below from the comfort of the easy chairs. While the early *Schwaben* had wicker furniture, and the *Bodensee* light wood, the furniture on the *Graf Zeppelin* was upholstered.

Dining-room service was as elaborate as on the finest surface ocean liners. Specially designed porcelain by Heinrich had an LZ insignia and a blue-and-gold border. The food was excellently prepared and specially catered by world-famous chefs. On the trip from Los Angeles to Lakehurst, at the time of the world cruise, the Los Angeles Biltmore Hotel furnished the menu.

First Day Luncheon: Honey Dew Melon au Citron
                            Hungarian Goulash
                            Cold Asparagus Vinaigrette
                            Eclairs — Coffee

On the Atlantic portion of that same trip, from New York to Friedrichshafen, Lewis Sherry of New York catered:

Second Day Luncheon: Buffet Sherry, Cream of Tomatoes
                              Breast of Duckling Bigarde with
                                  Fresh Fruits
                              New Succotash
                              Cherries Jubilee, Sherry Dry Cakes
                              Coffee

Of the twenty-five passenger and mail flights made from the Friedrichshafen base to Rio de Janeiro, twenty of them lasted from ninety to ninety-nine hours, and only five were of shorter or longer duration. Of the twenty-three flights made in the opposite direction, fifteen took from 100 to 110 hours, two were slightly longer, and six were shorter.

While the *LZ 126* (later the *Los Angeles*) had covered the distance from Friedrichshafen to Lakehurst in eighty-one hours, averaging sixty-two miles per hour, the *Graf Zeppelin* (the *LZ 127*) under most unfavorable weather conditions on its initial crossing, had required 111 hours, averaging but fifty-five miles per hour.

Generally, however, the flight across the Atlantic in the easterly direction was favored by winds, and the flights from Lakehurst took seventy-one, fifty-five, sixty-seven, and eighty-seven hours; from

The *Graf Zeppelin* in flight. (Courtesy, Lufthansa).

Akron, 102 hours, averaging fifty-eight to eighty miles per hour. The average time was seventy-six hours, but the flights in the westerly direction to the United States averaged ninety-six hours, nearly one day more.

After the first flight to North America, it was evident that the *Graf Zeppelin* was not efficient enough to maintain a regular schedule. A larger and stronger commercial airship would have to be designed and built to make such a run profitable.

From 18 September 1928 to 10 December 1935, the *Graf Zeppelin* had made 505 flights. Nearly all were uneventful. But in 1935, on a return flight to Friedrichshafen, the *Graf Zeppelin* could not land at Pernambuco because of a revolution raging there at the time. Captain Lehmann decided to remain in the air until the violent disturbances would be over and the revolutionary elements subdued. Flying in a wide circle about the area, he stayed aloft for a total of 118 hours and 40 minutes. While hovering he had taken on some needed provisions from the steamer *Espana* at sea near the shore. After the five-day flight, on 27 November the airship landed at the Giquia base.

By then, in the United States, in the field of

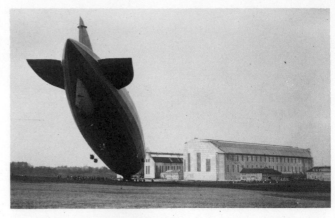

Rear view of the *Graf Zeppelin* at her hangar. (Courtesy, Luftschiffbau Zeppelin).

heavier-than-air craft, Pan American clippers made transatlantic flights, carrying mail and some passengers. In January 1935, Amelia Earhart made the first woman solo flight from Honolulu to San Francisco, and a clipper in November was the first seaplane to fly airmail from San Francisco to Manila and back. Yet, transoceanic flights were still hazardous. On 15 August 1935, Wiley Post with his passenger Will Rogers crashed on their projected round-the-world flight at Point Barrow, Alaska.

15

THE FINAL DISASTER

The projected airship was to be a considerable improvement over the *Graf Zeppelin,* especially in size and consequent carrying ability. The increased size would allow for a profitable operation on the America flights, and with another sister ship of similar proportions, it was calculated that a regularily scheduled weekly flight would be possible.

The *LZ 129* had a capacity of 190,000 cubic meters (7,063,000 cubic feet) of gas, but was only 804 feet long with a maximum diameter of 135 feet, giving the new airship a much stubbier appearance than the long, elegant form of the *Graf Zeppelin.* The weight of the airship was 430,950 pounds. But the actual net payload was 41,990 pounds, allowing 15,470 pounds for passengers and 26,520 pounds for mail and freight.

The four Mercedes-Benz diesel engines, each developing 1,300 horsepower, gave the airship a cruising speed of 84.5 miles per hour, decreasing by one-third the flying time to America. The use of heavy fuel oil reduced the fire hazard, and so did the contemplated use of helium gas in the outer cells. However, most of the sixteen cells were to be filled with the cheaper hydrogen gas, which also could lift 16.5 tons more than helium. But helium never became available.

The airship would carry seventy passengers. Most of the cabins were inside the airship, all had showers, and were much roomier than those on the

The *Hindenburg:* the construction of the skeleton for the *LZ 129.* (Courtesy, Luftschiffbau Zeppelin).

Graf Zeppelin. Twenty luxury staterooms were located on the outside of B-deck in the center of the airship, connected with A-deck above by two stairways. Here was a spacious fifteen by thirty foot dining room, seating thirty-four passengers, a writing and reading room, and a bar and smoking room. A specially designed Blüthner piano was installed, weighing only 112 pounds. The fifty-foot promenade decks ran along the outsides of A-deck, and the wide, slanted windows afforded a splendid view of the ground below. The chef and five assistants prepared the epicurean food in an all-electric galley, and 250 bottles of fine wines were carried.

The passengers were amazed at the tranquil quietness in the public rooms of the zeppelin. When scientists measured the sound value they found it to be fifty-one decibles. This was considerably lower than the fifty-nine found on ocean liners, or the seventy-one for an airplane, or the high eighty for the inside of a railroad coach. Turbulence had no effect and there was consequently no air sickness problem.

Passenger comfort was of prime concern. When compared with one of the first passenger-carrying airships, the *LZ 7* (the *Deutschland*), these figures are especially startling. The *Deutschland* allowed a total area of twenty square meters for passenger rooms, while the new ship, the *LZ 129,* provided 520 square meters. These 11.2 square meters for each passenger compared with only 1.7 square meters in an airplane. And the thirty-two cubic meters of cabin space on the zeppelin for each passenger compared most favorably with the 4.2 cubic meters allowed on a commercial airplane of that day.

The *LZ 129* had the five intertwining rings, the Olympic insignia, painted on both sides of the hull when the first flight was made on 4 March 1936, with eighty-seven persons aboard. The airship rose gracefully into the air, and when the engines were turned on at an altitude of three-hundred feet, observers in the control cabin were surprised by their unusual quietness. After making various tests over the Bodensee area for three hours, the airship returned to its hangar.

Another test flight was made the next day. After a short cruise over the lake, the airship flew to Bad Tölz, Munich, and Augsburg, and, after an eight-hour flight, landed at Friedrichshafen. A short third flight concluded all tests, but Captain Ernst

Application of the hull-covering material. (Courtesy, Luftschiffbau Zeppelin).

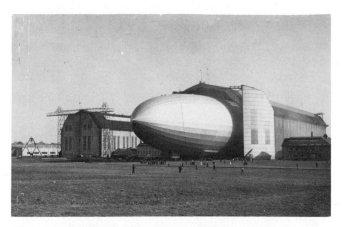

The completed *LZ 129* being brought out of her hangar. (Courtesy, Luftschiffbau Zeppelin).

Lehmann made another flight over the Allgäu and southern Germany—staying aloft for thirty hours — before taking 101 passengers and officials on a demonstration flight. This terminated at the new home for the *LZ 129,* a special hangar located at Löwenthal, a short distance from the other Friedrichshafen base.

The *LZ 129* being guided out of her hangar. (Courtesy, Daimler-Benz).

The galley of the *Hindenburg*. (Courtesy, Goodyear).

The grand salon, with baby grand piano, of the *Hindenburg*. (Courtesy, Luftschiffbau Zeppelin).

The *LZ 129* on the landing mast at Löwenthal. (Courtesy, Luftschiffbau Zeppelin).

The *LZ 129 Hindenburg,* with the Olympic Games insignia, aloft. (Courtesy Daimler-Benz).

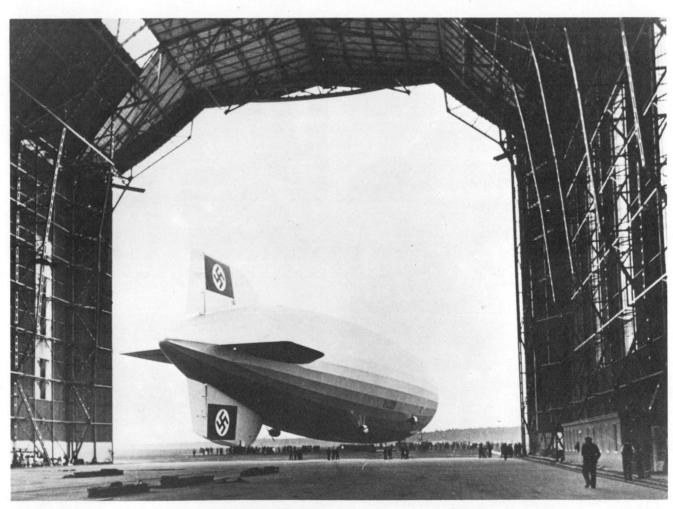

The *Hindenburg* leaves the hangar at Frankfurt Rhein-Main airport. (Courtesy, Lufthansa).

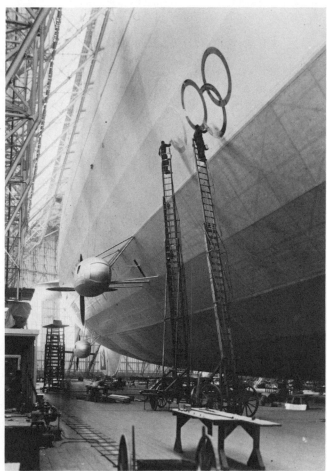

Painting the Olympic games insignia on the hull. (Courtesy, Luftschiffbau Zeppelin).

lay buried in the impressive monument at Tannenberg, the namesake hovered low and dropped a wreath to honor the great military hero.

The weather was clear along the Baltic coast over East Prussia and Pommerania and over the North Sea cities. Over Lower Saxony the weather was also favorable, and the two zeppelins crossed the country again, flying over the Rhineland, Saarland, Hesse, and Württemberg. Huge crowds gathered in every city to cheer their airships and, when at night torchlight parades moved along brightly lighted streets, spotlights illuminated the *Graf Zeppelin* and the *Hindenburg* cruising slowly above.

Immense crowds of people had seen the airships overhead, and when the zeppelins landed at their base, a large crowd greeted them. The *Hindenburg* had been aloft for seventy-five hours and had covered 4,110 miles, while the *Graf Zeppelin* had flown 4,375 miles.

For the 1936 season the *Deutsche Zeppelin Reederei* planned in close cooperation with the *Deutsche Lufthansa* and the *Condor Syndikat* to use the two airships in passenger and mail service for regular flights to South America, operating the *Hindenburg* and the *Graf Zeppelin* on a two-week schedule, beginning with the larger airship leaving Germany on 31 March. Landings were made on the newly constructed airfield at Santa Cruz, thirty-five miles from Rio de Janeiro. On this first return flight the *Hindenburg* was purposely flown through a heavy rain, so that the water could be caught by the troughs on the edges of the hull into ballast tanks. For this journey more powerful engines

On 22 March 1936, the *Graf Zeppelin* and the newer airship, with the name *Hindenburg* painted on its bow in large letters, took off on an election-campaign propaganda flight for the National Socialist Party to urge the German people to vote for Adolf Hitler as chancellor. Aloft for four days and three nights, the airship dropped millions of leaflets, and loudspeakers repeated marches and election speeches whenever one of the zeppelins flew over a populated area.

The *Graf Zeppelin*, commanded by Hans von Schiller, had preceded the larger *Hindenburg*, under the command of Ernst Lehmann, on this long *Deutschlandflug*, but both airships were usually in sight of each other. Communications were, however, maintained by radio.

When over Saxony on the way to Silesia heavy fog obscured everything below them, the captains decided instead to fly north and eastward. Near Allenstein, where Fieldmarshall von Hindenburg

The *LZ 129* over Friedrichshafen. (Courtesy, Luftschiffbau Zeppelin).

The *LZ 129 Hindenburg* anchored to the mooring mast. (Courtesy, Goodyear).

Same location from the other side. (Courtesy, Goodyear).

The *Hindenburg* aloft, showing the windows of the public rooms in the center of the airship. (Courtesy, Goodyear).

The *Hindenburg* being towed out of the Lakehurst hangar. (Courtesy, U.S. Navy).

The *Hindenburg* rising from the landing area. (Courtesy, Goodyear).

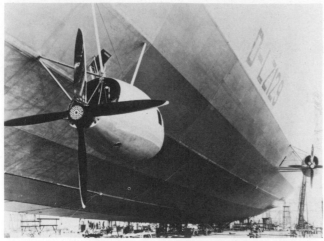

The engine nacelle of the *LZ 129*. (Courtesy, Daimler-Benz).

Construction details of the engine compartment. (Courtesy, Daimler-Benz).

The engines are easily reached and serviced while in flight. (Courtesy, Daimler-Benz).

were used. The four sixteen-cylinder, eighty-eight-liter, diesel engines each developed 1,320 horsepower at 1,620 revolutions per minute and weighed only 1.8 kilogram per horsepower. The *Hindenburg* landed at Löwenthal on 10 April having covered 13,500 miles in 216 hours of flight. In the meantime, the *Graf Zeppelin* made its 112th ocean-crossing flight.

For the trip to North America, after a short engine overhaul, the *Hindenburg* took off from the Rhein-Main *Welt-Flughafen,* the world airport, near Frankfurt am Main. Located at an altitude of 350 feet above sea level, departure from the airport allowed the zeppelin 13,200 pounds more lifting capability than its own one-thousand-foot-high Löwenthal base. The flight to Lakehurst took sixty-two hours and thirty-eight minutes, beating the time of the *LZ 126* by eighteen hours and thirty-six minutes, and setting a new record for the North Atlantic crossing by airship.

After a series of gay celebrations and receptions for Captain Lehmann and his officers after this first *Amerikafahrt* of the *Hindenburg,* the airship made its return flight. Carrying fifty-five passengers and 155,000 pieces of mail and 2,640 pounds of freight, the flight from Lakehurst was made in forty-nine hours and fourteen minutes, beating the record of the *LZ 127* by six hours and nine minutes.

Details of engine construction of the *LZ 130*. (Courtesy, Daimler-Benz).

The *LOF 6* airship engine (DB 602), sixteen cylinders and 1,300 horsepower. (Courtesy, Daimler-Benz).

That year, the *Hindenburg* made eight more flights to Lakehurst, averaging for the east-to-west flights sixty-three hours and forty-two minutes, and for the return trips fifty-one hours and forty-six minutes, or eighty-eight miles per hour. On one trip, on 9 to 11 August, with a strong tail wind, the airship set a new record of forty-two hours and fifty-three minutes, and the speed indicator actually showed 188 miles per hour briefly. In 1936, the *Hindenburg* carried a total of 3,530 passengers, compared with 841 the previous year, and sixty-six-thousand pounds of mail and freight. The basic fare from Frankfurt to Lakehurst and return was $720 per passenger, and to Rio de Janeiro, $1,500.

Regular passenger service between the Americas and Germany was well established, and the future of transatlantic airship transportation indeed looked great.

The year 1937 promised to be even better than the previous one. The first round-trip flight of the season to Rio de Janeiro by the *Hindenburg* had been completed and that airship was to inaugurate the regular service between Frankfurt and Lakehurst. The zeppelin left the Rhein-Main airport on 3 May on its flight to the United States. The *Hindenburg* had carried 1,002 passengers on its ten trips to the United States, but on this flight only thirty-six persons had booked passage on it. The crew consisted of sixty-one officers and men, many of whom were aboard to train for service on the *LZ 130,* sister ship to the *Hindenburg,* now being built at the Friedrichshafen works. In fact, besides the experienced commander, Captain Max Pruss, three other licensed airship captains, including Ernst Lehmann, rode along.

On the first day out, over the English Channel, the weather was bad and this storm caused some loss of time. Then over the Atlantic more stormy weather impeded the progress on this first of the eighteen scheduled trips for that season. And, when the airship reached Newfoundland, after flying slightly northerly of its regular course, weather reports indicated a delayed landing at Lakehurst because of heavy rains and a thunderstorm.

The *Hindenburg* flew over Boston and along the coast to appear over Manhattan at about three o'clock that afternoon and over the Lakehurst naval air base at about a quarter after four, then made a wide circle over the area to return for a

landing at six o'clock. However, at that time, the weather was still bad, and the landing was delayed for another hour until the weather cleared and the steady rain subsided. The *Hindenburg* was then ten hours behind schedule.

It was 7:25 when the *Hindenburg* was ready to land. The manila landing ropes were dropped, a small cloud of dust rising as they fell onto the wet ground. Although a slight drizzle fell, Commander Charles E. Rosendahl, the American Navy's airship expert, who stood at the base of the seventy-five-foot-high mooring mast, observed that "everything was proceeding in an entirely normal manner."

Captain Max Pruss had made about nine-hundred flights and many landings in severe, stormy weather, and especially so during a violent thunderstorm in the *L 11* during the war. Thus, the landing was not an unusual experience for the veteran commander of the *Hindenburg.*

Then, suddenly, Rosendahl saw "a small burst of flame" just ahead of the upper fin. "A yellowish flash, followed by a bright explosion," as Henry Roberts, radio editor of the *Aero Digest,* saw it. The fire was like "a million magnesium flares," Herbert Morrison broadcast in his amazing eye-witness account of the terrible disaster.

Within thirty-two seconds the huge airship, now a fiery inferno, collapsed into a heap of twisted metal ruin. The fire burned for more than three hours because of the heavy fuel oil.

Miraculously, sixty-one persons escaped the

The *Hindenburg,* afire, falls to the ground. (Courtesy, U.S. Navy).

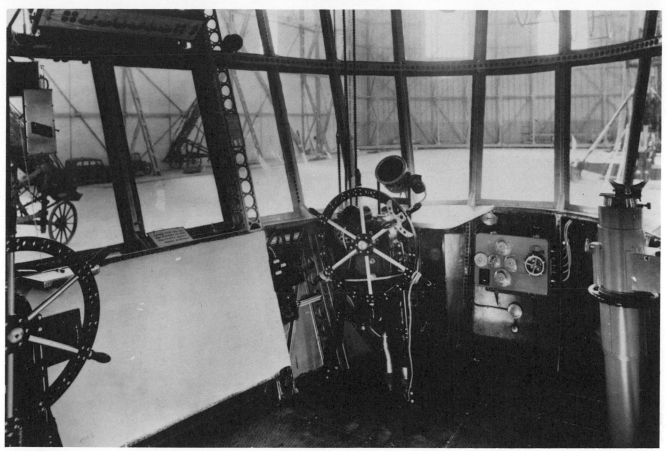

The pilot's compartment of the *Hindenburg*. (Courtesy, Luftschiffbau Zeppelin).

The wireless operators' room on the *Hindenburg*. (Courtesy, Lufthansa).

holocaust, but thirty-six passengers and crew lost their lives in this tragedy. Among those victims was Ernst Lehmann, then director of the *Reederei*, who died later in the hospital.

As to the cause of the catastrophe, Lehmann had said, *"Aber das kann ich nicht verstehen,"* but that I cannot understand. The only possibility was, to him, that a bolt of lightning had struck the airship and ignited escaping hydrogen gas. Yet, none of the hundreds of persons on the airfield had seen a lightning bolt strike the zeppelin during the landing operation.

Wernher von Braun called the disaster, "one of the most tragic and mysterious accidents in the pre-war history of air travel."

Anton Wittemann, one of the captains who had been in the *Führergondel* of the *Hindenburg,* concluded that "it is a complete mystery to me." He had, once during the war, landed his airship while lightning actually struck the hull, then already punctured by enemy bullets and shrapnel fragments. Wittemann had come to the United States with the *Los Angeles* and had stayed for three years as instructor. Subsequently he had flown with the *Graf Zeppelin* for almost a million miles. Thus, he was well experienced and had a good knowledge of English.

Testifying before the investigation committee appointed by the Bureau of Air Commerce at a public hearing, Commander Rosendahl, commandant of the Lakehurst naval station, stated that the *Hindenburg* had made a normal approach and that the handling of the bow line by the ground crew had definitely grounded the zeppelin, thus discharging what static electricity it contained. And it would have been most unlikely that a spark could have traveled from the ropes to the stern of the airship.

Hugo Eckener came from Germany with a group of zeppelin experts for the hearings, but neither he nor his aides could add anything that would shed light to this mystery.

Hans Luther, the German ambassador to Washington, had received hundreds of letters and calls threatening the destruction of the *Hindenburg,* or any other German airship that would land at Lakehurst. A letter from Kathie Rauch was specially handled and sent to the *Deutsche Zeppelin Reederei.* But the political situation at that time was such that bomb threats were constantly made against ocean liners or anything

that symbolized Nazi Germany, as did the airships with their huge swastikas painted on the rudders.

In *Collier's* magazine, W.B. Courtney had written at the conclusion of an article on airships: "It is the firm conviction of this skeptical reporter after close first-hand watching, that only a stroke of war or an unfathomable act of God will ever mar this German dirigible's safety record."

The zeppelin's designer, Ludwig Dürr, was convinced that it was not an accident.

Vice Admiral T.G.W. Settle, who had set an altitude record for free balloons in 1913, said, "It had to be sabotage. Any other cause must be eliminated."

And the writer A.A. Hoehling in his book *Who Destroyed the Hindenburg?* makes a good case for sabotage. He suggests that an incendiary device was used to destroy the airship. A regular time bomb was ruled out because of the delay in landing, although such a device could have been set to go off several hours after the airship had landed and was being serviced for the return flight. One of the riggers, with a rather curious background, had an excellent opportunity to place a device into the folds of the number four gas cell, where the first flash of fire was observed by some of the crew. In fact, the Bureau of Explosives of New York analyzed portions of a dry battery, which could well have been part of the device used to ignite the hydrogen gas. Since the ignition temperature of hydrogen is between six- and seven-hundred degrees Centigrade, a spark would have been necessary to ignite the gas. The exhaust sparks from the engine were only 200 to 250 degrees, and thus insufficient to set it ablaze, but a sparking device could indeed accomplish ignition.

It has been suggested that the Nazi government was actually convinced that an act of sabotage had destroyed the *Hindenburg,* but that to admit such subversive action would be tantamount to admittance of failure to protect any of its own vessels. This would have been intolerable to any regime.

At the time of the *Hindenburg* disaster, the *Graf Zeppelin* was flying homeward near the Canary Islands, at about the same spot where a year before both of these airships had met on their flight to and from South America. After Captain von Schiller landed his airship at the end of this seventieth South Atlantic crossing at Friedrichshafen, the *Graf Zeppelin* was grounded. Helium was unavailable from the United States. And it is doubtful that the airship would have carried a full list of passengers on any flights so soon after the catastrophe.

After having flown 1,053,618 miles in 590 flights and carried 12,443 passengers during nine years of service, the *Graf Zeppelin* as a museum was kept for a time at Frankfurt. The *Hindenburg* had flown 209,527 miles in 3,088 hours on sixty-three trips and had carried 3,059 passengers. Both airships had made 173 Atlantic crossings on the Germany to America route. A total of 47,008 kilograms of mail and 38,272 kilograms of freight had been carried by them.

The *LZ 130,* named *Graf Zeppelin II,* sister ship of the *Hindenburg,* was being completed in its hangar at Friedrichshafen. It was to enter the transatlantic service that fall of 1937. The maiden flight was made on September 14, 1939. Thirty test flights were made under Captain Hans von Schiller, but the airship was never used publicly and remained inactive throughout the Second World War. Then, together with the *Graf Zeppelin,*

both airships were dismantled and the salvaged material was used for other purposes.

The hangars and all airship construction facilities were totally destroyed during that war, and in 1945 the liquidation of the *Zeppelin-Bau* was ordered by the victorious Allies.

When on 20 October 1938 the aviation pioneer and expert, Colonel Charles A. Lindbergh, visited Friedrichshafen, he saw in the huge hangar the *Graf Zeppelin II.* In his book, *The Wartime Journals,* Lindbergh wrote that he saw the great ship, "shining new and clean, held floating stilly at the cables." He felt depressed looking at it, feeling that the airship seemed so capable of life and of movement, yet was held inactive in that hangar by intangible forces. Representing the result of all the years of development of lighter-than-air, the airship became like a last member of a once proud and influential family to Lindbergh. He could see no future for the airship, for it was inherently too slow, only about half the speed of an airplane at that time. Lindbergh believed that it might have a

The *LZ 130* on a test flight at Friedrichshafen. (Courtesy, Daimler-Benz).

163

The *LZ 130* at the mooring mast. (Courtesy, Lufthansa).

The *LZ 130* ready for another test flight. (Courtesy, Lufthansa).

few more years of life, but then it would probably become ever rarer than the squarerigger and the tea clipper — for sailing exists as a sport. Yet, the free balloon and the small blimp might live on to remind people of the days when the future of transoceanic air travel seemed to belong to the dirigible. Thus concluded this keen observer of the aviation situation in the various countries of the world at that crucial time.

Indeed, the zeppelins had their time of glory.

When airplanes were still handicapped by their limited cruising range, the airships already spanned wide oceans and could fly around the world without stopping. They pioneered world air transportation, affording passengers comforts unknown to airplane travelers.

The airships had contributed what Count Ferdinand von Zeppelin had written in his diary on 3 March 1911: "Each new means of transportation unites still further the nations upholding common goals." His zeppelins had done just that.

164

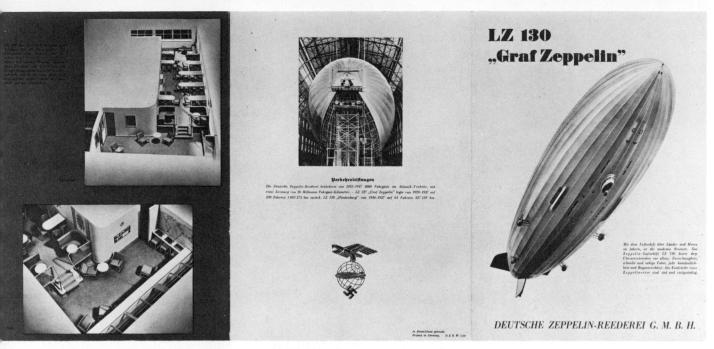

A brochure from the German Zeppelin Reederei (Shipping Company): "To cover countries and oceans with the airship is the modern travel style. The Zeppelin LZ 130 particularly offers the overseas traveler dependability, fast and quiet cruising, and every convenience and comfort. The impressions of a Zeppelin trip are lasting and varied."

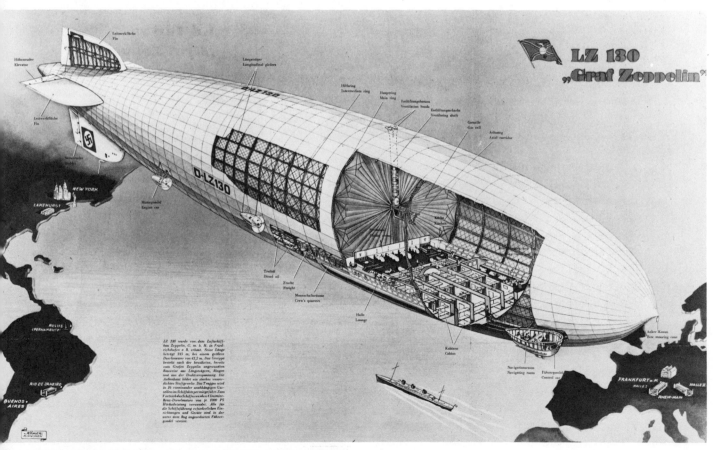

A schematic drawing of the zeppelin: "The German Zeppelin Shipping Company carried from 1935-1937, 3,000 passengers in the Atlantic traffic, equal to a performance of 26 million traveler-kilometers. The LZ 127 'Graf Zeppelin' made 590 trips and 1,695,272 kilometers in 1928-1937, and the LZ 129 'Hindenburg' 63 trips and 337,129 kilometers in 1936-1937.

16

DESIGN AND TECHNIQUE

A multitude of difficult problems had been encountered and solved, and much progress had been made in the span of thirty-five years, from the first airship that Count Zeppelin built in 1899 to the *LZ 129* constructed in 1934.

In his report, which the Count had sent to his king in 1887, he stated that if airships were to be of any real value for military purposes they had to be navigated against very strong air currents, they had to remain in the air for at least twenty-four hours, and they had to be built to carry a heavy load of men, supplies, and ammunition, And consequently, they had to be large.

The *LZ 1* had the largest possible load-carrying capability, the greatest possible dependability, and the highest possible speed, based on the technical knowledge of that time. The capacity of 11,300 cubic meters was believed then to be gigantic. The airship was 128 meters long and had a diameter of 11.7 meters. The cylinderlike shape simplified the construction problems because all of the skeleton rings used were of the same diameter and shape and thus were exchangable. Both ends had a bullet-type form. The skeleton consisted of sixteen rings and twenty-four flat surfaces. The lifting gas was carried in seventeen separate cloth bags located between the rings, but an air space was left as an insulation between these cells and the outer skin, so that the sun would not effect the expansion of the gas inside. The two engines of fifteen horsepower each with four propellers, giving the ship a top speed of 7.5 miles per hour, were placed in separate gondolas; these individual cars were attached to the airship body by means of trusses and cables. Steering was achieved by horizontal and vertical surfaces on the front and the rear of the airship hull. A movable weight on the underside of the airship regulated the rising or lowering in altitude. The open gondola cars were watertight so that the airship could rise or land on the water. For landings on solid ground a rubber bumper with springs was attached to the bottom of the gondola cars to dampen the sudden contact with the hard ground.

Six basic construction features of the first airship were constantly improved, refined, and perfected in subsequent airships, but they were never entirely changed. These were, first, the rigid skeleton frame of the airship form of light metal and covered with cloth; second, the placing of the lifting gas in a large number of completely separate containers; third, the engines divided into several independent units; fourth, the carrying load arrangement in several divided places in the interior of the airship; fifth, the separate elevators and rudder mechanism; and sixth, a central command center.

Ludwig Dürr, one of the closest associates of

Count Zeppelin, and for many years the chief of design and construction, said: "We cannot change the idea or add anything to it. We can only provide some refinements."

Principally because of its lightness, pure aluminum was used in constructing the girders for the *Traggerippe,* or skeleton, of the first airship. Already in the building of the second airship an improved material, a zinc-aluminum and zinc-aluminum-copper alloy was utilized. However, this combination proved to have serious imperfections because of different properties involved, and the supplier kept researching for a material with more stability than pure aluminum. Eventually, a combination of aluminum and copper was found with the desired qualities, and a duraluminum, invented by Alfred Wilm in 1909, was successfully employed in parts of the manufacture of the frames in the construction of the *LZ 7.* This metal was finally utilized first in 1915 in the entire construction of the *LZ 26.* At first, heavy T-beams and L-reinforcements had been employed, but later, in 1919, pressed ⌒ shapes were used.

It was mainly because of the use of this material, duraluminum, as *Werkstoff,* that the zeppelins were able to increase their performance as much as they did. In fact, the entire aircraft industry benefited from this strong material, which combined greater stability with considerably less weight; and the technical procedures and applications first pioneered in zeppelin construction actually opened the vast expanse of high performance airplane building. Duraluminum consisted of: 3.5 to 4.5 percent copper, 0.2 to 0.75 percent magnesium, 0.4 to 1.0 percent manganese, and a minimum of 92 percent aluminum.

The design of the skeleton was constantly improved. The main rings, which had been placed five meters apart in the first airship, were set ten meters apart in the *LZ 26,* and finally were placed fifteen meters apart in the constructions from the *LZ 100* on. The original twenty-four flat sides of the first airship were reduced to sixteen in the second one and, eventually, a type of slightly rounded segment was used, giving the appearance of still-smaller side panels and bestowing on the airship a rounder and much smoother-looking shape.

The runway on the underside of the airship was originally simply an open plank with a guide rope, attached to the frame, and used as companionway

between the gondolas. The second airship had a solidly attached runway, and from the *LZ 7* on, this was enclosed in the body of the airship, but still attached. In the *LZ 8,* however, the keel was a part of the inside of the airship and subsequently remained an integral part.

The hull-covering material of the first airship was an expensive Macco-cotton cloth, impregnated to make it waterproof. As protective material a combination of aztec-cellulose preparation was later used. This preparation was first painted on, the coat was rubbed down for smoothness, and then the next coat was applied. During the war, an aniline black was added to the paint to make detection by the enemy more difficult. And after the war, aluminum powder was added to improve the insulation against heat and to ensure a lowering of the damaging ultraviolet rays of the sun. The covering cloth was attached to the light metal frame in strips by means of hooks and eyes, and these strips were laced together. The seams were then pasted over with a strip of similar material. To correct the unevenness of the hull covering, wider strips were attached horizontally, from the building of the *LZ 92* on.

Since the early low power of the engines allowed only very moderate airship speeds, the simple torpedolike form was of little importance. It was an easy uncomplicated construction shape. Only when engine power increased appreciably was the shape of the airship changed to a more advantageous streamlined form. To find the best aerodynamic form, the testing laboratories, the *Aerodynamische Versuchsanstalt,* at Göttingen, later undertook wind-tunnel tests with models of airships; the Zeppelin works at Friedrichshafen also built a wind tunnel, then the largest in Germany, to make its own investigations of air pressure in different areas, streamline conditions, and limits of stresses on all parts in the airship. From the cigar-shaped *LZ 1,* a definite streamlined form evolved. The *LZ 40* of 1915 was thicker in the bow, the *LZ 62* (1916) was shorter, the *LZ 104* (1917) longer, and the *LZ 120 (Bodensee)* much smaller and shorter than previous airships built. The *LZ 126, LZ 127,* and *LZ 129* were again longer and larger and had more streamlined forms than the stubby *Bodensee.*

The size of the airship was consistently increased. It was considered to be the most critical consideration in the entire construction. What at first appeared truly tremendous soon faded into insignificance. Capacity increased gradually, but especially so in the military zeppelins, which, of course, demanded different requirements than did the commercial airships. The *LZ 5* type of 1909 (the *Z 11* of the army) had a capacity of fifteen-thousand cubic meters, diameter of thirteen meters, and was 136 meters long; and when the type *LZ 18* was built for the navy in 1913, that ship had a capacity of twenty-seven-thousand cubic meters, a diameter of 16.6 meters, and a length of 158 meters. The type *LZ 40* of 1915 (and the naval airship *L 10*) had a capacity of 31,900 cubic meters; the *LZ 62* type of 1916 had a capacity of 55,200 cubic meters; the *LZ 104* type of 1917 (actually the modified *L 59*) had reached a capacity of 68,500 cubic meters, a diameter of 23.9 meters, and a length of 226.5 meters, but it was built for a special purpose. On the other hand, when the military airships were completed and airships for passenger service were again constructed, the *Bodensee* had a capacity of only twenty-thousand cubic meters. The emphasis was no longer on altitude and load-carrying capability, but on safety, comfort, and, especially, improvement of performance. This small zeppelin had a diameter of 18.7 meters (the same as the *LZ 40* type) and a length of only 120.8 meters, actually 42.7 meters less than the *LZ 40.*

The *LZ 126,* built in 1924 for the United States Navy, had a capacity of seventy-thousand cubic meters, a maximum diameter of 27.64 meters, and a length of two-hundred meters. The *LZ 127,* the *Graf Zeppelin* was of 105,000 cubic-meter capacity, and the *LZ 129,* the *Hindenburg,* had a capacity of 190,000 cubic meters of gas.

In the first airship, the *Traggaszellen,* or gas cells, consisted of a heavy cotton material covered with a rubber coating. But when this material proved too porous and to eliminate the danger of any gas seeping into the hull of the huge airship, two layers of fine cotton cloth with heavier rubber coating were used thereafter. In 1908, tests with *Goldschlägerhaut* were made. Shingled on silk, this goldbeater's skin is actually the outer membrane of the large intestine of cattle, used by goldsmiths to beat out the gold into thin surfaces. Although rather sensitive, this material proved most satisfactory for the purpose, and a sevenfold material was then used with excellent results. When during the war the supply of this product from Russia and the United States stopped entirely, other material

was again tested, but after the short time that a silk product had been used for this purpose, an improved cotton material was again used for the gas cells.

The number of cells utilized also varied from type to type airship. The earliest one had seventeen separate cells, then the number was increased by one, decreased by two, increased by three again to reach a high of nineteen cells for the *LZ 62* series of 1916. It was believed that a larger number of cells would increase the safety of the military airships, so that when several cells were punctured by enemy action, sufficient lifting power would remain for the zeppelin to reach the home base. However, the *LZ 59* had only sixteen cells, and finally the *Bodensee* had but twelve. But this commercial airship was only less than one-third of the size of the previous *LZ 112* type, which had fifteen separate gas cells, thus the twelve were considerably smaller than any used on the earlier types of zeppelins. The *LZ 129* had sixteen cells.

The gas cells always used over ninety percent of the entire available space in the hull, and each individual cell had an automatic pressure valve and another, a *Manöverventil,* or maneuvering valve, controlled only from the command gondola.

The engines used for the *LZ 1* were built by the *Daimler Motorengesellschaft,* developed fifteen horsepower at 680 revolutions per minute and weighed 385 kilograms, or 25.7 kilogram per horsepower. These four-cylinder units used four-hundred grams of fuel per horsepower per hour. In the years following, the output of the engines rose to 90, 100, 115, and in 1910 to 120 horsepower at 1,100 revolutions per minute. These four-cylinder engines weighed 3.75 kilograms per horsepower and used 225 grams of fuel per horsepower per hour.

But when greater demands were made, it was decided to found a special company for the construction of airship engines, and the *Maybach Motorenbau G.m.b.H.* was created. The first Maybach engine, a six-cylinder unit built in 1909 and placed in the *LZ 9,* had 145 horsepower at 1,100 revolutions per minute and weighed 3.1 kilograms per horsepower, but used 240 grams of fuel per horsepower per hour. Improved over the years, to 180 horsepower by 1913 and by 1914 to 210 horsepower, by 1915 to 240, these engines weighed 1.52 kilograms per horsepower. The last military airships, the *LZ 105* to *LZ 114* had six-cylinder engines installed, which developed 240 to 260 horsepower at 1,400 revolutions per minute and weighed 1.6 kilograms per horsepower. They used two-hundred grams of fuel per horsepower per hour.

All of these airship engines had been designed especially for their purpose, because a mechanic had to be able to change the valves, or the cylinders, or the pistons, while the zeppelin was in flight. Thus, at first, the excellent racing-car engine, which Karl Maybach had designed, could not be used, and another, equally as light and as powerful, had to be built.

The Maybach engines installed in the *Schwaben* proved so successful that the other airships, the Gross-Basenach, the Parseval, and the Schütte-Lanz designed dirigibles, also used them. And in 1916 Karl Maybach designed an aero engine that reached its maximum power output of 245 horsepower at an altitude of 1,800 meters. This model *Mb IV* was widely used in aircraft and over two-thousand units were built during the war.

For the *LZ 126,* the *Los Angeles,* a twelve-cylinder V-type (VLI 12) engine was developed with an output of four-hundred horsepower at 1,400 revolutions per minute, weighing 2.35 kilograms per horsepower, and using 190 grams of fuel per horsepower per hour. The *LZ 127,* the *Graf Zeppelin,* had Maybach engines that developed 530 horsepower each, but the *LZ 129,* the *Hindenburg,* was equipped with engines built by Daimler-Benz. These models LOF6, or DB 602, diesel units of 88.5 liters, had sixteen cylinders and developed 1,300 horsepower at 1,600 revolutions per minute and weighed 1.8 kilogram per horsepower.

The gondola cars in which the engines were mounted were first constructed of a sturdy frame covered with cloth. Later, duraluminum was used for this purpose for lightness and greater stability. In the first airship, two gondola cars carried one engine each, which in turn drove the propeller attached to the upper sides of the hull. The military-type airships at first had four engines, placed in two gondola cars, and, when only three engines were installed, two were placed in the aft gondola car and drove the propellers on the sides, while the third was in the fore gondola. Minor changes were made in the drive of the *LZ 26* and, in the construction from the *LZ 38* on, three engines were placed in the aft gondola car. Eventually, to improve the weight distribution of the entire airship to best advantage, two engines were placed in the aft gondola car and the propellers installed at the center of the hull on the sides. Some airship types carried six, five, or, as in the *LZ 112,* which was the *L 70,* even seven engines, the fastest zeppelin during the war.

Finally, for easier service the engines were placed in roomy nacelles attached to the airship hull. The three-bladed propellers were driven directly from the engine by a short shaft from the rear of the engine. The ideal placement of the engines inside the hull was, of course, only possible in the American airships that used helium. A spark might have ignited the hydrogen gas.

The entire fuel supply for the first airship was carried in the gondola car with the engine. From the *LZ 6* on, the fuel supply was stored in barrels in the interior of the airship and forced by pressure to the engines, but later the flow was simply by gravity. Carried in aluminum barrels of one-hundred-liter capacity at first, the size was increased until the barrels held usually four-hundred liters each. While using generally seventy barrels of fuel for regular flights, the *LZ 126* carried 114 barrels of fuel and five barrels of lubricating oil, each holding 420 liters, on its transatlantic flight. The total fuel supply for the *LZ 2* weighed but 220 kilograms, but eventually the fuel load would weigh as much as thirty-thousand kilograms.

The propellers used were also of many various types. The first airship had the well-tested, small, four-wing ship propellers installed, which soon developed into three-wane screw propellers in 1905 to 1908. A two-wing paddlelike metal propeller was then used, only to be discarded for a similar type with a longer paddle. Then came a four-wing propeller, used in airships until 1914, but this was again replaced with a two-wing type. In a much refined form, this type remained in use and became the well-known wooden airplane propeller in 1915, with metal caps and edgings attached. (The *LZ 130* used three-bladed and four-bladed propellers.)

The carrying load and range of operation of the first airship were rather minimal but, by 1909, the airships could carry a load of 4,650 kilograms. The *Viktoria Luise* of 1912, which had a capacity of 18,700 cubic meters, could carry a payload of 6,500 kilograms, and with the *Bodensee,* the *LZ 120* of 1919, this had increased tremendously. The airship had a capacity of twenty-thousand cubic meters and the payload was ten-thousand kilograms. The range was 1,700 kilometers (about 1,050 miles). But these being passenger-carrying zeppelins, the design emphasis was quite different from that of the military airships. The first military zeppelins had already a greater payload capacity (11,100 kilograms) and range (2,100 kilometers). These two factors increased immensely. By 1915 (LZ 40) they were 15,900 and 4,200 respectively. The following year, the LZ 62 could carry 28,000 kilograms and had a range of 7,400 kilometers, while the LZ 70 was able to lift 44,500 kilograms with a flying range of twelve-thousand kilometers.

The *Viktoria Luise* carried during the 1912 to 1914 service 9,738 passengers, including her crew, on 489 flights totaling over 54,300 kilometers and 981 flying hours, while the *Bodensee* in the fall of 1919 carried aloft 4,050 passengers on 103 trips totaling over 51,200 kilometers in 532 flying hours. The last commercial airships naturally had longer ranges. The *LZ 127* had a maximum range of ten-thousand kilometers (6,250 miles) and the *LZ 129*, the *Hindenburg*, had a flying range of 13,500 kilometers (about 8,400 miles). The payload capabilities were for the former thirty-thousand kilograms and for the latter, twice that amount.

The military airships were constructed to reach higher altitudes than was necessary for the commercial ships to attain. The exception was the Africa ship, the *L 59*, which carried a fifteen-ton load and covered 6,500 kilometers, and could have flown another three-thousand kilometers when the airship landed after one-hundred hours with sufficient fuel to last another thirty-five hours. The *LZ 102*, for example, was built to reach an altitude of about 25,000 feet, an absolutely unnecessary feat for a commercial zeppelin.

For steering, the first airship used simple surfaces, a small boxlike device attached at the stern and larger flat surfaces on the tail of the zeppelin. With greater speeds, larger surfaces became necessary, and the *LZ 3* used a more elaborate system, consisting of several layers of surfaces, at the stem. The *LZ 10*, the *Schwaben*, carried a huge boxlike contraption of horizontal and vertical surfaces attached to the regular surfaces of the tail assembly, an improvement over the device used in the *LZ 4*. Eventually, the *LZ 25* of 1914 used as steering devices just plain surfaces, actually a part of the regular finlike stabilization arrangement, and

even the *Bodensee* had this structure improved into a neater-appearing integration on a sharper-pointed elongated tail. These completely redesigned steering surfaces were smooth and an immense improvement over the earlier systems.

The *LZ 1* used as elevator a simple weight on a wire, which ran along the bottom of the airship. To keep the rolling motion to a minimum, small rudder surfaces were placed on each side, at the center of the airship hull. This led eventually to the entire steering system to be combined in the tail assembly. For navigation, the *LZ 1* was equipped with only a compass and a barometer to indicate the altitude. The *LZ 4* carried larger navigational instruments — a compass, three-inches in diameter, and a barometer about five to six inches wide, both still in existence and at display in the museum at Friedrichshafen. Subsequently, airships were equipped with lightweight, but modern navigational aids similar to those used by ships at sea. The *LZ 127* and the *LZ 129* had, of course, the newest navigational devices available.

The gondola car of the first airship was roomy enough to accommodate the engine, the crew, and the equipment needed for the *Luftschiff*. As time went on, actually three distinct types of gondola cars were developed. The earliest type, attached below the runway, was a watertight boxlike space, rounded at the front and pointed at the rear. On the airships from the *LZ 36* on the *Führergondel*, or command gondola car, was enlarged about threefold, and included the pilot room, the wireless operator's room, and an officer's room. A place for a machine-gun mounting was also provided and all was entirely enclosed to protect against the elements. The third type of gondola car, actually a shorter version, was used in airships from the *LZ 95* on. In the *Bodensee*, an elongated gondola included the pilot room and, for the passengers, the *Fahrgasträume* consisted of the parlor and auxiliary rooms. The utilization of duraluminum frames for the construction of these gondola cars had also improved considerably, for when at one time the *Bodensee* hit the ground forcefully while landing during a storm, the damage inflicted was so slight that the zeppelin could continue the voyage without any delay.

The crew was quartered simply in austere spaces in the corridor running along the inside base of the airship. A man's quarters were wherever there was space to hang a hammock, or wherever there was a spot where he could sit or lie down to rest, between the gas bags and the girders in the immense hull of the zeppelin. Regular sleeping rooms and sitting rooms for officers and crew were not furnished until the transoceanic airships were built. But by then the passenger accommodations were also considerably more spacious and comfortable.

Lighting was supplied for the earliest airships by battery only. But when a powerful spotlight was demanded for the *L1 (LZ 14),* the first electric system was installed. A generator, which developed 120 watts at 12 volts, was placed in the forward gondola car. The sixty-five-watt lamp searchlight was supplied by a generator of three kilowatts. Continuous improvements in the system were made, so that the *LZ 47* had a generator of three-hundred watts and a Morse spotlight of five-hundred watts, and toward the end of the war an eight-hundred-watt generator supplied the one-thousand-watt spotlight.

Orders by the zeppelin commander were generally transmitted by a code system using electric bells. A basket on a wire stretched between the forward command gondola car and aft gondolas carried the written messages. But a speaking tube was used instead from the *LZ 26* on, and in all later airships a system of telephonic communication was established.

Count Zeppelin decided to install a wireless station in the *LZ 6* when on 25 August 1909 a trip to Berlin was planned. Tests were conducted before that actual flight during two months of that year with an antenna lowered from the gondola during flight to achieve transmissions. The Count had been interested in the tests with wireless telegraphy which the inventor Adolf Slaby had made in Berlin in 1898. The airship detachment of the army, under Captain von Sigsfeld, had assisted in raising antennas with balloons, which they later equipped with this new means of communication. The *LZ 6* made 73 flights, totaling over 8,698 kilometers (5,401 miles), using the wireless system extensively.

Based on the new experiences gathered with the zeppelin, the Telefunken company installed in 1910 a new wireless station in the *Z 11* built for the army, and achieved distances of 100 to 150 kilometers, while the airship was in flight. Considerable difficulties were encountered by the magnetizing of the equipment, but these problems were solved later by using simple wind engines. Tests in the *Viktoria Luise* in 1912 led to the construction of a wireless station, specially designed for airships. The system was perfected for the military forces in the airships of 1915, but it reached a high degree of sophistication for the *Bodensee,* and appreciably more so for the *LZ 126* and the *LZ 129.*

As Ludwig Dürr had said, "We can only provide some refinements." These were indeed provided in every field over the years.

NOTES

Chapter 1

1.Margaret Goldsmith. *Zeppelin: A Biography.* New York: William Morrow and Company, 1931, p. 7.

2. Ibid., p. 25-26.
3. Ibid., p. 27.

Chapter 2

1. Count Ferdinand von Zeppelin. *Aus dem Amerikanischen Kriegsjahre 1863.(From the American War Year 1863) Der Greif;* Cotta'sche Monatsschrift (periodical). Berlin: Volume 1, 1913-14. Book 4. January 1914.
2.Translated by the author.
3.*Paris Temps,* 1927.
4.Carl Schurz. *The Reminiscences of Carl Schurz.* Volume 2. New York: The McClure Company, 1907-08.

Chapter 3

1.*St. Paul Daily News,* February 9, 1915.
2.Maria Bach Dunn. *Zeppelin in Minnesota.* The Count's own Story. *Minnesota History,* published quarterly by Minnesota Historical Society. St. Paul: Summer, 1967. p. 277.
3.Ibid., p. 275.
4.*Minneapolis Journal,* February 9, 1915.
5.*Photographic History of the Civil War.* Volume 1. New York: Published by Review of Reviews, 1912.
6.Ibid.
7.Maria Bach Dunn. *Zeppelin in Minnesota,* p. 277.

Chapter 4

1.Count Ferdinand von Zeppelin. *Die Eroberung der Luft (The Conquest of the Air)* Stuttgart and Leipzig: Deutsche Verlagsanstalt, 1908.

Chapter 5

1.Otto Lilienthal. *Der Vogelflug als Grundlage der Flieger-kunst (The Birdflight as Basis for the Flying-art)* München und Stuttgart: R. Oldenbourg, 1910.
2.Count Ferdinand von Zeppelin in a speech before the Society of German Engineers in 1896.

Chapter 6

1.*Frankfurter Zeitung,* July 3, 1900.
2.Count Ferdinand von Zeppelin. *Erfahrungen beim Bau von Luftschiffen (Experiences when building Airships)* Berlin: Julius Springer, 1908.
3.*No author given, Die Woche* (periodical), October 1903.

Chapter 7

1.Count Ferdinand von Zeppelin. *Erfahrungen beim Bau von Luftschiffen (Experiences when building Airships)* Berlin: Julius Springer, 1908.
2.Ibid.
3.*Neues Wiener Tagblatt,* June 1908.
4.*Thüringer Zeitung,* July 2, 1908.
5.Margaret Goldsmith, *Zeppelin: A Biography.* New York: William Morrow and Company, 1931, p. 159-60.

Chapter 8

1.Margaret Goldsmith. *Zeppelin: A Biography.* New York: William Morrow and Company, 1931, p. 170-71.
2.Ibid., p. 176.
3.*Schwäbischer Merkur,* October 1908.

Chapter 9

1.*Berliner Tageblatt,* August 23, 1909.

2. Margaret Goldsmith. *Zeppelin: A Biography*. New York: William Morrow and Company, 1931, p. 196.

Chapter 10

1. Ernst Lehmann and Howard Mingos. *The Zeppelins. The Saturday Evening Post,* April 30, 1927, p. 46.

Chapter 11

1. Ernst Lehmann and Howard Mingos. *The Zeppelins. The Saturday Evening Post,* April 30, 1927, p. 25.
2. Ibid., p. 25.
3. *Frankfurter Zeitung,* May 17, 1915.
4. Ernst Lehmann and Howard Mingos. *The Zeppelins. The Saturday Evening Post,* April 30, 1927, p. 130.
5. Margaret Goldsmith. *Zeppelin: A Biography*. New York: William Morrow and Company, 1931, p. 220-21.

Chapter 12

1. Ernst Lehmann and Howard Mingos. *The Zeppelins. The Saturday Evening Post,* May 28, 1927, p. 47.
2. *St. Paul Daily News,* February 8, 1915.
3. Ibid.
4. Ibid.
5. Ibid.
6. Ibid.
7. Ibid.
8. Ibid.
9. Ibid.
10. *St. Paul Daily News,* February 9, 1915.
11. Ibid.
12. Ibid.
13. Ibid.
14. Paul von Hindenburg. *Aus meinem Leben (Of my Life)* Leipzig: S. Hirzel, 1920.
15. August von Parseval. *Graf Zeppelin und die Deutsche Luftschiffahrt (Count Zeppelin and the German Airship Travel)* Berlin-Grunewald: Hermann Klemm Verlad (no date given).
16. *Frankfurter Zeitung,* March 8, 1917.

APPENDICES

Appendix 1

Details of Airships built by the Luftschiffbau Zeppelin

YEAR BUILT	DESIGNATION AND NUMBER	CONSTRUCTOR'S TYPE	BUILT AT (SEE BELOW)	LENGTH (METERS)	DIAMETER (METERS)	NUMBER OF GAS CELLS	GAS CAPACITY (CUBIC METERS)	ENGINES AND MAKE	TOTAL HORSEPOWER (DIN)	NUMBER OF PROPELLERS
1899	LZ 1	a	M	128	11.25	17	11,300	2 Dai	28.4	4
1905	LZ 2	b	M	128	11.25	16	11,300	2 Dai	170	4
1906	LZ 3	b	M	128	11.65	16	11,300	2 Dai	170	4
	as Z I			136	11.65	17	12,200	2 Dai	200	4
1907	LZ 4	c	M	136	13	17	15,000	2 Dai	210	4
1908	LZ 5 (Z II)	c	M	136	13	17	15,000	2 Dai	210	4
1909	LZ 6	d	M	136	13	17	15,000	2 Dai	230	4
	rebuilt			144	13	18	16,000	2 Dai	230	4
1910	LZ 7 Deutschland	e	F	148	14	18	19,300	3 Dai	360	4
1911	LZ 8 Deutschland II	e	F	148	14	18	19,300	3 Dai	360	4
	LZ 9 (Z II)	f	F	132	14	18	16,550	3 My	435	4
	rebuilt			140	14	17	17,800	3 My	435	4
	LZ 10 Schwaben	f	F	140	14	17	17,800	3 My	435	4
1912	LZ 11 Viktoria Luise	g	F	148	14	18	18,700	3 My	510	4
	LZ 12 (ZIII)	f	F	140	14	17	17,800	3 My	435	4
	LZ 13 Hansa	g	F	148	14	18	18,700	3 My	510	4
	LZ 14 (L1)	h	F	158	14.9	18	22,500	3 My	495	4
1913	LZ 15 (Z I)	h	F	142	14.9	16	19,500	3 My	510	4
	LZ 16 (Z IV)	h	F	142	14.9	16	19,500	3 My	510	4
	LZ 17 Sachsen	h	F	140	14.9	16	19,500	3 My	510	4
	rebuilt			148	14.9	17	20,900	3 My	540	4
	LZ 18 (L 2)	i	F	158	16.6	18	27,000	4 My	720	4
	LZ 19 (Z I)	h	F	140	14.9	16	19,500	3 My	495	4
	LZ 20 (Z V)	h	F	140	14.9	16	19,500	3 My	495	4
	rebuilt			148	14.9	17	20,900	3 My	540	4
	LZ 21 (Z VI)	k	F	148	16.6	17	30,900	3 My	540	4

SPEED (MILES PER HOUR)	SPEED (METERS PER SECOND)	RANGE (KILOMETERS)	LOAD CAPACITY (KILOGRAMS)	MAIDEN FLIGHT (DATE)		FATE OF AIRSHIP
17	7.5	—	—	7.2.	1900	dismantled in 1901
24.5	11	—	2,800	1.17.	1906	wrecked in 1906 at Kisslegg
24.5	11	—	2,800	10.9.	1906	
24.5	11	—	2,900		1908	dismantled in 1913 at Metz
30.1	13.5	—	4,600	6.20.	1908	burned up in 1908 at Echterdingen
34.6	15.5	—	4,650	5.26.	1909	wrecked and dismantled in 1910 at Weilburg
30.1	13.5	2,000	4,500	8.25.	1909	
30.1	13.5	2,000	4,370		1910	burned up in hangar in 1910 at Oos
37.5	16.7	1,600	6.800	6.19.	1910	wrecked in 1910 in Teutoburger Wald
37.5	16.7	1,600	6,800	3.30.	1911	damaged and dismantled in 1911 at Düsseldorf
48.4	21.7	1,600	4,600	10.2.	1911	
48.4	21.7	1,600	6,000		1911	dismantled in 1914 at Gotha
48.4	21.7	1,600	6,000	6.26.	1911	wrecked in 1912 at Düsseldorf
49.5	22.2	1,100	6,500	2.19.	1912	wrecked and dismantled in 1915
48.4	21.7	1,600	6,700	4.25.	1912	dismantled in 1914 at Metz
49.5	22.2	1,100	6,300	7.30.	1912	dismantled in 1916 at Johannisthal
47.2	21.2	2,300	9,500	10.7.	1912	lost in storm in 1913 off Helgoland
48.6	21.8	2,700	8,200	1.16.	1913	lost in storm in 1913 at Karlsruhe
48.6	21.8	2,700	8,200	3.14.	1913	dismantled in 1916 at Jüterbog
47.9	21.5	2,700	7,400	5.3.	1913	
46.8	21	2,800	7,400		1914	dismantled in 1916 at Düren
44.6	20	2,800	7,200	6.6.	1913	wrecked and dismantled in 1914 at Johannisthal
45.7	20.5	2,800	7,200	8.1.	1913	wrecked and dismantled in 1914 at Diedenhofen
44.6	20	2,800	7,600		1914	burned in 1913
46.8	21	2,100	11,100	9.9.	1913	landed in enemy territory in 1914, Mlava, Poland
46.8	21	1,900	8,800	11.10.	1913	wrecked in 1914 near Bonn

YEAR BUILT	DESIGNATION AND NUMBER	CONSTRUCTOR'S TYPE	BUILT AT (SEE BELOW)	LENGTH (METERS)	DIAMETER (METERS)	NUMBER OF GAS CELLS	GAS CAPACITY (CUBIC METERS)	ENGINES AND MAKE	TOTAL HORSEPOWER (DIN)	NUMBER OF PROPELLERS
1914	LZ 22 (Z VII)	l	F	156	14.9	18	22,100	3 My	540	4
	LZ 23 (Z VIII)	l	F	156	14.9	18	22,100	3 My	540	4
	LZ 24 (L 3)	m	F	158	14.9	18	22,500	3 My	600	4
	LZ 25 (Z IX)	m	F	158	14.9	18	22,500	3 My	630	4
	LZ 26 (Z XII)	n	Fk	161.2	16	15	25,000	3 My	630	3
	LZ 27 (L 4)	m	F	158	14.9	18	22,500	3 My	630	4
	LZ 28 (L 5)	m	F	158	14.9	18	22,500	3 My	630	4
	LZ 29 (Z X)	m	F	158	14.9	18	22,500	3 My	630	4
	LZ 30 (Z XI)	m	P	158	14.9	18	22,500	3 My	630	4
	LZ 31 (L 6)	m	F	158	14.9	18	22,500	3 My	630	4
	LZ 32 (L 7)	m	F	158	14.9	18	22,500	3 My	630	4
	LZ 33 (L 8)	m	F	158	14.9	18	22,500	3 My	630	4
	LZ 34 (LZ 34)	m	P	158	14.9	18	22,500	3 My	630	4
	LZ 35 (LZ 35)	m	F	158	14.9	18	22,500	3 My	630	4
1915	LZ 36 (L 9)	o	F	161.4	16	15	24,900	3 My	630	3
	LZ 37 (LZ 37)	m	P	158	14.9	18	22,500	3 My	630	4
	LZ 38 (LZ 38)	p	F	163.5	18.7	15	31,900	3 My	630	3
	LZ 39 (LZ 39)	o	F	161.4	16	15	24,900	3 My	630	3
	LZ 40 (LZ 10)	p	F	163.5	18.7	15	31,900	4 My	840	4
	LZ 41 (L 11)	p	L	163.5	18.7	15	31,900	4 My	840	4
	LZ 42 (LZ 72)	p	P	163.5	18.7	15	31,900	4 My	840	4
	LZ 43 (L 12)	p	F	163.5	18.7	15	31,900	4 My	840	4
	LZ 44 (LZ 74)	p	L	163.5	18.7	15	31,900	4 My	840	4
	LZ 45 (L 13)	p	F	163.5	18.7	15	31,900	4 My	840	4
	LZ 46 (L 14)	p	L	163.5	18.7	15	31,900	4 My	840	4
	LZ 47 (LZ 77)	p	F	163.5	18.7	15	31,900	4 My	840	4
	LZ 48 (L 15)	p	L	163.5	18.7	15	31,900	4 My	960	4
	LZ 49 (LZ 79)	p	P	163.5	18.7	15	31,900	4 My	960	4
	LZ 50 (L 16)	p	F	163.5	18.7	15	31,900	4 My	960	4
	LZ 51 (LZ 81)	p	L	163.5	18.7	15	31,900	4 My	960	4
	rebuilt (Dresden)			178.5	18.7	17	35,800	4 My	960	4
	LZ 52 (L 18)	p	L	163.5	18.7	15	31,900	4 My	960	4
	LZ 53 (L 17)	p	F	163.5	18.7	15	31,900	4 My	960	4
	LZ 54 (L 19)	p	F	163.5	18.7	16	31,900	4 My	960	4
	LZ 55 (LZ 85)	p	P	163.5	18.7	16	31,900	4 My	960	4
	LZ 56 (LZ 86)	p	P	163.5	18.7	16	31,900	4 My	960	4
	rebuilt (Dresden)			178.5	18.7	18	35,800	4 My	960	4
	LZ 57 (LZ 87)	p	L	178.5	18.7	18	35,800	4 My	960	4
	LZ 58 (LZ 88 L 25)	p	P	178.5	18.7	18	35,800	4 My	960	4
	LZ 59 (L 20)	g	F	178.8	18.7	18	35,800	4 My	960	4
	LZ 60 (LZ 90)	p	P	163.5	18.7	16	31,900	4 My	960	4
	rebuilt (Dresden)			178.8	18.7	18	35,800	4 My	960	4
	LZ 61 (L 21)	g	L	178.8	18.7	18	35,800	4 My	960	4
1916	LZ 62 (L 30)	r	F	198	23.9	19	55,200	6 My	1,440	6
	LZ 63 (LZ 93)	p	P	178.8	18.7	18	35,800	4 My	960	4
	LZ 64 (L 22)	g	L	178.8	18.7	18	35,800	4 My	960	4

SPEED (MILES PER HOUR)	SPEED (METERS PER SECOND)	RANGE (KILOMETERS)	LOAD CAPACITY (KILOGRAMS)	MAIDEN FLIGHT (DATE)		FATE OF AIRSHIP
44.6	20	1,900	8,800	1.8.	1914	wrecked and dismantled in 1914, St. Quirin, France
44.6	20	2,000	8,800	5.11.	1914	wrecked and dismantled in 1914, Badonviller, France
49.0	22.4	2,200	9,200	5.11.	1914	wrecked in 1915, on Fanö Island, Denmark
50.2	22.5	2,200	9,200	7.13.	1914	bombed in hangar in 1914, at Düsseldorf
50.2	22.5	3,300	12,200	12.14.	1914	dismantled in 1917, at Jüterbog
50.2	22.5	2,200	9,200	8.18.	1914	wrecked in 1915, at Blaavands Huck, Denmark
50.2	22.5	2,200	9,200	9.24.	1914	wrecked and dismantled in 1915 at Dunamünde, Russia
50.2	22.5	2,200	9,200	10.13.	1914	wrecked and dismantled in 1915 at St. Quentin, France
50.2	22.5	2,200	9,200	11.15.	1914	burned in 1915, at Posen
49.0	22.4	2,200	9,200	11.3.	1914	burned in 1916, at Fuhlsbüttel
49.0	22.4	2,200	9,200	11.20.	1914	shot down in 1916, off Horns Reef
49.0	22.4	2,200	9,200	12.17.	1914	wrecked and dismantled in 1915, at Tirlemort, Belgium
49.0	22.4	2,200	9,200	1.6.	1915	wrecked and burned in 1915, at Insterburg
49.0	22.4	2,200	9,200	1.11.	1915	burned in 1916, at Fuhlsbüttel
52.6	23.6	2,800	11,100	3.8.	1915	shot down in 1915, at Ghent, Belgium
49.0	22.4	2,200	9,200	3.4	1915	wrecked in 1915, at Poperinghe, Belgium
55.8	25	4,300	15,000	4.3.	1915	bombed in hangar in 1915 at Evere
50.2	22.5	2,800	11,100	4.24.	1915	wrecked and dismantled in 1915, near Kovno, Russia
59.5	26.7	4,300	15,000	5.13.	1915	burned in 1915, off Neuwerk Island
59.5	26.7	4,300	15,000	6.7.	1915	dismantled in 1917, at Hage
58.6	26.3	4,000	14,000	6.15.	1915	dismantled in 1917, at Jüterbog
59.5	26.7	4,300	16,200	6.21.	1915	burned when dismantled in 1915, off Ostende
59.5	26.7	4,300	16,200	7.8.	1915	wrecked in 1915, in Schnee Eifel mountains
59.5	26.7	4,300	16,200	4.23.	1915	dismantled in 1917, at Hage
59.5	26.7	4,300	16,200	8.9.	1915	wrecked in 1919, at Nordholz
59.5	26.7	4,300	16,200	8.24.	1915	shot down in 1916, at Revigny
60.2	27	4,300	16,200	9.9.	1915	sunk in 1916, in the Thames estuary
60.2	27	4,300	16,200	8.2.	1915	shot down and dismantled in 1916, at Ath, Belgium
60.2	27	4,300	16,200	11.23.	1915	wrecked and dismantled in 1917, at Nordholz
60.2	27	4,300	16,200	10.7.	1915	
59.1	26.5	4,900	17,900		1916	wrecked and dismantled in 1916, at Tirnova, Bulgaria
60.2	27	4,300	16,200	11.3.	1915	burned in 1915, at Tondern
60.2	27	4,300	16,200	10.20.	1915	burned in 1915, at Tondern
60.2	27	4,300	16,200	11.19.	1915	sunk in 1916, in the North Sea
60.2	27	4,300	16,200	9.12.	1915	lost in 1916, at Salonika, Greece
60.2	27	4,300	16,200	10.10.	1915	
58.4	26.2	4,900	17,900		1916	wrecked in 1916, at Temesvar, Rumania
58.4	26.2	4,900	17,900	12.6.	1915	dismantled in 1917, at Jüterbog
58.4	26.2	4,900	17,900	11.14.	1915	dismantled in 1917, at Potsdam
59.1	26.5	4,300	17,900	12.21.	1915	destroyed in 1916, in Norway
60.2	27	4,300	16,200	1.1.	1916	
59.1	26.5	4,300	17,900		1916	wrecked in 1916, at Wittmundhaven
59.1	26.5	4,300	17,900	1.10.	1916	shot down in 1916, off Yarmouth
64.0	28.7	7,400	32,500	5.28.	1916	dismantled in 1917, at Seerappen
59.1	26.5	4,300	17,900	2.23.	1916	dismantled in 1917, at Trier
59.1	26.5	4,300	17,900	3.3.	1916	shot down in 1917, off Terschelling

YEAR BUILT	DESIGNATION AND NUMBER	CONSTRUCTOR'S TYPE	BUILT AT (SEE BELOW)	LENGTH (METERS)	DIAMETER (METERS)	NUMBER OF GAS CELLS	GAS CAPACITY (CUBIC METERS)	ENGINES AND MAKE	TOTAL HORSEPOWER (DIN)	NUMBER OF PROPELLERS
	LZ 65 (LZ 95)	g	F	178.5	18.7	18	35,800	4 My	960	4
	LZ 66 (L 23)	g	P	178.5	18.7	18	35,800	4 My	960	4
	LZ 67 (LZ 97)	g	L	178.5	18.7	18	35,800	4 My	960	4
	LZ 68 (LZ 98)	g	L	178.5	18.7	18	35,800	4 My	960	4
	LZ 69 (L 24)	g	P	178.5	18.7	18	35,800	4 My	960	4
	LZ 70 was not built									
	LZ 71 (LZ 101)	g	P	178.5	18.7	18	35,800	4 My	960	4
	LZ 72 (L 31)	r	L	198	23.9	19	55,200	6 My	1,440	6
	LZ 73 (LZ 103)	g	P	178.5	18.7	18	35,800	4 My	960	4
	LZ 74 (L 32)	r	F	196.5	23.9	19	55,200	6 My	1,440	6
	LZ 75 (L 37)	r	S	196.5	23.9	19	55,200	6 My	1,440	6
	LZ 76 (L 33)	r	F	196.5	23.9	19	55,200	6 My	1,440	6
	LZ 77 (LZ 107)	g	P	178.5	18.7	18	35,800	4 My	960	4
	LZ 78 (L 34)	r	L	196.5	23.9	19	55,200	6 My	1,440	6
	LZ 79 (L 41)	r	S	196.5	23.9	19	55,200	6 My	1,440	6
	LZ 80 (L 35)	r	F	196.5	23.9	19	55,200	6 My	1,440	6
	LZ 81 (LZ 111)	g	P	178.5	18.7	18	35,800	4 My	960	4
	LZ 82 (L 36)	r	F	196.5	23.9	19	55,200	6 My	1,440	6
	LZ 83 (LZ 113)	r	S	196.5	23.9	19	55,200	6 My	1,440	6
	LZ 84 (L 38)	r	L	196.5	23.9	19	55,200	6 My	1,440	6
1917	LZ 85 (L 45)	r	S	196.5	23.9	19	55,200	6 My	1,440	6
	LZ 86 (L 39)	r	F	196.5	23.9	19	55,200	6 My	1,440	6
	LZ 87 (L 47)	r	S	196.5	23.9	19	55,200	6 My	1,440	6
	LZ 88 (L 40)	r	F	196.5	23.9	19	55,200	6 My	1,440	6
	LZ 89 (L 50)	r	S	196.5	23.9	19	55,200	6 My	1,440	6
	LZ 90 (LZ 120)	r	L	196.5	23.9	19	55,200	6 My	1,440	6
	LZ 91 (L 42)	s	F	196.5	23.9	18	55,500	5 My	1,200	5
	LZ 92 (L 43)	s	F	196.5	23.9	18	55,500	5 My	1,200	5
	LZ 93 (L 44)	t	L	196.5	23.9	18	55,500	5 My	1,200	4
	LZ 94 (L 46)	t	L	196.5	23.9	18	55,500	5 My	1,200	4
	LZ 95 (L 48)	u	F	196.5	23.9	18	55,500	5 My	1,200	4
	LZ 96 (L 49)	u	L	196.5	23.9	18	55,500	5 My	1,200	4
	LZ 97 (L 51)	u	F	196.5	23.9	18	55,500	5 My	1,200	4
	LZ 98 (L 52)	u	S	196.5	23.9	18	55,500	5 My	1,200	4
	LZ 99 (L 54)	u	S	196.5	23.9	18	55,500	5 My	1,200	4
	LZ 100 (L 53)	v	F	196.5	23.9	14	56,000	5 My	1,200	4
	LZ 101 (L 55)	v	L	196.5	23.9	14	56,000	5 My	1,300	4
	LZ 102 (L 57)	w	F	226.5	23.9	16	68,500	5 My	1,200	4
	LZ 103 (L 56)	v	S	196.5	23.9	14	56,000	5 My	1,300	4
	LZ 104 (L 59)	w	S	226.5	23.9	16	68,500	5 My	1,200	4
	LZ 105 (L 58)	v	F	196.5	23.9	14	56,000	5 My	1,300	4
	LZ 106 (L 61)	v	F	196.5	23.9	14	56,000	5 My	1,300	4
	LZ 107 (L 62)	v	L	196.5	23.9	14	56,000	5 My	1,300	4
	LZ 108 (L 60)	v	S	196.5	23.9	14	56,000	5 My	1,300	4
1918	LZ 109 (L 64)	v	S	196.5	23.9	14	56,000	5 My	1,300	4
	LZ 110 (L 63)	v	F	196.5	23.9	14	56,000	5 My	1,300	4

SPEED (MILES PER HOUR)	SPEED (METERS PER SECOND)	RANGE (KILOMETERS)	LOAD CAPACITY (KILOGRAMS)	MAIDEN FLIGHT (DATE)		FATE OF AIRSHIP
59.1	26.5	4,300	17,900	2.1.	1916	wrecked in 1916, at Namur
59.1	26.5	4,300	17,900	4.8.	1916	shot down in 1917, off Lyngvig
59.1	26.5	4,300	18,200	4.4.	1916	dismantled in 1917 at Jüterbog
59.1	26.5	4,300	18,400	4.28.	1916	dismantled in 1917 at Schneidemühl
59.1	26.5	4,300	18,400	5.20.	1916	burned in 1916, at Tondern
59.1	26.5	4,900	18,400	6.29.	1916	dismantled in 1917 at Jüterbog
64.0	28.7	7,400	32,500	7.12.	1916	shot down in 1916, at Potters Bar
59.1	26.5	4,900	18,400	8.23.	1916	dismantled in 1917, at Königsberg
64.0	28.7	7,400	32,500	8.14.	1916	shot down in 1916, at Billericay
64.0	28.7	7,400	32,500	11.9.	1916	dismantled in 1917, at Seddin
64.0	28.7	7,400	32,500	8.30.	1916	lost in 1916, at Little Wigborough
59.1	26.5	4,900	18,400	10.16.	1916	dismantled in 1917, at Darmstadt
64.0	28.7	7,400	32,500	9.22.	1916	shot down in 1916, off West Hartlepool
64.0	28.7	7,400	32,500	1.15.	1917	destroyed in 1918, at Nordholz
64.0	28.7	7,400	32,500	10.12.	1916	dismantled in 1918 at Jüterbog
59.1	26.5	4,900	18,400	12.20.	1916	dismantled in 1917, at Dresden
64.0	28.7	7,400	32,500	11.1.	1916	destroyed in 1918, at Rehben an der Aller
64.0	28.7	7,400	32,500	2.22.	1917	wrecked in 1917, at Maubeuge
64.0	28.7	7,400	32,500	11.22.	1916	dismantled in 1916, at Seemuppen, Russia
64.0	28.7	7,400	32,500	4.12.	1917	captured in 1917, at Sisteron, France
64.0	28.7	7,400	32,500	12.11.	1916	shot down in 1917, at Compiègne, France
64.0	28.7	7,400	32,500	5.1.	1917	destroyed in 1918, at Ahlhorn
64.0	28.7	7,400	32,500	1.3.	1917	dismantled in 1917, at Neuenwald
64.0	28.7	7,400	32,500	6.9.	1917	wrecked in 1917, in the Mediterranean
64.0	28.7	7,400	32,500	1.31.	1917	to Italy in 1920, dismantled at Ciampino 1921
64.0	28.7	10,400	36,400	2.22.	1917	destroyed in 1919, at Nordholz
64.0	28.7	10,400	36,400	3.6.	1917	shot down in 1917, off Vlieland
64.4	28.9	11,500	37,800	4.1.	1917	shot down in 1917, at St. Clement
64.4	28.9	11,500	37,800	4.24.	1917	destroyed in 1918, at Ahlhorn
66.7	29.9	12,200	39,000	5.22.	1917	shot down in 1917, at Theberton
66.7	29.9	12,200	39,000	6.13.	1917	captured in 1917, at Bourbonne-les-Bains
66.7	29.9	12,200	39,000	7.6.	1917	destroyed in 1918, at Ahlhorn
70.9	31.8	13,500	39,000	7.14.	1917	destroyed in 1919, at Wittmund
70.9	31.8	13,500	39,000	8.13.	1917	bombed in 1918, at Tondern
70.9	31.8	13,500	40,000	8.8.	1917	shot down in 1918, off Terschelling
70.9	31.8	13,500	40,000	8.1.	1917	dismantled in 1917, at Tiefenort an der Werra
63.8	28.6	16,000	52,100	9.26.	1917	dismantled in 1917, at Jüterbog
70.9	31.8	13,500	40,000	9.24.	1917	destroyed in 1919, at Wittmund
63.8	28.6	16,000	52,100	10.25.	1917	wrecked in 1918, at Straits of Otranto, Italy
70.9	31.8	13,500	40,000	10.29.	1917	destroyed in 1918, at Ahlhorn
70.9	31.8	13,500	40,000	10.29.	1917	to Italy in 1920, wrecked at Ciampino 1921
70.9	31.8	13,500	40,000	1.19.	1918	shot down in 1918, off Helgoland
70.9	31.8	13,500	40,000	12.18.	1917	bombed in 1918, at Tondern
70.9	31.8	13,500	40,000	3.11.	1918	to Britain in 1920, dismantled at Pulham 1921
70.9	31.8	13,500	40,000	3.9.	1918	destroyed in 1918, at Nordholz

YEAR BUILT	DESIGNATION AND NUMBER	CONSTRUCTOR'S TYPE	BUILT AT (SEE BELOW)	LENGTH (METERS)	DIAMETER (METERS)	NUMBER OF GAS CELLS	GAS CAPACITY (CUBIC METERS)	ENGINES AND MAKE	TOTAL HORSEPOWER (DIN)	NUMBER OF PROPELLERS
	LZ 111 (L 65)	v	L	196.5	23.9	14	56,000	5 My	1,300	4
	LZ 112 (L 70)	x	F	211.5	23.9	15	62,200	7 My	1,820	6
	LZ 113 (L 71)	x	F	211.5	23.9	15	62,200	6 My	1,560	6
	LZ 114 (L 72)	x	L	211.5	23.9	15	62,200	6 My	1,560	6
	LZ 115 to LZ 119 were not completed									
1919	LZ 120 Bodensee	y	F	120.8	18.7	12	22,500	3 My	780	3
	rebuilt			130.8	18.7	13	22,500	3 My	780	3
1920	LZ 121 Nordstern	y	F	130.8	18.7	13	22,500	3 My	780	3
	LZ 122, 123, 124, and 125 were designed but not built									
1924	LZ 126 (Los Angeles)		F	200	27.6	13	70,000	5 My	2,000	5
1928	LZ 127 Graf Zeppelin		F	236.6	30.5	16	105,000	5 My	2,650	5
	LZ 128 was not built									
1936	LZ 129 Hindenburg		F	245	41.2	17	200,000	4 D-B	4,200	5
1938	LZ 130 Graf Zeppelin II		F	245	41.2	17	200,000	4 D-B	4,200	5
	LZ 131 construction barely started									

Manufacturing facilities were M – Manzell
F – Friedrichshafen
Fk – Frankfurt
P – Potsdam
L – Löwenthal
S – Staaken

SPEED (MILES PER HOUR)	SPEED (METERS PER SECOND)	RANGE (KILOMETERS)	LOAD CAPACITY (KILOGRAMS)	MAIDEN FLIGHT (DATE)		FATE OF AIRSHIP
70.9	31.8	13,500	40,000	4.17.	1918	destroyed in 1919, at Nordholz
81.4	36.5	12,000	43,500	1.1.	1918	shot down in 1918, off Cromer
81.2	36.4	12,000	44,500	7.29.	1918	to Britain in 1920, dismantled at Pulham 1923
81.2	36.4	12,000	44,500	7.9	1918	to France in 1920, lost off Sicily 1923
82.1	36.8	2,000	10,000	8.20.	1919	
78.9	35.4	2,200	11,200		1919	to Italy in 1921, dismantled in 1928
78.9	35.4	2,200	11,200	6.13.	1921	to France in 1921, dismantled in 1926
76.9	34.5	8,500		8.27.	1924	in service until 1936 by U.S. Navy, dismantled in 1939
68.2	30.6	12,000	30,000	9.18.	1928	in service until 1937, dismantled in Frankfurt 1940
81.2	36.4	16,500	60,000	3.4.	1936	burned in 1937, at Lakehurst
81.2	36.4	16,500	60,000	9.14.	1938	dismantled in 1940, at Frankfurt

Appendix 2

Engines

YEAR	MAKE	HORSEPOWER	REVOLUTIONS PER MINUTE	WEIGHT (KILOGRAMS)	KILOGRAMS PER HORSEPOWER	CYLINDERS	FUEL CONSUMPTION IN GRAMS PER HORSEPOWER/HOUR
1899	Daimler N/L1	14.2	680	385	25.7	4	400
1905	Daimler H41/L	85	1050	360	4.0	4	265−240
1907	Daimler H4L/Ls	105	1080	400	4.0	4	265−240
1909	Daimler H4L/GP	115	1100	420	3.65	4	265−240
1910	Daimler	120	1100	450	3.75	4	225
1911	Maybach AZ	145	1100	450	3.1	6	240
1913	Maybach CX	170	1200	462	2.56	6	225
1914	Maybach CX	210	1250	414	1.97	6	225
1915	Maybach HSLu	240	1400	365	1.52	6	200
1917	Maybach Mb IVa	240+260	1400	400	1.66+1.54	6	200
1918	Maybach MbIVa	240−260	1400	390	1.62−1.50	6	200
1924	Maybach VL1	400	1400	950	2.375	12	200
1928	Maybach VL2	530	1600	1210	2.2	12	195
1936	Daimler-Benz LOF6, Diesel	1050	1600	2285	2.6	16	160

APPENDIX 3

Airships turned over to the Allies after the War

LZ 62   (L 30) to Belgium (dismantled)
LZ 75   (L 37) to Japan (dismantled)
LZ 106 (L 61) to Italy
LZ 109 (L 64) to Britain
LZ 113 (L 71) to Britain
LZ 114 (L 72) to France (became the *Dixmude*)
LZ 83   (LZ 113) to France (dismantled)
LZ 90   (LZ 120) to Italy (became the *Anzonia*)
LZ 120 *(Bodensee)* to Italy (became the *Esperia*)
LZ 121 *(Nordstern)* to France (became the *Méditerranée*)
LZ 126 to the United States (became the *Los Angeles*)

Appendix 4

Wartime Activities of Airships

	ARMY AIRSHIPS	IN USE	NAVY AIRSHIPS	IN USE
Zeppelins	43	30	67	65
Schütte-Lanz	10	5	8	7
Parseval	6	1	3	1
Gross-Basenach	1	0	1	1

The Navy airships flew 325 attack missions, 1,205 reconnaissance flights, and 2,984 other missions for a total of 2.4 million kilometers.

The Army airships flew a total of 323 main missions and others for a total of 600,000 kilometers.

The Army and Navy had in service in:

1914 an average of 9 airships, and maximum of 12
1915 an average of 14 airships, and maximum of 25
1916 an average of 22 airships, and maximum of 29
1917 an average of 22 airships, and maximum of 26

Appendix 5

PEACETIME ACTIVITIES OF AIRSHIPS

	IN SERVICE	KILOMETERS FLOWN	HOURS FLOWN	PASSENGERS CARRIED	TRIPS MADE
LZ 6	June 1910 to Sept. 1910	3,132	66:00	1,100	34
LZ 7 Deutschland	June 1910 to June 1910	1,035	20:30	220	7
LZ 8 Deutschland II	March 1911 to May 1911	2,379	47:00	458	22
LZ 10 Schwaben	June 1911 to June 1912	27,321	479:30	4,354	218
LZ 11 Viktoria Luise	Febr. 1912 to July 1914	54,312	981:20	9,738	489
LZ 13 Hansa	July 1912 to July 1914	44,437	840:40	8,321	399
LZ 17 Sachsen	May 1913 to July 1914	39,919	741:00	9,837	419
LZ 120 Bodensee	Aug. 1919 to Dec. 1919	51,258	532:00	4,050	103
LZ 127 Graf Zeppelin	Aug. 1928 to June 1937	1,695,272	17,177:48	34,000	590
LZ 129 Hindenburg	March 1936 to May 1937	337,129	3,088:36	7,305	63
TOTALS		2,256,194	23,973:84	79,383	2,344

Appendix 6
Chronology

Ferdinand von Zeppelin

8 July 1838	born in Konstanz
21 October 1853	enters the Military Academy
6 May 1863	arrives in New York
21 May	visits President Lincoln
28 June	leaves the Union army
17 August	arrives in St. Paul
19 August	makes balloon ascension with Prof. Steiner
18 November	embarks at New York for London
14 July 1866	volunteers for patrol at Aschaffenberg
22 March 1869	made adjutant to Prince Wilhelm in Berlin
7 August	marries Freiin Isabella von Wolff
23 July 1870	leads patrol into France: Scheuerlenhof episode
24 April 1874	makes first entry on "balloon vehicles" in his diary
28 September 1882	appointed regimental commander
21 October 1887	becomes minister in the Bundesrat
13 January 1890	appointed commander of brigade at Saarburg
29 November	retires from active military service
31 August 1895	receives a patent for his balloon vehicle
31 December 1896	The Society of Engineers publishes Appeal of Support
17 June 1899	start of construction of first airship at Manzell
2 July 1900	first flight of airship *LZ 1*
17 January 1906	emergency landing of *LZ 2* near Kissleg
30 September 1907	eight-hour flight of *LZ 3*
1 July 1908	twelve-hour flight over Switzerland in *LZ 4*
5 August	the airship is destroyed at Echterdingen
31 May 1909	The *LZ 5* completes a flight of over thirty-seven hours
8 March 1917	death of Count Ferdinand von Zeppelin
31 July	the *LZ 120* remains in air for 101 hours
19 October	the *LZ 55* sets altitude record of 7,600 meters
20 August 1919	the *Bodensee* begins regular passenger service
15 October 1924	the *LZ 126* reaches Lakehurst after crossing the ocean
15 October 1928	the *Graf Zeppelin* completes flight to Lakehurst
4 September 1929	the *Graf Zeppelin* completes round-the-world trip
6 June 1930	the *Graf Zeppelin* completes first tri-angular flight (Friedrichshafen-Rio de Janeiro-Lakehurst-Friedrichshafen)
31 March 1936	the *Hindenburg* begins South America service
6 May 1937	the *Hindenburg* burns at Lakehurst
14 September 1939	the *Graf Zeppelin II* makes its first test flight

BIBLIOGRAPHY

Black, Archibald. *The Story of Flying*. New York: Whittlesley House, 1940.

Blücher, Princess Evelyn. *An English Wife in Berlin*. London: Constable and Company, 1920.

Büdenkapp, Georg, and Alt, Hans. *Unser Graf Zeppelin und sein Werk (Our Count Zeppelin and his Work)*. 1933.

Davy, M.J.B. *Aeronautics*. London: His Majesty's Stationery Office, 1950.

Dettmann, Fritz. *Zeppelin, Gestern und Morgen (Zeppelin, Yesterday and Tomorrow)*. 1936.

Dommett, William E. *Aeroplanes and Airships*. London: Whittaker & Co. 1915.

Dürr, Ludwig. *25 Jahre Zeppelin-Luftschiffbau (25 Years Zeppelin-Airship Construction)*. Berlin: V.D.I. Verlag, 1924.

Eckener, Hugo. *Der Lenkbare Ballon (The Steerable Balloon)*. Chapter in *Die Eroberung der Luft (The Conquest of the Air)*. Stuttgart: Union Deutsche Verlagsgesellschaft, 1909.

———.*Graf Zeppelin (Count Zeppelin)*. Stuttgart: J.G. Cotta'sche Buchhandlung, 1938.

Encyclopedia Americana. Volume 1. New York: Americana Corporation, 1968.

Engberding, Marinebaurat. *Luftschiff und Luftschiffahrt (Airship and Airship Travel)*. Berlin: Udi Verlag, 1928.

Fischer, Ludwig. *Graf Zeppelin: Sein Leben, Sein Werk (Count Zeppelin: His Life, His Work)*. Munich: R. Oldenbourg, 1930.

Fraser, Chelsea. *The Story of Aircraft*. New York: Thomas Y. Crowell, 1933.

Glines, G.V., Editor. *Lighter-than-Air Flight*. New York: Franklin Watts, 1965.

Goebel, J. and Förster, Walter. *Afrika zu unseren Füssen (Africa at our Feet)*. Leipzig: K.F. Koehler, 1925.

Grieder, Karl. *Giganten der Lüfte. (Giants of the Air)*. Zurich: Orell Füssli Verlag, 1971.

Higham, Robin. *The British Rigid Airship, 1908-1931*. London: G. T. Foulis & Co., 1961.

Hildebrandt, Hans. *Zeppelin: Denkmal für das Deutsche Volk (Zeppelin: Monument for the German People)*. Stuttgart: Germania Verlag, 1925.

Hindenburg, Paul von, Generalfeldmarschall. *Aus meinem Leben (Out of my Life)*. Leipzig: S. Hirzel, 1920.

Hoeling, A.A. *Who Destroyed the Hindenburg?* Boston: Little, Brown and Company, 1962.

Horton, Edward. *The Age of the Airship*. London: Sidgwick & Jackson, 1973

Jackson, Robert. *Airships in Peace and War*. London: Cassell & Co., 1971

Kirchner, Wilhelm. *Zeppelin-Luftschiff (Zeppelin-Airship)*. 1933.

Kirschner, Edwin J. *The Zeppelin in the Atomic Age*. Urbana: University of Illinois Press, 1957.

Klitzing, Friedrich Wilhelm von. *Zeppelin, Marsch! (Zeppelin March!)*. Berlin: Ullstein, 1936.

Laswell, H.D. *Propaganda Technique in the World War*. New York: Alfred A. Knopf, 1927.

Lehmann, Ernst A. and Mingos, Howard L. *The Zeppelins*. New York: Sears Publishing Co., 1927.

Lilienthal, Otto. *Der Vogelflug als Grundlage der Fliegerkunst (The Birdflight as Basis for the Flying-art)*. München and Stuttgart: R. Oldenbourg, 1910.

Lindbergh, Charles A. *The Wartime Journals of Charles A. Lindbergh*. New York: Harcourt Brace Jovanovich, Inc., 1970.

Luftschiffbau-Zeppelin. *Das Werk Zeppelins: Eine Festgabe zu seinem 75. Geburtstag (The Work of Zeppelin: A Festival gift for his 75th Birthday)*. Stuttgart: Julius Hoffmann, 1913.

Mayer, Joseph. *Graf Ferdinand von Zeppelin (Count Ferdinand von Zeppelin)*. Stuttgart: Verlags und Druckerei Gesellschaft, 1925.

Miller, Francis T. *The World in the Air*. New York: G.P. Putnam's Sons, 1930.

Miethe, A. and Hergesell, H. *Mit Zeppelin nach Spitzbergen: 1911 (With Zeppelin to Spitsbergen: 1911)*. Berlin, Wien: Deutsches Verlagshaus Bong & Co., 1911.

Michell, William. *Skyways*. Philadelphia: J. B. Lippincott Co., 1930.

Nitske, W. Robert and Wilson, Charles Morrow, *Rudolf Diesel*. Norman: University of Oklahoma Press, 1965.

Parseval, August von. *Graf Zeppelin und die Deutsche Luftschiffahrt (Count Zeppelin and the German Airship Travel)*. Berlin-Grunewald: Hermann Klemm Verlag.

Photographic History of the Civil War, Volume 1. New York: Review of Reviews, 1912.

Poolman, Kenneth. *Zeppelins against London*. New York: Charles Scribner's Son, 1938.

Robinson, Douglas H. *Giants in the Sky*. Seattle: University of Washington Press, 1973.

Robinson, Douglas Hill. *The Zeppelin in Combat 1912-18*. London: G.T. Foulis, 1962.

Rolt, L.T.C. *The Aeronauts*. London: Longmans, Green and Co., 1966.

Rosendahl, Charles E. *Up Ship*. New York: Dodd, Mead, 1931.

————.*What about the Airship?* New York: Charles Scribner's Son, 1938.

Rosenkranz, Hans. *Ferdinand Graf von Zeppelin (Count Ferdinand von Zeppelin)*. Berlin: Ullstein, 1931.

Sanger, Adolf. *Zeppelin: Der Mensch, der Kämpfer, der Sieger (Zeppelin: The Man, the Fighter, the Winner)*. Umschlag, 1915.

Santos-Dumont, Alberto. *My Airships*. New York: The Century Co., 1904.

Sass, Friedrich. *Geschichte des deutschen Verbrennungsmotorenbaues (History of the German Combustion Engine Construction)*. Berlin: Springer Verlag, 1962.

Schiller, Hans von. *Zeppelin: Wegbereiter des Weltluftverkehrs (Zeppelin: Pathfinder of the World Air Travel)*. Bad Godesberg: Kirschbaum, 1967.

Schurz, Carl. *The Reminiscences of Carl Schurz*. Volume 2. New York: The McClure Company, 1907-08.

Siebertz, Paul. *Gottlieb Daimler*. Stuttgart: Reclam Verlag, 1950.

Smith, Richard K. *The Airships Akron and Macon*. Annapolis: U.S. Naval Institute, 1965.

Stephen, Heinrich von. *Weltpost und Luftschiffahrt (World Mail and Airship Travel)*. Berlin: Springer, 1873.

Schwengler, Johannes. *Der Bau der Starrluftschiffe (The Building of the Rigid Airships)*. Berlin: Springer, 1925.

Vaeth, J. Gordon. *Graf Zeppelin*. New York: Harper & Brothers, 1958.

Wachsmuth, Richard. *Wissenschaftliche Vorträge (ILA) [Scientific Lectures (ILA)]*. Berlin: Julius Springer, 1910.

Werder, Markus. *Graf Ferdinand von Zeppelin und sein Werk (Count Ferdinand von Zeppelin and his Work)*. Langeusalza: Julius Beltz Verlag.

Whitehouse, Arthur G. *The Zeppelin Fighters*. Garden City: Doubleday, 1966.

Wilson, G.L. and Bryan, Leslie A. *Air Transportation*. New York: Prentice-Hall, 1949.

Zeppelin, Graf Ferdinand von. *Aufruf an das Deutsche Volk, mit Geldbeiträgen den Bau eines Luftschiffes finanzieren zu helfen (Call on the German People, to help finance with money donations the construction of an airship)*. Stuttgart: 1895.

————.*Erfahrungen beim Bau von Luftschiffen (Experiences when Building Airships)*. Berlin: Julius Springer, 1908.

————.*Die Eroberung der Luft (The Conquest of the Air)*. Stuttgart and Leipzig: Deutsche Verlagsanstalt, 1908.

Zeppeline über England. Ein Tagebuch von . . (Zeppelins over England. A diary of . . .). Berlin: Ullstein & Co., 1916.

PERIODICALS

"Air Tickets Around the World," *Popular Mechanics,* March 1935.

"The Ascension of Count Zeppelin's Airship." *Scientific American,* August 11, 1900.

Berliner Tageblatt, August 23, 1909.

"Count von Zeppelin's Airship," *Scientific American,* May 26, 1900.

"Death of a Dirigible," *Westways,* November 1966.

Die Woche, (periodical) October 1903.

"The Disaster of the Shenandoah," *Science Supplement,* September 1925.

Dunn, Maria Bach. "Zeppelin in Minnesota. The Count's Own Story." *Minnesota History,* Summer 1967.

Eckener, Dr. Hugo. "The Remodeled Zeppelin III Airship," *Scientific American Supplement,* December 12, 1908.

"The First Airship Flight around the World," *The National Geographic Magazine,* June 1930.

"The First two Trial Trips of Von Zeppelin's Airship," *Scientific American Supplement,* October 27, 1900.

Frankfurter Zeitung, July 3, 1900; May 17, 1915; March 8, 1917.

Gilman, Rhoda R. "Zeppelin in Minnesota. A Study in Fact and Fable," *Minnesota History,* Fall 1965.

"The Graf Zeppelin," *Science Supplement,* October 26, 1928.

"Into the Arctic Wastes with the Graf Zeppelin," *Popular Mechanics,* November 1931.

Lampe, David. "The Great Airship Revival." *True Magazine,* September 1971.

"The Latest European Airships." *Scientific American,* November 21, 1908.

Minneapolis Journal, February 9, 1915.

Modebeck, H.W.L. "The Termination of the Trials of Count von Zeppelin's Airship." *Scientific American Supplement,* April 13, 1901.

Mutter, Alexander Karl von. "Zeppelin." *Süddeutsche Monatshefte,* April 1917.

Neues Wiener Tagblatt, June 1908.

"Nuclear Power for Airships?" *Nucleonics,* December 1965. New York: McGraw-Hill.

Paris Temps, 1927.

"Recent Airship Experiments in Europe." *Scientific American,* May 26, 1900.

Rosendahl, C.E. "Inside the Graf Zeppelin." *Scientific American,* March 1929.

Schwäbischer Merkur, October 1908.

St. Paul Daily News, February 8, 1915; February 9, 1915; August 14 to August 20, 1863.

Stahl, Friedrich. "Die Starrluftschiffe." *Illustrierte Flugwelt,* Volume 2, Leipzig, 1920.

Stratz, Rudolph. "Graf Zeppelin." *Vellhagen und Klassings Monatshefte,* August 1930.

Thüringer Zeitung, July 2, 1908.

Walzer, Franz. "Die Zeppelin Luftschiffe seit 25 Jahren." ("The Zeppelin Airships of 25 Years.") A series of articles in the *Seeblatt* 1925.

Zeppelin, Graf Ferdinand von. "Aus dem Amerikanischen Kriegsjahre 1863." ("From the American War Year 1863.") *Der Greif; Cotta'sche Monatsschrift.* Volume 1, 1913-14. Book 4. January 1914.

"Zeppelin and his Achievement." *The Nation.* Volume 104, no. 2698, March 15, 1917.

"Zeppelin's Schwaben." *Scientific American,* November 25, 1911.

"The Zeppelin III Airship and its Trip to Berlin." *Scientific American,* October 2, 1909.

INDEX

NOTE: Page numbers in italics indicate illustrations.